The Graduate Career Guidebook

Palgrave Study Skills

Business Degree Success
Career Skills
Cite Them Right (9th edn)
Critical Thinking Skills (2nd edn)
e-Learning Skills (2nd edn)
The Exam Skills Handbook (2nd edn)
The Graduate Career Guidebook
Great Ways to Learn Anatomy and Physiology
How to Begin Studying English Literature (3rd edn)
How to Study Foreign Languages
How to Study Linguistics (2nd edn)
How to Use Your Reading in Your Essays (2nd edn)
How to Write Better Essays (3rd edn)
How to Write Your Undergraduate Dissertation
Improve Your Grammar
Information Skills
The International Student Handbook
The Mature Student's Guide to Writing (3rd edn)
The Mature Student's Handbook
The Palgrave Student Planner
Practical Criticism
Presentation Skills for Students (2nd edn)
The Principles of Writing in Psychology
Professional Writing (3rd edn)
Researching Online
Skills for Success (2nd edn)
The Student's Guide to Writing (3rd edn)
The Student Phrase Book
Study Skills Connected
The Study Skills Handbook (4th edn)
Study Skills for International Postgraduates
Study Skills for Speakers of English as a Second Language
Studying History (3rd edn)
Studying Law (3rd edn)
Studying Modern Drama (2nd edn)
Studying Psychology (2nd edn)
Teaching Study Skills and Supporting Learning
The Undergraduate Research Handbook
The Work-Based Learning Student Handbook
Work Placements – A Survival Guide for Students
Write it Right (2nd edn)
Writing for Engineers (3rd edn)
Writing for Law
Writing for Nursing and Midwifery Students (2nd edn)
You2Uni: Decide.Prepare.Apply.

Pocket Study Skills

14 Days to Exam Success
Blogs, Wikis, Podcasts and More
Brilliant Writing Tips for Students
Completing Your PhD
Doing Research
Getting Critical
Planning Your Dissertation
Planning Your Essay
Planning Your PhD
Reading and Making Notes
Referencing and Understanding Plagiarism
Reflective Writing
Report Writing
Science Study Skills
Studying with Dyslexia
Success in Groupwork
Time Management
Writing for University

Palgrave Research Skills

Authoring a PhD
Getting to Grips with Doctoral Research
The Foundations of Research (2nd edn)
The Good Supervisor (2nd edn)
The Postgraduate Research Handbook (2nd edn)
The Professional Doctorate
Structuring Your Research Thesis

For a complete listing of all our titles in this area please visit **www.palgrave.com/studyskills**

Also by Steve Rook

Legal Skills
Various sections of the Graduate Prospects website: www.prospects.ac.uk

The Graduate Career Guidebook

Steve Rook

palgrave

First published 2013 by
PALGRAVE

Palgrave in the UK is an imprint of Macmillan Publishers Limited, registered in England, company number 785998, 4 Crinan Street, London N1 9XW

Palgrave Macmillan in the US is a division of St Martin's Press LLC, 175 Fifth Avenue, New York, NY 10010.

Palgrave is a global imprint of the above companies and is represented throughout the world.

Palgrave® and Macmillan® are registered trademarks in the United States, the United Kingdom, Europe and other countries.

ISBN 13: 978–0230–39175–8

This book is printed on paper suitable for recycling and made from fully managed and sustained forest sources. Logging, pulping and manufacturing processes are expected to conform to the environmental regulations of the country of origin.

A catalogue record for this book is available from the British Library.

A catalog record for this book is available from the Library of Congress.

Brief Contents

Contents

Preface

I have written this guide because I am passionate about helping people find fulfilling careers. This is because I faced a massive struggle to get my own career going and I want to pass on what I've learnt along the way.

I found it almost impossible to get started because I got a third-class degree during a recession and had no idea what career planning involved (or anything else for that matter!). Consequently, I decided to apply for a hundred jobs. I received 50 rejections and the rest didn't even respond!

Therefore, I drifted around the world for many years and only started to appreciate how I could turn my career around in my mid-thirties. A light suddenly went on in my head and I realised that, instead of just looking for jobs, I should focus more on what I wanted to do in life and carefully plan my journey. Since then I have emigrated to Australia, worked as a primary school teacher, run my own recruitment company, counselled numerous students as a university careers adviser and now write books.

In recent years I have come to see life as one big opportunity where anything is possible, and I want to pass on this confidence to my readers. I sincerely hope you are able to successfully navigate your way through my guide and find a successful path in life. Please feel free to contact me on steventhomasrook@yahoo.co.uk for any reason at all.

Steve Rook

Acknowledgements

A great number of people have made it possible for me to write this guide and I want to say thanks.

My mother ensured that I gained a sound education in difficult circumstances and my sister Caroline has recently given me the support and guidance that I have needed to realise my writing ambitions.

The careers advisers in Perth, particularly Marilyn Prestage, helped me get into the careers field and Ann Collins at Southampton gave me my first opportunity. Since then, I have also been lucky enough to have worked with some incredibly dedicated and proficient colleagues in the field, especially Ann Berry and Catherine Gregory who have continued to provide support and encouragement.

My GP, Dr Jonathan Griffin, and Sharon Brooks at the Sheffield Asperger Syndrome Service have recently given me the wonderful opportunity to find peace and contentment for the first time ever as an autistic person.

However, greatest thanks must go to the two Suzies in my life. Suzannah Burywood at Palgrave kept an open mind about my proposals, welcomed me into the fold and patiently helped me put the book together, whilst my wife Susan and her family encouraged me, supported me and gave me the confidence to help thousands of students and graduates who currently face such a daunting journey in life.

Introduction: Help! Where do I start?

"Begin at the beginning," the King said, very gravely, "and go on till you come to the end: then stop." *Lewis Carroll*

So, what now?

Getting into a graduate career nowadays can be more daunting than ever before because there are so many directions to take and factors to consider. Nevertheless, you shouldn't be overwhelmed. Once you work out a plan and take your first steps, things tend to take care of themselves and become a great deal easier.

What 'career' means to you

Career > **Job**

Careers encompass so much more than just finding a job and clocking on for the next 50 years, but it's very hard to come up with a universal definition because we all have our own unique hopes, plans and aspirations. Therefore, before you can plan your career, you need to identify what the term specifically means to you. A good way to do this is to reflect on what you personally think differentiates careers from jobs. Try this in the two-minute test below.

The two-minute test

Take two minutes to list five things that you think differentiate 'careers' from 'jobs'.

Careers are...
•
•
•
•
•

Many students and new graduates see careers as being more long term than jobs; something they enjoy; something they're good at and where there are good long-term prospects. You may also be attracted to good pay, professional kudos and a good work–life balance. These elements can be summarised in terms of finding a fulfilling path that matches your skills, what you enjoy and your motivations in life.

Whatever you thought of when you completed the test, keep it in mind so you can maintain your drive for what's truly important to you in life.

Are you sitting comfortably?

Before you start planning your next steps in life, make sure you're in a safe, comfortable environment and ready to face the inevitable challenges. Avoid putting yourself under too much pressure and...

- Allow yourself plenty of time.
- Research a wide a range of roles. You don't want to miss your perfect career just because you've never heard of it!
- Find a role that excites you – you will have a much greater chance of success.
- Ensure that you can support yourself financially while you plan your next steps (you may have to get a part-time or temporary job).
- Get support from friends and family.

Then let's begin (using this guidebook)

The guidebook systematically divides the career planning process into four discrete sections to help you take control of your next steps in life, as follows:

Part I – Finding your way: An outline of career planning, employability and a model of guidance plus advice and guidance for choosing a career path and making it happen.

Part II – The stepping stones: An outline of the three key steps that most students and graduates should consider to get their careers off the ground, namely, experience, internships and networking, plus a few words on taking time out.

Part III – Getting a job: How to find vacancies and put together effective applications. Specific chapters focus on promoting yourself effectively, targeting your CVs, application forms, cover letters, interviews, psychometric tests, assessment centres, as well as what to do once you start work.

Part IV – Entrepreneurship: An introduction to setting up in business with chapters on becoming an entrepreneur and setting up your own business.

Finally, the book finishes by answering some frequently asked questions and referring readers to the appropriate sections of the guide that deal with their specific concerns.

You can either follow these discrete, manageable steps from start to finish or dip into them according to your needs. Either way, at the end of each chapter you will find links to more information and guidance on where to go next. If you're not sure where to start, just turn to the opening chapter and take it from there. Hopefully, before long you'll feel more positive and in control of your own career journey.

The companion website

This guide also comes with a companion website available at www.palgravecareerskills.com. On this site you'll find resources for both students/graduates and educators.

All that's left to say now is 'Good luck and enjoy the trip!'

Part

I

FINDING YOUR WAY

This guide is for all students and graduates who are wondering what to do once they leave university, especially those who are completely lost and don't know where to turn (you are not alone!).

This section of the guide helps you determine what you want from a career and identify the route you need to take to get there.

Chapter

1

Understanding employability and career planning

"Never look back unless you are planning to go that way." *Henry David Thoreau*

Contents

What you will gain from this chapter:

- **Decision making:** An awareness of the key decisions involved in career planning.
- **Opportunity awareness:** An appreciation of the key skills required by employers.
- **Transition learning:** An introduction to what's involved in finding work.
- **Self-awareness:** The foundations of personal career reflection.

Taking control

This chapter defines employability and career planning and establishes a theoretical foundation and framework for the rest of this guide. You will quickly see that the career journey is both an intellectual and an emotional process, which everyone can master by getting out there and taking control.

What is employability?

'Employability' means your ability to get a job and keep it. In the words of Hillage and Pollard (1998), it is:

> the capability to move self-sufficiently within the labour market to realise potential through sustainable employment. For the individual, employability depends on the knowledge, skills and attitudes they possess, the way they use those assets and present them to employers.[1]

Therefore, employability is down to three factors – your knowledge, commitment and especially your skills. Whether you want to be a publican or a politician, you need an understanding of what you're doing, the desire to succeed and the ability to perform. You can develop these qualities throughout your experience and qualifications. All experience gives you a chance to promote yourself but paid employment is especially attractive to employers because the knowledge, commitment and skills you gain are easily transferable. You will need both technical competencies related to your specific post and transferable abilities that can be used in a range of fields. These classifications are outlined below.

Technical skills

These are specific competencies related to particular jobs and are therefore fundamental to your success, so relevant experience is highly regarded. Technical skills required in one job/industry are not generally very transferable. For example, an ability to make cocktails may help you get a job in a posh bar but probably won't help you become an automotive engineer!

Transferable skills

As the name suggests, these are skills/competencies, such as teamwork and organisation, that can be used in a wide range of roles. They are highly prized by graduate employers because they are a crucial element of success in every industry. There are numerous transferable skills and every industry/recruiter will have unique requirements, but the table below lists the most common competencies that are required. You should certainly be proficient in each of these areas. You can identify what's involved in each of these skills on the companion website where there are also more details on the skills required in specific industries and roles.

Common transferable skills required by employers	
• Enthusiasm and self-reliance	• Management
• Numeracy	• Creativity
• Teamwork	• Problem solving
• Research	• IT
• Organisation	• Commercial awareness
• Leadership	• Customer service

What about career planning?

Career planning can be seen as a subcategory of employability. It comprises a set of metacognitive competencies which enable you to reflect on your commitment, knowledge and skills, identify appropriate roles and take control of your next steps in life. Various theories have developed over the last century to describe how individuals go about finding and choosing appropriate careers. It's worth quickly running through these to gain a useful understanding of the specific model of guidance used in this book.

Trait and factor theories

Vocational guidance theories were first established at the start of the last century. In 1909, Frank Parsons introduced talent matching by linking students with particular qualities to supposedly appropriate roles. In The 1930s, Edmund Williamson built on this pioneering work to develop a full-blown trait and factor theory. This model focused on testing students to identify their unique capabilities and potentialities (traits) so they could make rational vocational choices. In the early 1970s, Professor Alec Rodger developed a trait and factor working framework, which was widely adopted in the UK, called the Seven-Point Plan. This was used to build personal profiles of clients according to their:

- Physical makeup
- Attainments
- General intelligence
- Special attributes
- Interests
- Disposition
- Circumstances

Personality theories

Personality-based occupational theories emerged in the 1950s; these were largely based on the work of Sigmund Freud (1856–1939). In the late 1950s, Anne Roe, and also John Holland, stressed the importance of early childhood experiences. Holland's Theory of Career Choice postulates that people find fulfilment in jobs by searching for work environments that fit their personality types. He categorised these as follows:

- Realistic
- Investigative
- Artistic
- Conventional
- Social
- Enterprising

Try the exercise below to reflect on your own abilities and aspirations.

Self-assessment: What are you like?

Describe your personality in three words and consider some relevant careers.

You in three words	Some relevant careers
•	
•	
•	

Keep these ideas in mind for the next chapter on choosing a career role.

Developmental theories

Shortly after the Second World War, much of the research into career planning and development focused on the process of personal development. In 1951, Eli Ginzberg concluded that people decide on occupations in three stages as they get older. Thirty years later, Donald Super moved this theory on by demonstrating that people gradually develop their vocational maturity in five clear stages as follows:

1 Growth (from birth to 14 years of age): When we become increasingly conscious of who we are and what's involved in the world of work.
2 Exploration (from 15 to 24): When we try out new experiences at school/university/work and during our hobbies.
3 Establishment (from 25 to 44): At which point we perfect our skills and establish ourselves in our roles.
4 Maintenance (from 45 to 64): When we focus on promotion and moving up in our field.
5 Decline (65 years of age and over): As we reduce output and prepare for retirement.

Post-1968, K. Roberts refined Ginzberg's and Super's development theories with an 'opportunity structure' model which highlights the restraints on young people in freely developing occupational choices because of difficulties connected to their home lives, environments, educational institutions, peer groups and the job market. For example, you may find the whole process too daunting, have limited aspirations or drink too much.

Self-assessment: What's holding you back?

Identify what's holding you back in your career and what you could do about it.

What's holding you back in your career?	What can you do about it?

Keep these reflections in mind for Chapter 3 on planning your career journey.

Recent viewpoints

Two more recent theories are John Kumboltz's Theory of Planned Happenstance and the narrative theories developed by Michael White, David Epsom and Gregory Bateson. These theories relate particularly well to university students and new graduates. John Kumboltz's theory propagates the benefits of putting yourself in beneficial situations and taking full advantage. He stresses the need for curiosity, persistence, flexibility, self-reflection, openness to feedback, networking and a positive attitude. Narrative theories stress the advantages of taking a step back from your life and interpreting your own career through the stories of others which give you the necessary perspective to trace a logical and fulfilling path.

The guidance model used in this book

In recent years a number of career guidance models have been developed to represent the various strands and theories of vocational choice within educational programmes. This guide broadly follows the DOTS/New DOTS model first postulated by Bill Law and A. G. Watts in 1977 and then updated in 1999,[2] because it encompasses elements of trait and factor, personality and development theories, and is very flexible in order to account for diversity.

What's involved?

DOTS stands for the following four skills and understandings that Law sees as being at the heart of successful career planning and development:

Decision making: Choosing suitable career options and navigating the appropriate route to get you where you're going.

Opportunity awareness: Appreciating your full range of job options and the possible stepping stones to your destination.

Transition learning: Understanding the job market, finding jobs and making successful applications.

Self-awareness: Assessing your skills, commitment and knowledge.

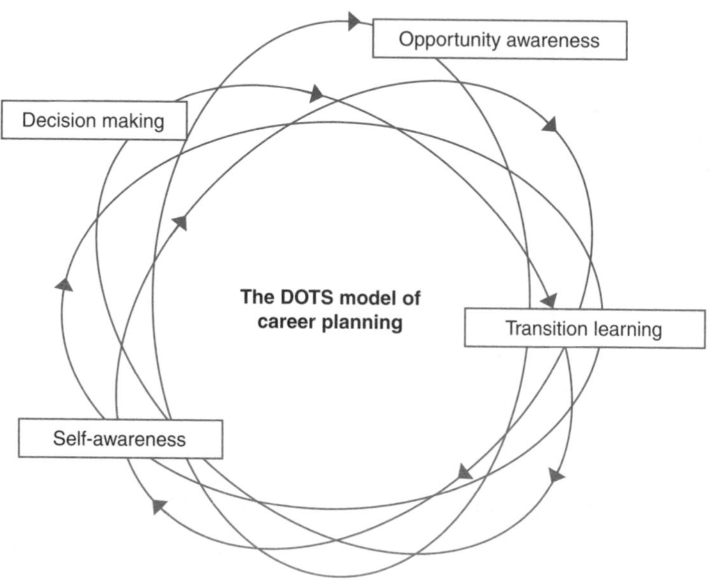

The DOTS diagram portrays career planning as a constant lifelong process of 'sensing, shifting and focusing on' each of the four elements of personal growth outlined above. The four individual strands of development are interwoven in the diagram to demonstrate that this is not a straightforward cycle where you sequentially make decisions; learn about your opportunities; transit into a new position; and then learn more about yourself. It is, in fact, a dynamic, ongoing process in which each of us constantly and simultaneously addresses and readdresses each of these four core elements that drive our journey. This fluid DOTS model forms the backbone of this guide, so, by the end of the book, you will have a valuable skill that will help you throughout your life.

Practise your DOTS-related career reflection now by listing some of the key problems you have with each of the model's four elements of growth so you can look back at your answers when you've finished the guide and see if they have all been addressed.

Self-assessment: Your DOTS problems?

What are your key problems with each aspect of the DOTS model?

The DOTS architects of growth	Where you struggle with each one
• Decision making	
• Opportunity awareness	
• Transition learning	
• Self-awareness	

Finding out more

In this guide

- Choosing a role – Chapter 2.
- Planning your journey – Chapter 3.

On the companion website

- Skills linked to a wide range of graduate occupations.
- Examples of how and where you can develop specific skills.

On the web

On the companion website you will find up-to-date links for the websites of:

- The careers centres at Bradford and Kent Universities, which have excellent resources on employability skills.
- Careers New Zealand, which has a good summary of career development theories.
- The Open University's pages on the DOTS model of career planning as used in this guide.

What to do next

The following chapters of the guide show you how to use the guidance model to develop your employability and secure fulfilling positions. Start by focusing as clearly as possible on the specific career path you want to take, as this will help you systematically plan your next steps.

Summary

- Employability is your ability to get a job and keep it, so it's down to your skills, commitment and knowledge.
- Career development theories have developed over the last century, focusing on linking traits and factors, personality and personal development.
- This guide employs the DOTS model of career planning, which focuses on decision making, opportunity awareness, transition learning and self-awareness.

Chapter

2

Choosing a role

"Choose a job you love, and you will never have to work a day in your life." *Confucius*

Contents

What you will gain from this chapter:

- **Decision making:** The ability to choose appropriate career options.
- **Opportunity awareness:** Familiarity with graduate recruitment trends and a wide range of career options.
- **Transition learning:** The confidence to dream of fulfilling roles.
- **Self-awareness:** The ability to relate your personal attributes to interesting occupations.

The world is your oyster

As a graduate you have a wealth of career opportunities. You can go into roles linked to your studies and employment experience or try something completely new. However, many students and graduates are daunted by this choice and just don't know how to start. This chapter helps you resolve this dilemma by showing you how to systematically research all your choices and find a fulfilling role.

Graduate jobs

What do you know already?

Test your knowledge of graduate jobs in this short quiz. The answers are provided below.

A quick graduate employment quiz

1 What percentage of graduates go into roles directly related to their degrees?

2 What's the percentage growth in HE numbers since the early 1960s?
10% ☐ 100% ☐ 400% ☐ 600% ☐ 6000% ☐

3 Degrees cost so much – what are your chances of getting your money back by earning a higher salary?
Extremely unlikely ☐ Unlikely ☐ Possible ☐ Likely ☐ Probably ☐

4 When do you need to apply for student internships?

Consider the answers carefully and reflect on how they could affect your future plans:

1 Only about 30–40 per cent of graduates end up in careers that are directly related to their degrees.[1] This is because your grades and skills are better indicators of your potential than your knowledge.

2 Student numbers in Higher Education have grown by 6000 per cent! In the early 1960s only a few people went on to HE and they were mostly white and male.[2]

3 The answer is 'probably'. Research indicates that graduates still earn more over their careers than non-graduates.

4 Although internships are offered to students and graduates at every stage of their studies and beyond, most major recruiters hire students at the end of their penultimate year of study and start taking applications as soon as they come back to university in September/October of that year.

A story of growth

About two-thirds of new graduates go straight into full-time work, many others go travelling, take up some sort of postgraduate study or just take some time out from all the hassle. They go into a massive range of careers and find work in every part of the country, but over 60 per cent of vacancies with larger employers are based in the South East. Some new graduates on training programmes take home over £30,000 but many will only earn about £15,000 for the first few years after leaving university (but afterwards their salaries tend to rise quicker than those without degrees).

Over the last 50 years, HE student numbers have grown from 25,000 to 1.5 million but the supply of graduate jobs has also expanded accordingly. However, few of these fresh opportunities have been in traditional graduate positions, but instead are in 'new', 'niche' and 'modern' graduate roles as outlined below:

- *New roles*: Occupations that have recently become more 'professional', require greater technical skills, or have seen an influx of graduates with relevant skills. Examples include marketing and sales positions, management accountants and therapists.
- *Niche roles*: Jobs that necessitate a high level of expertise and the ability to manage within employment sectors that do not generally require graduates. For example, agricultural consultants, detectives and graphic designers.

- *Modern roles*: Professions that have increasingly required a degree. For example, managers, software engineers, primary school teachers and journalists.

Since the recession

The UK economy went into a steep decline in 2008 after a prolonged period of growth. At the height of the recession graduate vacancies at major recruiters fell by 17.8 per cent and many small and medium-sized enterprises (SMEs) made drastic cutbacks, causing a graduate unemployment rate of 20 per cent. However, as of 2012 there were significant signs of a recovery – you can find an up-to-date outline of current trends on the companion website.

So, in general, the picture is positive. There are numerous opportunities for ambitious and proactive graduates. You have more job options than ever before, more routes into fulfilling occupations and greater scope to manage your own career. Therefore, you should consider as wide a range of careers as possible, and allow yourself to dream. After all, if a role exists then someone has to do it – so why shouldn't it be you?

Daring to dream

Graduate horizons

The proportion of occupations that most graduates consider

All graduate occupations

Unfortunately, most of us only ever consider a few of our potential career options. For example, most psychology graduates will think about becoming a counsellor or psychologist but few look into less common roles such as media production, direct marketing or drama therapy. Don't fall into this trap. If you want to find an interesting career, take the time to assess as many job options as you can and remain open to new ideas.

To see how comprehensively you've researched your career preferences so far, complete the two-minute test below and assess your answers. Most of us only discover career options in five limited ways – through our friends, family, university, TV and job pages on the Internet. If this sounds like you, read on to see how you can widen your horizons.

The two-minute test

List five occupations you've considered at some time in your life (even as a child) and identify how you first discovered that they actually exist.

Five occupations you've considered	How you first discovered them
•	
•	
•	
•	
•	

Researching your options

Use the following tools to come up with as many interesting career options as you can in the table provided. Don't just focus on the obvious occupations such as teaching and accountancy (although there's nothing wrong with these), and take your time to find truly inspiring roles, even if they're not mainstream, such as drama therapy or working as a park ranger. Also, don't feel too pressured about making such a life-changing decision because, nowadays, you can change your career any time you wish! List 15 career ideas that come to you in the table below.

Self-assessment: Possible career options

Use the strategies outlined below to identify 15 attractive occupations

Possible careers	Possible careers	Possible careers
•	•	•
•	•	•
•	•	•
•	•	•
•	•	•

Brainstorm

Just find a quiet place, sit down and see what comes to mind. Don't be afraid to list anything that comes to mind, however peculiar or unexpected.

Find your careers service

Pop into your university's careers centre, ask for help, and attend relevant events. Most services will also see graduates, so don't be shy.

Look up some graduate career websites

Look for interesting occupations on sites such as www.prospects.ac.uk and www.targetjobs.co.uk. Prospects also has a great facility in its 'Types of jobs' section where you can look up a particular role and click on a button to reveal 'related jobs'. Doing this repeatedly over the course of evening is a great way to widen your search.

Identify what people do with your degree

See Prospects and ask your careers service (or former careers service) to show you what specific graduates on your course have done after graduation.

Ask for help

Find out what your friends, family and colleagues think you'd be good at and get help on social networks.

Other creative strategies

Students and graduates also find millions of unique personal strategies for identifying careers, so don't be afraid to try any creative approach that comes to mind, for example:

- Look at the vacancies on offer at temp agencies and identify interesting roles.
- Research postgrad courses and see what interesting careers they lead to.
- See what comes up when you search on your browser for 'alternative careers' or 'exciting jobs'.
- Get busy and just keep your eyes open for new ideas. For example, get involved in new activities and see what comes to mind.
- Watch TV and see what roles you'd enjoy.
- Try to remember all your career dreams, even when you were a child, and see if they are still feasible or there are some similar roles that look interesting. For example, if you once dreamed of being a footballer, you might be too old and wobbly now to make the big time, but you could still become a football coach or a sports journalist.
- Think of opportunities linked to your interests. For example, if you enjoy helping friends with their problems, you could consider counselling; or, if you like cooking, why not become a chef?

Personality types

You can also identify potentially fulfilling careers by assessing what sort of person you are and considering relevant roles. A wide range of tests have been developed to help you do this, such as:

- Prospects Planner: www.prospects.ac.uk/planner – Graduate-focused test with a comprehensive report – take your time!
- Windmills: www.windmillsonline.co.uk/interactive – Various interactive exercises.

Myers Briggs

One of the more reputable personality profiles is the Myers Briggs Type Indicator (MBTI®). This test was developed shortly after the Second World War in the USA by Katherine Briggs and her daughter Isabel Briggs Myers, who extrapolated Carl Jung's earlier work in the area. In essence, it allocates people to one of 16 different patterns of behaviour based on how they interact, process information, make decisions and organise their lives, as follows:

How people interact: People can either be primarily 'I' for Introverted or 'E' for Extroverted, where...

- Introverts prefer being alone; they think things through internally and tend to be private with their feelings.
- Extroverts tend to be energised by others; they think out loud and share their feelings.

How people process information: People can either be 'S' if they tend to Sense things or "N' if they use their iNtuition, where...

- People who sense things tend to focus on what they can actually see, hear, touch, taste and smell. They trust concrete concepts; base their opinions on established facts; and prefer to use established skills so they are often described as being 'well grounded'.
- Intuitive people tend to trust their instincts; search for new solutions; interpret facts and continually develop their skills.

How people make decisions: People can either be primarily 'T' for Thinkers or 'F' for Feelers, where...

- Thinkers tend to be logical; objective; analytical; highly motivated and often uncaring about other people's feelings.
- Feelers tend to make decisions according to their instincts and the feelings of others. Therefore, they enjoy pleasing people and finding compromise.

How people organise their lives: People can either be 'J' if they prefer to carefully Judge their next steps in life or 'P' if they rely on Perception, where...

- People who use judgement strive to learn as much as they can about things before taking action. They work hard to achieve goals and enjoy the feeling of finishing projects, so they often appear to be organised.
- Perceptive people prefer to keep their options open and are therefore remain flexible about taking up new paths, learning new things and gaining new experiences.

In the following exercise, make an approximation of your particular Myers Briggs/Jungian type based on the information provided.

Self-assessment: Your personality profile

What's your personality type?

Place an 'I' in the box if you think you are more of an introvert or an 'E' if you're an extrovert.	Place an 'S' in the box if you tend to use your senses to interpret things or an 'N' if you use your intuition.	Place a 'T' in the box if you like to think your decisions through or an 'F' if you go with your feelings.	Place a 'J' in the box if you focus on achieving goals or a 'P' if you prefer to keep your options open.
☐	☐	☐	☐

Now you have an idea of your specific personality type you can research it in more depth to identify appropriate careers and career paths. You can do this via a wealth of websites such as www.kiersey.com and www.personalitypage.com. Two highly recommended books on the subject are also listed in the references section at the end of this guide: *Do What You Are* by Tieger and Barron and *What's Your Type of Career?* by Donna Dunning.

Finding the perfect fit

Once you've identified a shortlist of potential careers you can narrow down your search by identifying the roles that most closely match your skills (what you can do), your interests (what you enjoy doing on a day-to-day basis) and your motivations (what you want from life). You can do this in the exercise below.

“You must look forward to going to work. If you dread Monday mornings you will be unhappy and fail. Keep money at the bottom of your wish list.”
Godfrey Bloom, MEP for Yorkshire and the Humber

Self-assessment: Your favourite occupations

Enter three stimulating occupations you've identified in this chapter and see which one most closely matches your skills, interests and motivations.

Three exciting careers you've discovered:	Role 1 ______	Role 2 ______	Role 3 ______
Your relevant skills (why you'd be any good)	• •	• •	• •
Your relevant interests (what you'd enjoy)	• •	• •	• •
Your life motivations the role will deliver (such as security, money, flexibility and a good work–life balance)	• • •	• • •	• • •

The hidden message from this exercise

Obviously, this exercise is designed to help you identify suitable career options, but there is also a hidden learning outcome. Namely, your approach to the question can reveal a great deal about your current career planning strategies and how they can be improved, as follows:

- If you didn't do the exercise, are you engaging deeply enough with the process?
- If you only assessed one role, are you rushing things and not looking widely enough?
- If you found it easiest to fill in the skills section but struggled with the others, are you so worried about getting a job you're forgetting to dream?
- If you found it easier to complete the interests section, are you being mature enough about finding a long-term fulfilling role or are you just looking for a bit of fun?
- If you found it easier to complete the motivations section, are you dreaming too much and not giving enough time to what you can actually do?

Only you can answer these questions and identify whether you need to slightly rearrange your focus.

But I still haven't found what I'm looking for

Don't panic if you've tried everything possible to identify a wonderfully fulfilling carer, but you're still confused. This is quite understandable because there are just so many options for anyone with a decent amount of education and intelligence (i.e. you!). There are a number of things you can do, such as any, or all, of the following:

- Ease the pressure off and just take your time.
- Take a break and return to the issues when you're refreshed.
- Aim for any role that meets a fair number of your skills, interests and motivations, but keep your options open. After all, the modern graduate recruitment market is so flexible you can refocus your career at any stage, as realised by Ann Widdecombe after her appearance on Strictly Come Dancing.

> "Remember, the whole of your life is before you. What you do now does not have to be what you are doing in ten years' time. I began in industry, moved to university administration, ended up in parliament and have now been on stage at the Royal Opera House!"
> *The Rt Hon Ann Widdecombe*

- Just jump in and try anything but keep your eyes open for interesting roles.

> "If you're not sure what you want to do with your life, just jump in and see what happens. Sometimes doing the wrong thing can help you figure out what the right thing is."
> *Louis Theroux, Broadcaster*

- Become a 'slasher', i.e. a portfolio careerist holding down a range of roles – e.g. a journalist/web editor/PR consultant. Many slashers combine paid employment with volunteering opportunities and even set up one or two businesses. This career route is exciting because you can try little bits of what you enjoy and avoid getting bored or typecast.

> "A portfolio careerist means never getting bored doing the same old 9–5 routine, never having to think that you will have to endure yet another day in the same office chair shuffling the same office papers! It is an option for the adventurous, the enterprising and the slightly mad. The thrill of not knowing where your next project might come from or what your next task might be or even whether there will be a next task is often exciting and even more often scary. You have to balance your books, worry about cash flow, network like crazy, put yourself forward, take risks and go with the flow. It beats the full-time routine any day for me."
> *Ann Berry, Careers adviser, postgraduate course leader, interim business coordinator, event florist, celebrant registrar (to name but a few of my jobs)*

Finding out more

On the companion website

- Up-to-date graduate labour market information and links.
- More examples of traditional, new, modern and niche roles in various sectors.

On the web

On the companion website you will find up-to-date links for a range of websites which outline graduate recruitment trends including sector-specific resources, such as the websites of Graduate Prospects, the Association of Graduate Recruiters (AGR), the *Guardian* and High Flyers Research.

What to do next

If you've managed to identify a few interesting career roles, the next step is to find out how to get your foot in the door. This involves researching the skills, knowledge and commitment that are required in your chosen field and finding the experience to demonstrate them.

The next chapter shows you how to plan your journey.

Summary

- Since the early 1960s the graduate job market has grown beyond all recognition and graduates now go into a massive range of traditional, new, modern and niche roles.
- There are numerous ways to look into career options, from research into lists provided on websites such as Prospects to more creative strategies and personality tests.
- You can learn a lot about your personal career planning strategies by linking your job ideas to your skills, interests and motivations.
- Don't panic if you still can't find an exciting path. There are numerous strategies you can employ, from taking a break to moving forward with a few rough ideas and keeping your eyes open.

“For as long as I can remember I had always wanted to be a dentist. I liked the idea of having the option to work for myself and work in the medical profession without having to work shifts. Also, dentists always seemed to drive nice cars and this was very appealing to me as a teenager.

I was always a hard-working student, not a natural academic, but I managed to maintain good grades throughout my school years, finally achieving As and Bs in my GCSEs.

I had done my research and knew that to study dentistry at university, I would need three A levels, two of which had to be science subjects and I would need to achieve at least two As and a B. With that in mind I chose to study biology, chemistry and modern history at Greenhead College, Huddersfield.

Throughout my time at Greenhead College I continued to work hard, but found it increasingly difficult to achieve the As and Bs I was used to gaining. I was finding that A levels were much tougher than I had anticipated and by the end of the first year it was quite evident I was not going to attain the grades I needed to study dentistry.

I was thrown into a state of panic! I had never considered doing anything else and I was supposed to apply for universities in a few months. I filled out questionnaires which were supposed to identify what type of career I was suited to, spoke to my careers adviser and spent hours researching different career pathways on the Internet. I was so preoccupied with finding myself an alternative profession that I found my grades were slipping further.

I thought I had looked into every possible career that was remotely involved in the health care profession until my dad suggested chiropractic and/or osteopathy. My initial response was "What's that?" However, once I had looked into it further and visited several chiropractors and osteopaths I decided it was something I could see myself doing and applied.

I did a further year at Greenhead College to improve my results, pick up a few AS levels and give myself I bit of time to confirm that I was making the right decision.

After that year I have never looked back. I started my chiropractic training in 2002, having the time of my life at university. In 2006 I graduated with an upper second-class qualification in chiropractic and got a job straight after university in my home town. I now have my own practice with an associate chiropractor and three reception staff working for me. I love my job and now when I look back I cannot imagine why I wanted to be a dentist. Why would I want to look in people's mouths all day?"

Elizabeth Hunt, Bsc (Hons) Chiropractic

Chapter

3

Planning your journey

"There is a tide in the affairs of men
Which, taken at the flood, leads on to fortune."
William Shakespeare

> General transferable skills are very important in the recruitment process but customer service and being a 'people person' are quickly becoming absolutely crucial.
>
> Graduates need to realise that most opportunities are not provided through traditional graduate recruitment programmes at large businesses. They need to be more proactive about finding alternative pathways including opportunities at SMEs.
>
> *James Johnston, Business Relationship Manager – Student Promotions, ACCA UK*

Contents

What you will gain from this chapter:

- **Decision making:** The ability to choose an appropriate career path.
- **Opportunity awareness:** An appreciation of the possible paths into your chosen career.
- **Transition learning:** The inspiration to take control of your journey.
- **Self-awareness:** The ability to reflect on your current career planning strategy and assess how it can be improved.

Taking control

Now you have an idea of what you want to do after university, you can start planning how to get there. At first, this can be quite a challenging process because your journey could take the form of a thousand different routes and steps depending on your unique attributes and aspirations. However, by breaking the process up into a sequence of discrete manageable tasks you can set yourself achievable goals as you progress and get to your destination before you even realise you've left.

What's involved?

The career journey starts with research into the skills, knowledge and commitment required in your chosen role and identifying the various paths to get there.

Whilst the following chapters go into detail about crossing each of your specific career stepping stones, this chapter focuses on planning ahead.

When to start planning

It's never too early to start planning your career (or too late!). It can really help to get going in your first year at university, but don't worry if you're just opening this guide during your graduation ceremony! You can only start from where you are now. However, it takes time to get the experience, networks and qualifications you typically need in today's graduate job market, so the sooner you start the better.

Researching what's required

Unfortunately, many graduates just follow the more common routes into their chosen careers without even considering any alternative paths that may be more suitable. For example, they often focus on:

- Graduate training programmes when they actually comprise only a small minority of graduate opportunities in a limited number of sectors.
- Popular courses such as the Postgraduate Certificate in Education (PGCE) when there are other options, such as School-centred Initial Teacher Training (SCITT) or the School Direct Training Programme (see details at www.education.gov.uk).

Therefore, it's up to you to identify all the possible paths into your chosen career and identify the route that best suits your particular skills and aspirations.

Your personal journey

Career planning is like a walk in the park. Imagine there's a map at the entrance with a big red arrow stating 'You are here'. In this situation you would find your destination, identify all your possible routes to get there and choose the one that suits you best.

Career planning follows much the same process. For example, two different routes for a first-year law student to become a commercial solicitor are shown below. You will see that many of the planned experiences are similar, particularly at the early stages of the process, whilst others are completely different.

After considering our example journeys into law, choose two different routes for yourself into your chosen occupation and identify your favourite path. Your different plans could involve aspects such as alternative postgraduate courses, a choice between further study or not, different graduate training programmes or working your way up from the bottom at an SME.

Obviously, if you've already moved on from your first year at university, start your plans from where you are now – even if you're a 46-year-old graduate like me embarking on his fourth career!

Two different action plans for a first-year law student to become a commercial solicitor

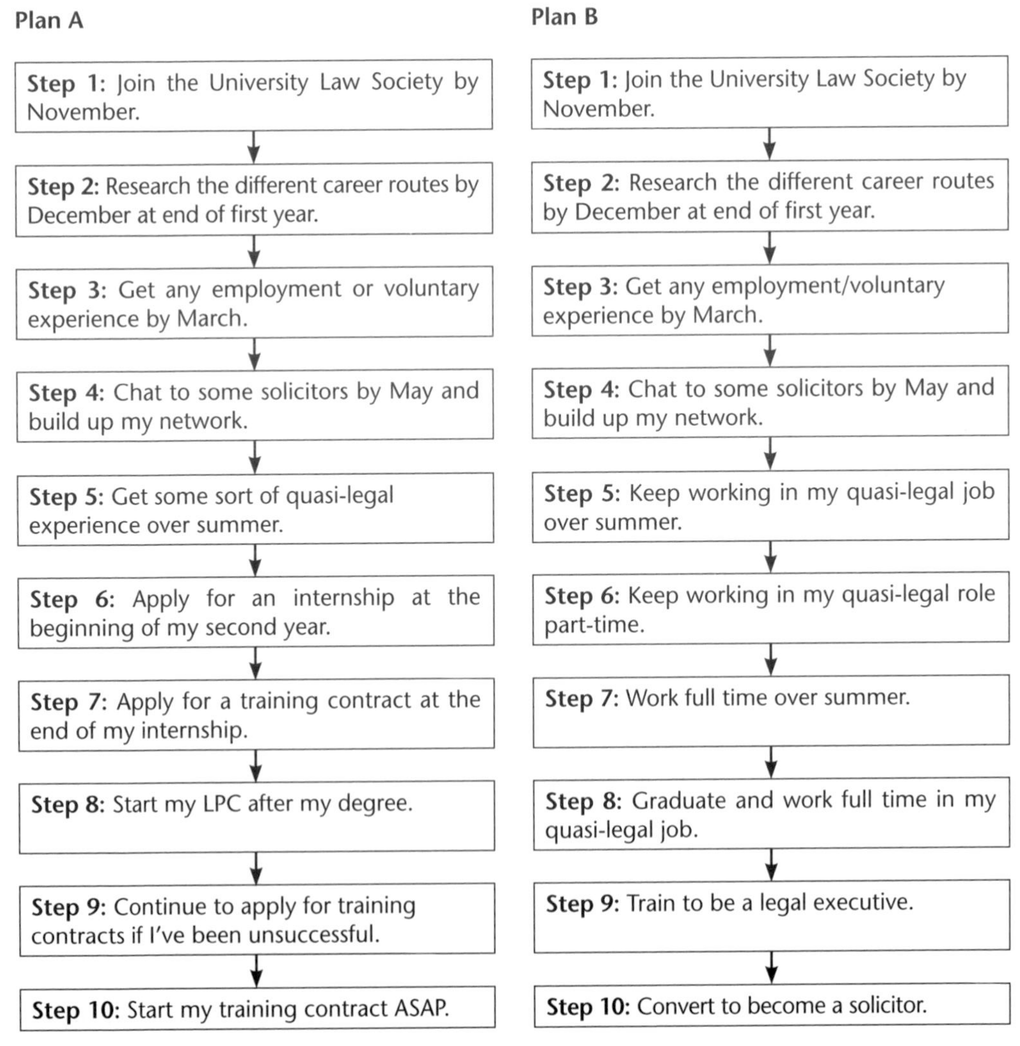

Self-assessment: Two possible career plans

Now try it for yourself. Come up with two possible plans for getting into your chosen career and explain why you've chosen your preferred route.

Plan A	Plan B
Step 1:	**Step 1:**
Step 2:	**Step 2:**
Step 3:	**Step 3:**
Step 4:	**Step 4:**
Step 5:	**Step 5:**
Step 6:	**Step 6:**
Step 7:	**Step 7:**
Step 8:	**Step 8:**
Step 9:	**Step 9:**
Step 10:	**Step 10:**

Which is your favourite route and why?

Perfecting your approach

Whether you're an old hand at career planning or you've just started the process, it can really help to assess how things have gone so far. Eight of the more common career planning strategies are outlined below. Identify your personal approach in the exercise at the end of the chapter and list some specific practical strategies to help you move on.

The systematic approach

Well-organised people tend to carefully plan their careers in advance, alter their plans as required and steadfastly focus on their goals. Of course, this strategy can be very successful but you need to be flexible, open to unexpected opportunities and happy to refocus when necessary.

Landing on your feet

Some people are just lucky and whatever they touch turns to gold. If you're one of these fortunate souls, buy a lottery ticket but make sure you're aiming high enough and are prepared to compete with battle-hardened graduates who've had to work hard for every break.

The mad rush

Many graduates are far too busy to carefully plan their next steps in life or commit to anything for long enough. Like the hare in the children's nursery rhyme, they excitedly jump from activity to activity without any sense of direction. If they're lucky they may stumble upon a fulfilling role but often get completely lost.

If this has been your approach to finding a fulfilling career, congratulate yourself on your energy and courage but pause for a while, research your next steps more carefully and ask for help. You just need to stick at things for a little longer!

What will be will be

A large number of graduates just drift into their careers totally unprepared. They might be lucky but, more often than not, they end up either unemployed or underemployed and feeling let down by the whole system. If this sounds like you then you need to reinvigorate your career plans. Even if you feel like you're in a deep hole, just take five minutes a day to dream of what jobs you could go into if you had a magic career wand. You could then research these roles and see what small steps you could take to get on track, such as some sort of training or a night course at the local college. Once you allow yourself to dream again and take the smallest steps to a new life, you'll quickly realise that the future is actually in your own hands.

Follow the leader

Some graduates are so dependent on advice from others that they just follow their friends into certain occupations or sign up for a role suggested by their parents. If you find yourself in this position, listen to advice but, also, make sure you research a wide range of roles for yourself and choose a career path that suits your personal skills and interests.

Learning as you go

This is the career path for everyone who puts their IKEA wardrobes together without looking at the instructions. Graduates with this approach tend to jump into their careers without hesitation and pick up useful tips and ideas as they progress. They often get lost at first but don't give up easily and eventually find the right path. One good thing about this approach is that you will probably have the chance to try a wide range of career paths. However, you could also spend a great deal of your life in the slow lane when there are far more direct routes to your destination. If this has been your approach, take stock of your position from time to time and target your chosen occupation more efficiently.

Seeing the light

This category describes graduates who are unsatisfied with their careers so far and suddenly realise that they need to start taking control. This phenomenon has recently been called a 'quarter-century crisis' because people in this situation are often in their mid-twenties and under a great deal of pressure to make the most of their careers. If you are in this position then don't panic: all your experiences (whether or not they're positive) will help you in your new search for a fulfilling role because you will have gained new skills, a chance to reflect and a renewed passion and determination.

A failure to thrive

Some people stall before they even get going. They search for inspiration and briefly try to get into some sort of graduate role, but it all seems too difficult and they just retreat into their own shells. Unfortunately we all find ourselves in this position from time to time on our career journeys, but you need to come back fighting because, even if you've taken the wrong steps until now, you'll eventually find the right path. If this sounds like you, you could reassess your career choice to make sure it is appropriate and/or establish smaller career steps so you can regain your confidence. For example, if you just can't find any work in your chosen sector, maybe you could start by looking for a voluntary position or similar work in a related area that will give you the skills, experience and contacts to get the job you want in the future.

Self-assessment: Your personal career path

Assess how you have planned your career so far and how you could improve things.

Provide an appropriate title for your current career planning strategy:

• ______________________________

Describe your strategy

____
____
____
____
____
____

How could you improve things?

• ______________________________
____
____
• ______________________________
____
____

Finding out more

In this guide

- The stepping stones: Chapters 4–7.

On the companion website

- Personal career stories.
- Summary of common routes into popular careers.

On the web

On the companion website you will find up-to-date links for a range of websites with advice on taking control of your career journey, including Target Jobs and Graduate Prospects.

What to do next

Once you've planned your way forward into your chosen career you need to make it happen. The next chapters in the guide show you how to get relevant experience, build your networks, sign up for further study and make the most of any time out.

Summary

- Once you know what you want to do in your career take some time to plan your next steps.
- There will be numerous paths into your chosen field – identify the one that best suits your particular abilities and aspirations.
- It can really help to reflect on your current career planning strategies so you can improve things in the future.

Part

THE STEPPING STONES

Now that you have a grounding in modern graduate employment and recruitment, you can move ahead and develop the building blocks of your career. Depending on where you are in the career planning process these could involve any or all of the chapters shown alongside.

How to prepare for the job hunt

“Beginning to hunt for jobs can be daunting for young people: many may be uncertain about what their ideal job looks like and unaware of the possibilities open to them, whilst others will have a more specific idea, but be concerned about how competitive their chosen field is.

However, those who use their time at university wisely will have ample opportunities to think through their goals, and build up an impressive portfolio of relevant experience. Students develop their employability skills all the time whilst taking part in extra-curricular activities, whether through team sports, taking a leadership role within a university society, or showing their creativity by writing for a student paper – they just need to present these skills in a clear and meaningful way to boost their CVs.

Work experience is an excellent way to prepare for job hunting. Taking on a casual job during university holiday, or volunteering for charity during a gap year helps to demonstrate drive and awareness of working environments. The more experience students gain, the better placed they will be to make decisions about which roles are likely to suit them.

When choosing what jobs to go for, students and graduates should focus on selecting the right roles and putting in high quality applications, rather than spending time filling out multiple cut-and-paste applications for roles that don’t suit them. Finally, it’s important to have long- as well as short-term career goals and value your first job as an important step on the career ladder.”

Carl Gilleard, Chief Executive of the Association of Graduate Recruiters (AGR)

Chapter

4

Experience and internships

"The only source of knowledge is experience."
Albert Einstein

Contents

What you will gain from this chapter:

- **Decision making:** The ability to identify and choose appropriate experience.
- **Opportunity awareness:** A sound appreciation of your experience options.
- **Transition learning:** Effective strategies for making the most of what you do.
- **Self-awareness:** The capacity to reflect on how your experience has developed your skills.

Why experience is important

Experience is central to the employment process because it helps you confirm your career decisions, prove your skills and identify your particular strengths. All experience is beneficial whether or not it's relevant to your chosen profession because you will have the chance to develop your key transferable skills.

> We look for candidates who have a good academic background but we are especially attracted to those who also have a wealth of experience – people who have gone out of their way to get wider experience and some general business awareness.
> *Laura Lodwick, Operations Manager BJSS Limited*

Complete the two-minute test below to get into the routine of relating your employment experience to your future career.

The two-minute test

List two of your recent experiences and outline the skills you demonstrated which are relevant to your future career.

Two recent experiences	The career-relevant skills you demonstrated

Making the most of your experience

There are certain things you can do to maximise the impact of all your hard work:

- Reflect on the skills and knowledge you've gained during your experience.
- Look for opportunities where you can develop your skills in a similar environment to your chosen career.
- Proactively look for extra opportunities to develop the requisite skills within your existing activities.
- Find opportunities that put you in touch with professionals in the field you want to enter so you can get advice and practise what you've learned.

Gradually moving on up

> You can impress employers by demonstrating an in-depth understanding of their organisations and what they bring to the market.
>
> Due to the expansion in the Internet and the range of social media, it's very easy to learn the basics about organisations and what they offer. Therefore, today's recruiters expect you to delve a little bit deeper. You should research the organisations that interest you and reflect deeply about what you discover in order to develop your own views, judgements and ideas.
>
> Start early. In your first year you should get some relevant experience and develop a real understanding of how businesses work. In your second year, try to get an internship. In this way, by the time you are looking for a graduate job, you will be ready to relate to interviewers and business contacts.
> *Graduate from 'Big 4' accountancy firm*

Relevant experience will greatly help you get into a graduate career, but many people find themselves in a pernicious catch-22 situation where they can't even get the experience they need because they don't have any experience! The trick to breaking this vicious circle is to start in relatively basic roles and gradually work your way up the 'greasy pole'. This is why you really need to start planning and developing your career as soon as possible The four-step process below outlines how you can incrementally develop your skills and become more employable.

- **Step 1:** Find any voluntary experience and some sort of casual work, plus sign up for any career-related modules at university or night courses where you live.
- **Step 2:** Gradually seek out activities at work and in your voluntary experience that demonstrate the skills you'll need in your career, and start to network.
- **Step 3:** Get a more relevant job, shadow your contacts (see the next chapter) and get some highly relevant employment experience.
- **Step 4:** Find an internship and continue to build your networks.

Activities at university

There are a number of things you can do to get experience during your studies:

- Pick activities/modules that will enhance your skills. For example, if you need to develop your team skills, you could target group-based assignments.
- Pick activities/modules that are related to your favoured career.
- Sign up for any career/entrepreneurship modules on your degree.
- See if your university runs an employability skills award, i.e. a module which links employability skills to a period of employment experience.

Expanding your interests

Employers are very attracted to applicants who have gone out of their way to get involved in extra-curricular activities. It's also a great way to meet new people and get the most out of your time at university (and once you've graduated). You can get involved in everything from archery to Zoroastrianism, and if a club hasn't yet been invented to suit your unique interests then why not set one up yourself? Some of the more popular activities are shown below. See what ideas come to mind and list them in the table below.

Student societies

All universities run a wide range of sporting and cultural clubs that are open to all students. Look up your student union website to see how you can get involved.

Local groups

Look out for interesting groups in your area. For example, if you live in Huddersfield you could get involved in the Halifax Amateur Radio Society, the Rothwell Shokotan Karate Club or the Skelmanthorpe Historical Society (or all three!).

Careers events

Visit university/local events related to your chosen career. For example, if you want to go into marketing you could see what the local branch of the Chartered Institute of Marketing is getting up to in your area.

Self-assessment: Non-work experience

Identify some groups and activities outside work where you could get experience and develop your skills.

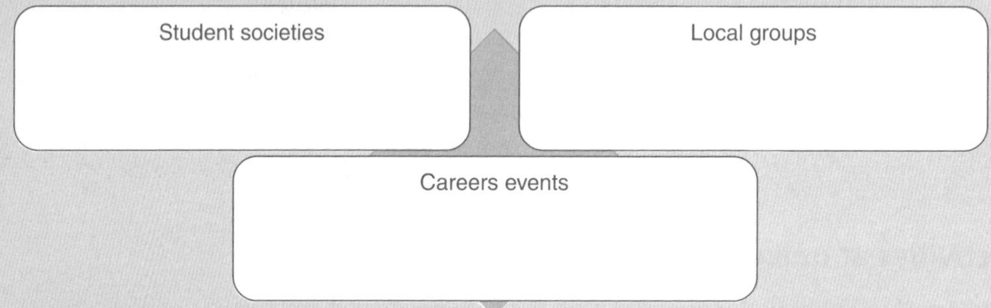

Volunteering

Volunteering is a great way to practise your skills, gain confidence and find the exact experience you need. Employers are attracted to candidates with voluntary experience because they value the skills you've gained and the commitment you've shown to get involved without any financial reward. Another advantage is that you can look for positions related to your chosen career and find your own niche.

Most universities have some sort of volunteer agency for students, or you could pop into the careers service and ask for help. You can also find opportunities in your area through Internet searches such as "volunteering in x" (the name of your town or chosen sector). You could also try speculative applications and asking your friends, family and contacts.

Here are some useful websites:

- Community Service Volunteers: www.csv.org.uk – A massive organisation offering opportunities in social or health care, education and youth justice.
- DirectGov: www.direct.gov.uk – Search for 'Volunteering' to find lots of useful information.
- Do-It: www.do-it.org.uk – Search volunteer opportunities by postcode.
- Timebank: www.timebank.org.uk – Volunteering focused on youth/social issues.
- Idealist: www.idealist.org – A massive database of volunteer opportunities, jobs and internships across the globe.
- Elevation Networks: www.elevationnetworks.org – Networking events, mentoring, internships and volunteer opportunities for students/graduates from minority ethnic backgrounds, women, and those affected by a disability.

- The *Guardian*'s Volunteering pages: http://www.guardian.co.uk/voluntary-sector-network – Articles and opportunities.
- i-volunteer: www.i-volunteer.org.uk – A range of interesting practical opportunities for people of any age.
- Vinspired: www.vinspired.com – Volunteering website for 14–25-year-olds.

Paid employment

Employment experience is especially valuable because it proves to employers that you have the skills and commitment to succeed in the workplace. Students and graduates have access to a number of job opportunities. Your university probably has a 'job shop' and, as with voluntary experience, you can make speculative applications and ask for help from contacts. Find out more about networking in Chapter 5.

Employment agencies

A number of local and multinational organisations advertise general vacancies or jobs in specific sectors and can be a good source of work in the holidays. You can find agencies in your local area on your local newspaper's website and the website of the Recruitment and Employment Confederation at www.rec.uk.com. You can also try the Jobcentre Plus website at www.direct.gov.uk.

Other seasonal work

Many organisations recruit students at certain times of the year, such as the Royal Mail, numerous retail outlets, the Royal Household and summer camps. Vacancies are usually advertised well in advance, so keep your eyes peeled, or approach organisations yourself. Some useful websites include:

- Employment4students: www.e4s.co.uk
- Just Jobs 4 students: www.justjobs4students.co.uk
- StudentJob: www.studentjob.co.uk
- Student-Jobs: www.student-jobs.co.uk

In order to identify busy, ethical agencies, look for those with an actual postal address, and a large number of vacancies. Also, avoid paying any fees upfront.

Shoe leather

Approach organisations you find really attractive and try to speak to the general manager or recruitment manager so you can quickly promote what you have to offer.

Internships

A broad overview

Internships are short-term, structured employment experience opportunities that operate at the interface between study and graduate employment. They have traditionally been designed for students nearing the end of their degrees but, in recent times, they have morphed into a range of diverse opportunities, from short-term menial tasks for little or no salary to lucrative summer-long placements. They are popular with employers, students and graduates. For employers they are cheap labour and a great opportunity to see if people are up to the mark. Interns themselves appreciate the chance to confirm a career choice, gain relevant skills, develop networks and find a potential pathway into graduate work.

> “During my first year I applied for jobs everywhere for the summer holidays and got an internship at Pershing, a financial services firm. At the end of my second year, I was invited back for an internship with their parent company, the Bank of New York Mellon, and now I am hoping to work there in a customer-facing role.
>
> My advice would be to try to get as much as work experience before graduating and be curious about what's outside the top 100s. Before my first year, I had never heard about Pershing, but thanks to the first internship I am now more clear on where I would like to work and what I would like to do in the future.”
>
> *Katerina Vlkova, Economics and History student*

Finding opportunities

You can use the following resources to find internships:

- Your academic department.
- General graduate employment websites such as www.prospects.ac.uk, www.milkround.com, and www.targetjobs.co.uk.
- The websites of professional organisations.
- Specialist internship websites such as www.interntown.com, www.step.org.uk, www.ratemyplacement.co.uk, www.topinternships.com, www.indeed.co.uk, www.simplyhired.co.uk and www.yini.org.uk (for industrial placements).
- Specialist graduate internship sites such as: http://graduatetalentpool.direct.gov.uk, www.inspiringinterns.com, and www.topemployers.co.uk.
- Your university's careers service.

You should also ask your contacts for help and send out speculative applications. A good approach with SMEs is to approach them with specific offers of help over the summer: for example, you might suggest that you could develop their website, write a marketing plan or improve their industrial processes.

Six common types of placements are outlined below.

1 Introductory events

A number of organisations offer short-term opportunities during the winter, spring and summer vacations that are open to first-year students who are considering certain careers. They typically last from a few days to a couple of weeks.

For example:

- JP Morgan offers a fortnight of activities to demonstrate what's involved in investment banking and risk management (see http://careers.jpmorgan.com).
- The City Solicitors' Educational Trust runs a one-week training scheme to encourage students from diverse backgrounds to consider a career in law (see www.cset.org.uk).

2 Vacation placements

Vacation placements are the customary internship option in the UK. They are typically structured to fit into the spring, summer or winter university vacations and last from a few weeks to two or three months during the summer break at the end of students' penultimate year of study, but many are also available at other times.

Summer internships at larger employers are usually advertised from October onwards for the following year's intake. Therefore, you'll need to apply as soon as you start your penultimate year at university. Applications are often viewed on a first come, first served basis. SMEs are more likely to accept applications throughout the year.

3 Internships as part of your study

An increasing number of undergraduate and postgraduate degree programmes now include academic placements in industry. On these courses you are typically asked to complete some sort of research for the organisation or undertake a specific project linked to your study.

For example:

- The BSc Computing degree at Edge Hill University offers a second-year module in 'Work related learning' during which you will work in industry with workplace mentors to solve a specific problem.
- The Communications Engineering Masters with Industrial Studies at the University of Birmingham offers a summer placement following your exams and includes a module to help you prepare.
- The Bank of England has a PhD internship scheme for people currently researching a PhD in fields related to monetary analysis and financial stability.

4 Skills modules

A number of universities now also offer modules specifically designed to improve your employability skills. For example, York University offers an employability certificate for undergraduates called the 'York Award' that provides internships and volunteering opportunities alongside skills training.

5 Sandwich courses (often called placements/industrial placements)

University sandwich courses offer undergraduates the chance to undertake an extended 'industrial placement' for a period of between six months and two years, usually in between their penultimate and final years of study. Some Masters courses also offer this opportunity. These extended internships confer extensive experience and the majority of interns are taken on permanently once they've graduated. During your time away from campus you are usually treated as a current student but your fees will be reduced. Examples of sandwich year opportunities are shown below:

- Over 50 per cent of undergraduates at Aston University take a placement year.
- All degrees in the Department of Business and Management at Sussex University.
- The MSc in Civil Engineering at the University of Southampton offers an 11-month industrial placement with UK companies and government organisations.

Funding for overseas industrial placements is available from Erasmus at www.britishcouncil.org/erasmus.htm.

6 Graduate internships

Graduate internship opportunities have grown massively in the UK over the last decade, and especially since the economy went south (literally and metaphorically). Expansion in this sector is primarily due to the fact that:

- Employers enjoy the chance to assess graduates over a sustained period of time.
- Employers currently have less money and a large supply of cheap talent.
- Recession-proof graduates are prepared to try anything to get into their careers.

These internships are usually short-term work opportunities where you'll carry out relatively routine tasks. Another group of internships that are increasingly available to graduates are vacation schemes that were traditionally only open to students, for example:

- Barnardo's offers a 12-week placement for students or graduates who are under 25 in various sectors of their business.
- Barclays Capital offers a variety of short-term and six-month internships at both Analyst and Associate level that are open to students and graduates.

Paid or unpaid?

UK internships have traditionally provided a living wage but employers are increasingly expecting interns to work for nothing, especially on graduate internships. This is simply due to the lack of demand for (and increased supply of) talent in an economic slowdown. Hopefully, when the economy turns around, salaries will return, but you shouldn't hold your breath! In fact, a number of websites, such as www.etsio.com, now even auction off the best opportunities!

If you're prepared to undertake an unpaid internship, there are a few things you can do to make sure it's a beneficial experience:

Before you start:

- Check out the specific internship on forums such as www.thestudentroom.com and http://internsanonymous.co.uk/.
- Clarify exactly what you'll be doing.
- Try to negotiate the payment for expenses.
- Set parameters such as how long the internship will last and the hours you will be expected to work.
- Make sure you will have an opportunity to develop the specific skills you require.

Once you get going:

- Maximise your learning opportunities and make good contacts.
- Talk your way into paid work.

What suits you?

In the following exercise, use the resources provided throughout this chapter to identify some interesting employment experience opportunities.

Self-assessment: What experience are you after?

List a range of specific activities you could undertake to develop your skills.

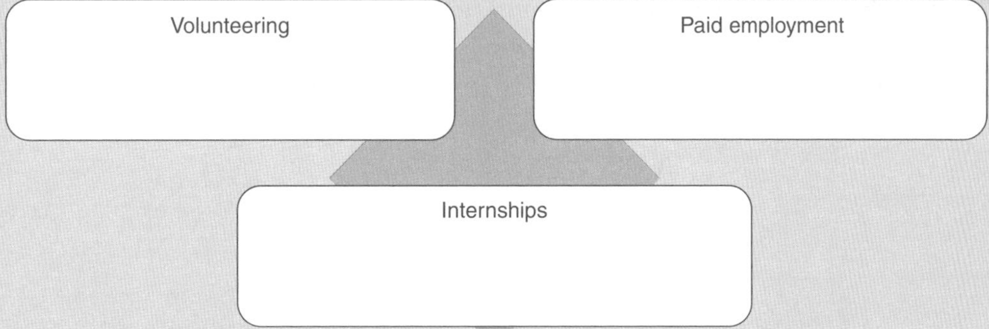

Finding out more

In this guide

- Planning your journey – Chapter 3.

On the companion website

- Further links to internships in a wide range of sectors.

On the web

A wide range of links are listed throughout this chapter, but you will also find additional up-to-date links on the companion website including links to Prospect's work experience section and various agencies such as Hotrecruit, Enternships and Anywork Anywhere.

What to do next

Leave your house and get busy. Try anything and everything (within reason) to get your foot in the door of your chosen career and make sure you proactively use your experience to improve your requisite skills.

Summary

- Experience is a crucial element of your career journey, even if it's not related to your chosen profession, because it will help you develop your requisite skills.
- You can get involved in activities at university, local groups, career-related events, interesting hobbies, volunteer work, paid work and internships.
- Employment experience is especially valuable because it demonstrates your skills in the workplace.
- Internships are becoming increasingly important and comprise everything from short introductory to year-long (or more) sandwich opportunities.
- Make sure you proactively and systematically use your experience to develop the specific skills you require.

Chapter 5

Effective networking

"Skill is fine, and genius is splendid, but the right contacts are more valuable than either."
Sir Arthur Conan Doyle

Contents

- Why networking is important
- Who do you know?
- Who do they know?
- Six degrees of separation
- How your contacts can help
- What you can do for them
- An effective strategy
- Networking online
- Your online presence
- Finding out more
- What to do next
- Summary

What you will gain from this chapter:

- **Decision making:** The knack of identifying your needs and choosing appropriate contacts.
- **Opportunity awareness:** The ability to find and identify possible contacts.
- **Transition learning:** An effective networking strategy.
- **Self-awareness:** The ability to reflect on the specific help you need.

Why networking is important

"We are always actively on the look-out for people who can talk openly and honestly about working with us as well as confidence and enthusiasm. It's absolutely crucial that we find graduates with whom we can build positive personal and professional relationships and who fit in with our teams."
David Griffiths, Graduate, AlphaSights

Ever since Julius Caesar became a Roman general on the back of his family link to the goddess Venus, contacts have been crucial. Today, this is as true as it ever was. Graduates who have grown up in a professional family with influential friends are far more likely to succeed, because they have what is called 'social capital'. This means they are comfortable and confident around professional people; aspire to great things and expect them to happen. They can also call on favours from people in high places.

Whether or not you were lucky enough to grow up in a privileged position, it is imperative that you feel comfortable around professionals in your chosen field and are able to dream of a successful future and make it happen. This is where networking comes in. For most students, 'networking' is an ugly word that conjures up images of cheap suits and greasy handshakes, but it's actually just about getting to know like-minded people with whom you can build longstanding friendships.

Who do you know?

Networking is all about contacting people and providing mutual support. Of course, you should start with the people you already know such as your extended family, colleagues at work, your boss, tutors, careers advisers and friends – but don't stop there. Take the time to think of all the people you come across in every aspect of your life and, before long, you will probably find someone worth contacting, such as a colleague in your evening job who knows someone in your chosen occupation, or your friend's aunt who once did some interesting training.

Who do they know?

Unfortunately, most students will only ever have a few useful contacts amongst the people in their immediate circle. This is quite natural but it doesn't mean you should give up! The real magic of networking is that it's not just about who you know, but also who they know and who they know, and so on. Therefore, if you get out there and start asking contacts to introduce you to others, you will soon realise that you actually have links to people in almost every situation.

Six degrees of separation

The power of networking was reinforced in 1929 by Frigyes Karinthy, who showed that everyone on earth is just six steps away, by way of introduction, from every other person. He called this phenomenon 'the six degrees of separation' and it's still true today. Look at how the students in the following diagrams might be connected to their heroes or useful career contacts and try to find similar paths for yourself. For example, your mum might have a friend in your chosen sector; your boss's cousin may know someone high up in graduate recruitment.

Self-assessment: Who could you meet?

Think of a personal hero and a key career contact you'd love to meet and identify the steps you could take to get in touch. Be creative! (Examples are provided for Bradley Wiggins, the cyclist, and the graduate recruitment manager at Ernst and Young.)

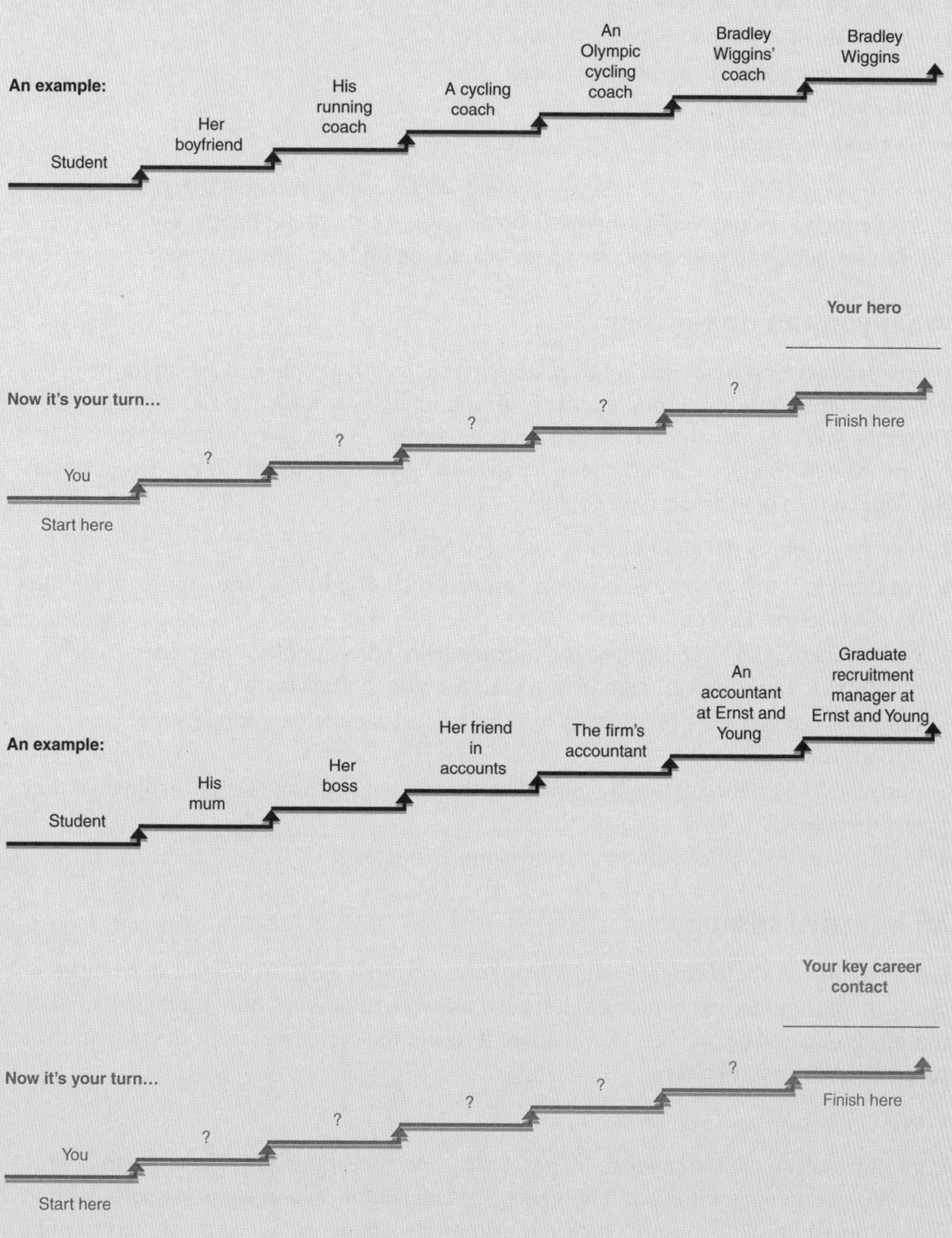

How your contacts can help

There are several ways your contacts can help you develop your career, limited only by your own creativity and imagination. For example, they could:

- Tell you what their careers are really like.
- Tell you what skills you'll need to succeed.
- Show you how to get your foot in the door.
- Let you shadow them at work or volunteer.
- Give you some employment experience.
- Offer you a graduate job.
- Give you more contacts.

Of course, only some of the people you contact will be willing and able to help but, if you contact enough people, you'll soon get a break. Even if a thousand people say no to your requests for help, you only need one to say yes, so the odds are always in your favour.

What you can do for them

Effective networking is not just about getting in touch with people and asking for help, it usually comes down to a simple process of 'you scratch my back and I'll scratch yours'. Therefore, you'll get much more help from your contacts if you give them an incentive to get involved. Before you contact them, try to creatively come up with some ideas for what you could offer. For example, you could:

- Help them with a difficult task on a voluntary basis.
- Put them in touch with other business contacts such as possible customers or academics running internship programmes.
- Provide them with a service in return for their help. For example, if they want to play more sport, you could let them play in your 5-a-side football team.
- Get involved with any projects they run to demonstrate their corporate social responsibility.
- Appeal to their better nature by reminding them of what it was like for them when they first graduated!
- Brighten up their office with your scintillating character.

An effective strategy

Just sending your CV to contacts and asking for a job rarely bears fruit because employers usually have thousands of similar requests and no work to offer! A more subtle networking strategy is outlined below. Feel free to adapt it to suit the sector you want to enter and your particular skills and interests.

1 Put out some feelers

Start off by asking your immediate friends, family and colleagues if they could help, then gradually get more ambitious and approach the acquaintances you know less well, such as your tutors and distant cousins. Once you gain more confidence ask your contacts to put you in touch with other people who might be able to help, and so on.

Another good approach is to get involved with activities and organisations where you have a good chance of meeting useful contacts. For example, you could:

- Join professional organisations connected to the career you want to enter and see what help they can provide. For example, the Chartered Institute of Marketing will put you in touch with mentors in your area and allow you to attend a range of networking events where you could rub shoulders with professionals in the field.
- Ask for help from relevant special interest groups such as the Royal National Institute of the Blind or the Women's Engineering Society.
- Join university student societies that have links with employers, such as your student law society.
- Get involved with any career-related activities at your university such as careers fairs and employer workshops and talks. These are usually advertised on your career service's website and are often open to graduates as well as students.
- Pursue your interests in relevant groups both on and off campus and see who you can meet. For example, if you're into wine, you could join some local wine-tasting groups and chat to wonderful contacts over a subtle Sancerre.

Don't worry if you struggle at first to network with new people; it takes practice. It's a great way to develop your professional communication skills and, on the whole, people are keen to help.

2 Ask for a chat

When you're introduced to new contacts or you meet people at events, ask if they can spare five minutes for a chat. Don't tell them you're looking for a job because this will probably scare them away; just say you're trying to find out more about their particular role. This is quite a simple request to grant and people will usually agree because they'll be flattered.

Don't just rely on your immediate contacts to talk to people on your behalf; you'll have much more success by getting people's details and taking the initiative yourself. This demonstrates your commitment and enables you to build closer relationships right from the start. It's also harder to say no to people in person! For example, if your friend's father is a barrister and you want to go into law, send his dad an email to ask if you can visit him in Chambers for a five-minute chat, and ask your friend to back you up.

One way to maximise your chances of success is to give your new contact various times when you could meet (but don't be too demanding). For example, you could say, 'I'm in London next week and can see you on Tuesday at 9.00 a.m., Wednesday at 2.00 p.m. or Thursday at 3.00 p.m. Which time works best for you?' This is an old salesman's technique to make your contacts think they don't have a choice!

During your meeting you could ask questions about what the job's like, what skills you'd need, how your contact got his or her career started and what he or she recommends for you. This last question can be very effective because they will probably suggest that you should get some employment experience and then won't be able to say no to your next request.

3 Shadow

Once you've met and impressed your new contact you could ask to shadow them for a day or two at work. This just involves hanging around to see what their job is really like. While you're at their workplace, be prompt, dress appropriately and demonstrate good manners with everyone you meet. Make sure you ask intelligent questions, help out where you can and show that you have a brain. Try to identify any specific tasks where you could lend a hand such as mundane jobs no one else wants to do or something related to your skills/degree. Then, you'll then be in a great position to make your next move.

4 Volunteer

"I decided to become a university careers adviser whilst running my own graduate recruitment agency in Perth, Western Australia. During this period I regularly liaised with all sorts of university personnel and thought the careers advisory role was fantastic. Therefore, I decided to join their ranks. However, instead of just immediately applying for jobs, I decided to plan and execute a strategy to get my foot in the door. My journey involved the following steps:

1. Building stronger relationships with the careers advisers I had got to know.
2. Shadowing them while they counselled students.
3. Volunteering to help.
4. Getting them to give me references.
5. Applying for a part-time position in the UK (where there were far more jobs). I chose Southampton because it's expensive and out of the way so I didn't think many people would apply.
6. I got the job.
7. I gained a full-time job up north.

This journey demonstrates my newfound wisdom at this stage in my life to take control of my next steps in life – not just look for interesting jobs and apply willy-nilly."

Steve Rook, author of this guide

Now you've formally met your contacts and seen what their businesses involve, offer to support them on a voluntary basis, especially if you've identified a specific project where you can make a difference. While you're there continue to impress and build rapport with colleagues so that, one day, they'll see you so often they'll offer you a pay cheque.

5 Employment experience/a graduate job

Of course, once you've got your foot in the door you can continue to impress and establish yourself as a valued member of the team, so that when a vacancy arises you will be in the right place at the right time and be offered the post.

This process is far more common than you might imagine and explains why over 50 per cent of jobs in the UK are never advertised.

And finally ...

Of course, every conversation you have won't lead to a graduate job, and more often than not you won't even get past stage 2, but every contact you make will help in some way and you never know when you'll get a lucky break. For example, you could have a five-minute chat with someone who can't help at all but knows a man who can. Whether an interaction is successful or not, ask everyone you meet to give you details of further contacts who might be able to help.

In the exercise below, develop your own network strategy, starting with your immediate current contacts and ending with a fulfilling career.

Self-assessment: Your networking strategy

Create your own specific networking strategy.

Who	What help you'll ask for
1	
2	
3	
4	
5	
6	

Networking online

Employers are increasingly putting more emphasis on social media in their graduate recruitment activities,[1] therefore it is becoming more and more important to build and maintain effective online contacts. After all, the links may be virtual, but the jobs are real!

It takes time to build up good online networks, so start early! This is because it takes a while to develop strong enough bonds with contacts so they'll be happy to lend a hand. Once you've developed some good contacts you can start asking for help in your career search. Advice on three key networking sites is provided below.

Facebook

This is primarily a social networking tool but it can also be used to establish some good job links. For example, it would be beneficial to join any groups linked to your past or current education (such as your school and university) and employers. You should also attempt to join any general student or graduate groups and employers/organisations linked to your chosen career where you can contact professionals. Make sure the groups are well used and popular by looking for activity on the recent news pages and the discussion board.

You can find interesting groups as follows:

- Look for local and national employers in your chosen sector.
- Join the groups to which your friends and existing contacts belong.
- Enter keywords such as "graphic designers", identifying the interesting groups that appear. If necessary, you can then also filter these groups according to particular categories such as "professional" or "common interest".
- Look at the related groups promoted by the Facebook groups you've already identified.
- Search on the Internet for "Facebook groups" "ANY KEYWORDS YOU WANT".

Once you've joined a group, don't just ask for a job straight out; start by gaining some rapport with active contributors by:

- Introducing yourself on the group's wall.
- Sharing interesting links.
- Gradually adding regular contacts as friends.
- Maintaining your high level of involvement.

LinkedIn

This is the key professional networking site and an especially useful tool for getting in touch with people from small and medium-sized enterprises, and therefore it's very surprising that fewer than 10 per cent[2] of students and graduates use it to get in touch with people![3]

The first thing you need to do on this site is create a profile. Maximise your input by ensuring that:

- You fill out all the sections and check that the site acknowledges you have done so (it will indicate that you have attained 100% completion).
- Your picture looks professional.
- Your profile is accurate, engaging and not too formal.
- There are no time gaps or spelling and grammar mistakes.
- Your goals are listed under your name if you're not currently in a relevant post.
- You include relevant keywords that get you noticed such as 'international nanny' or 'Corgi registered', but try to avoid clichés like 'extensive experience', 'dynamic' and 'motivated'.
- You effectively promote your university achievements and skills, using the 'More' tab and the 'Add Sections' bar.

You can also:

- Add your CV, any blogs you've written, relevant documents and presentations in order to get noticed and show off your work.
- Personalise your URL so it's more memorable.
- Make sure you regularly update what you've written. A good way to do this is to link your input to your professional Twitter account.

Once you've completed your profile you can make contacts by:

- Exporting your address book from your email account/s.
- Accepting the suggestions provided by LinkedIn.
- Identifying interesting connections amongst your existing contacts.

This approach should hopefully get you noticed by employers and recruiters. It is also beneficial to join relevant industry groups and organisations so you can:

- Contact interesting people without having to pass through human resources.
- Keep up to date with what's going on.
- Get involved with discussions.
- Identify interesting opportunities such as employment experience, conferences or networking events.

Twitter

The key attraction of Twitter in terms of networking is that it's an open network, i.e. you can contact anyone, anywhere. Many jobs and employment experience opportunities and internships are also advertised on the network. It is an especially useful tool for getting in touch with graduate employers and keeping up with what's going on and raising your profile, but make sure you connect your Twitter account to your professional LinkedIn profile so employers can find out more about you if they are so minded.

You can identify interesting employers, people and organisations through the search engine provided but, as with LinkedIn, you shouldn't just immediately ask for a job (however much you need one). Follow interesting people for a while so you can see what makes them tick, retweet interesting comments to raise your profile, and join in conversations, especially those that are relevant to graduate work opportunities.

Your online presence

Whether or not you decide to actively use your social networks to find a job, you should at least make sure that your online content isn't turning people off (at least – the right sort of people!). Here are some quick measures you can perform to clean up your image:

- Use a simple, conservative email address (not something like sexy_sue@...).
- As far as possible, separate your content into professional and personal profiles with different information (and pictures!). For example, on Facebook you could create two or more separate lists of friends with different levels of privacy.
- Look yourself up on Google and find any potentially offensive material, then do your best to get rid of it.

Finding out more

In this guide

- Searching for graduate jobs – Chapter 8.
- Cover letters that open doors – Chapter 12.
- This job's for you – Chapter 16.

On the companion website

- Extra networking suggestions.
- Extra networking exercises.

On the web

Extensive up-to-date links to further information in this area can be found on the companion website, including advice on using each of the major social networks.

What to do next

Get in touch with the most friendly – or least scary – contacts you can think of (or contacts of contacts) and see how easy it is to just say hello and ask for a chat. Take things easy and pretty soon you'll build up the confidence to contact anyone. Don't just approach clearly relevant people but say hello to as many contacts as you can think of and ask if they can recommend anyone who can help. After all, for all you know your old boss's paperboy's dad may be just the person you need to talk to, but you'll never find out if you don't ask!

Summary

- Networking is important as it gives you an idea of what your chosen career is like plus the skills to interact in that sector and unearth opportunities.
- All experience is beneficial, even if it isn't directly related to the career you want to break into, because you will develop key transferable skills.
- The key to networking is to realise that it's not just who you know that's important, but also, who they know.
- An effective strategy is to put out some feelers, then ask for a chat, shadow people at work, volunteer, gain employment experience and hopefully then secure a graduate job.
- Online networks are increasingly important – you should maximise your efforts using Facebook, LinkedIn and Twitter.

Chapter

6

Further study

"An investment in knowledge pays the best interest." *Benjamin Franklin*

Contents

- Is it right for me?
- Finding a course
- Choosing a course
- Funding
- Applying
- Making the most of the course
- Finding out more
- What to do next
- Summary

What you will gain from this chapter:

- **Decision making:** The capacity to decide whether further study is right for you and choose which course to take (if any).
- **Opportunity awareness:** The wherewithal to find appropriate courses.
- **Transition learning:** Some tips on finding and applying for courses and an appreciation of how further study may (or may not) lead to particular careers.
- **Self-awareness:** The ability to reflect on whether further study fits your career dreams and aspirations.

Is it right for me?

" I have studied two postgraduate courses – a Masters in Environmental Law and a Postgraduate Certificate in Education (PGCE).

I enjoyed my Masters and it has recently impressed employers but, at the time, I didn't use it effectively to further my career. I imagined the qualification would help me somehow but I put little thought into how. In retrospect, I should have networked more effectively with the leaders in the field who were teaching me and reflected on the skills I was gaining so I could target relevant roles.

I decided to become a primary school teacher after working for many years in the cash office of a music store in central London. I only got onto a PGCE course after volunteering for a year in a school during my time off from work. Now I'm a very happy and dedicated teacher.

Each of these experiences has given me a very favourable impression of further study, but also an appreciation of the benefits of planning how I'm going to make the most of the experience. ”

Susan Davies, Primary School Teacher

This chapter is designed to help you decide whether further study is right for you and plan your next steps accordingly.

The first key factor to appreciate is that postgraduate study does not automatically increase your chances of getting into a new career.

Further qualifications can certainly be a great way of developing your career – but only if they are part of a well thought through plan and strategy. If you're considering further study on the simple assumption that it's bound to help you get on, you're probably misleading yourself. For example, a Postgraduate Certificate of Education will help you get into teaching, or a Masters in Risk Assessment may help you find a relevant role in the City, but extra qualifications will not automatically improve your chances of gaining entry into many graduate training programmes. This is simply because, as stated throughout this guide, employers are generally more concerned with your grades, skills and employment experience than what you know.

Typical motivations for taking up further study are outlined below along with advice on what you should consider in each situation. Once you've read through the list, identify your personal motivations in the exercise provided and list the specific factors you need to consider in choosing whether further study is right for you.

Usual motivations

Studying a subject you love: This is a pure and noble reason for signing up for a new course, and it's hard to knock it. However, you should determine whether you can afford another course and whether it fits in with your career plans. You may also consider studying your chosen subject in your own time, for example on an evening course.

Buying more time: After a lifetime in education it can be very difficult to face your next steps but this should not be your deciding factor in staying put.

Studying at a favoured college/studying overseas: This is a lifestyle choice that may prove to be very fulfilling, but make sure the course is beneficial, especially if you want to use an overseas qualification back in the UK.

Refocusing your career: One reason for taking up postgraduate study is to go into a new field. This is a risky decision, so make sure your chosen qualification will actually help and that it is accredited by the appropriate professional body. Good conversion courses are a real plus if you want to enter some professional sectors such as journalism and IT; however, relevant employment experience is often more useful, even if the role you want to enter is unconnected to your first degree.

Freshening up your qualifications: This is a common motive for graduates who have been away from university for a while and are unhappy with their lot. They often sign up for a course in the hope that a further qualification will reboot their careers and give employers a new respect for what they have to offer. If this is your plan, make sure the extra qualifications will be useful and dedicate yourself to readjusting to the student life.

Getting a professional qualification: Many professions such as teaching and clinical psychology require further professional qualifications. If you're considering this route, make sure you're happy with your career choice before applying and consider whether it's worth taking some time out first to get some relevant experience.

Undertaking ongoing professional training: Further study can really help you to develop your career once you've already started. For example, you may want to study a certain aspect of your profession in greater detail. This can be a great way to move forward, especially if you agree your options with your managers.

Making up for a disappointing first degree: Further qualifications may persuade recruiters that your previous poor grades were a glitch, but most of the larger employers will not have the flexibility to consider your personal situation and will still focus on the marks you gained in your first degree. Some people even consider starting another undergraduate degree if they didn't enjoy their original course but, again, employers will still focus on your original grades. Furthermore, if you have already completed one and a half years of an undergraduate degree you'll be liable for the full fees up front.

Becoming an academic: If you are considering staying on at university to become a lecturer or researcher, make sure you look at the pros and cons of this career route as you would any other before making a decision. In other words, don't just start a PhD because an academic has told you how wonderful you are and asked for your help.

Studying overseas

There are many benefits to upping sticks and studying in another country, such as:

- Learning about another culture, lifestyle and educational system at first hand.
- Developing international experience, foreign language capabilities and a global perspective so that you stand out.
- Working in an internationally recognised faculty or institution.
- Moving lock, stock and barrel to another country (if this is your passion).
- Saving some money (overseas courses are often cheaper, as is the cost of living).

Obviously, English-speaking nations such as the USA and Australia teach in English as do many institutions across Europe and Asia.

If you're considering this route make sure you know exactly what you're letting yourself in for and, if possible, try to speak to British people who have already studied at the institution you are interested in. Also, check that you can use the qualification back in the UK. If you're still at university, you should also consider studying in Europe as part of your undergraduate course. You can find out more on the Erasmus website (www.britishcouncil.org/erasmus.htm).

Now you've seen the common motivations for taking up further study, identify yours in the following exercise.

Self-assessment: What's your motivation?

Identify your top three motivations for considering postgraduate study and the factors you should therefore consider before signing up.

Your top three study motivations	The factors you should consider
• ______________________ ______________________	• ______________________ ______________________
• ______________________ ______________________	• ______________________ ______________________
• ______________________ ______________________	• ______________________ ______________________

Finding a course

Postgraduate study in general

- Hotcourses Abroad directory of courses in the UK and overseas, including English-language courses in other countries: www.hotcoursesabroad.com/sitemap.html
- Prospects' course directory: www.prospects.ac.uk/search_courses.htm
- Target courses: http://targetcourses.co.uk
- Individual institution course directories, which are typically available on their websites.
- Courses overseas: www.prospects.ac.uk/country_profiles.htm

Taught courses

Taught Masters courses (MA, MSc, etc.) are the most common postgraduate study option. They generally last for one year, full time (or two years, part time). You can either focus on a favoured aspect of your undergraduate degree or take up a conversion course in a subject specifically related to a particular area such as magazine editing or human resources. Either way, most course providers will expect good grades in your initial degree. See the links above to find some that suit you.

Vocational courses

You can study professional courses in everything from acting to youth work. It is also possible to train for certain roles such as medicine through accelerated postgraduate courses. However, you should keep in mind that new qualifications do not automatically get you a job! Courses can be short if only a diploma or certificate is required but they usually take a year or more to complete.

Applications for work-related qualifications are usually made through central application bodies. Some of the bodies are listed below but you'll also find more on the companion website.

- Teaching: the Graduate Teacher Training Registry at www.gttr.ac.uk
- Becoming a solicitor: www.lawcabs.com
- Medicine/Dentistry/Social work: www.ucas.com
- Clinical psychology: the Clearing House for Postgraduate Courses in Clinical Psychology at www.leeds.ac.uk/chpccp
- Speech therapy: the Health and Care Professions Council at www.hpc-uk.org/apply
- Journalism: the National Council for the Training of Journalists at www.nctj.com/accredited/course-application-forms

Masters by Research (MRes)

These typically last up to two years and combine taught courses with intensive training in research methodology. They are often taken as a precursor to a career in research. You can usually find these opportunities on individual university websites or on the FindAMasters international masters directory: www.findamasters.com

Doctorates (PhDs)

PhDs take three years or more to complete and are usually the first step to a career in research. They involve new research in a specific field resulting in a thesis and oral exam (viva). New route PhDs combine research with discipline-specific and generic training in a wide range of subjects including biological sciences and political studies. You can find traditional PhDs by discovering where your favoured research is being undertaken and approaching academics (start at your own institution). You can also find them at FindAPhD international directory of research programmes: www.findaphd.com. Start looking for new route PhDs at www.newroutephd.ac.uk

Masters in Business Administration (MBAs)

One-year courses primarily tailored for graduates who already have experience and want to develop careers in management. You can start looking for them at:

- Top MBA directory: www.topmba.com/business-schools.
- *Financial Times* rankings: search on http://rankings.ft.com.

Short courses

Learn specific skills linked to the sector you want to enter, such as web authoring software or bookkeeping. Local councils organise a wide range of courses at different times and venues in your local area such as schools, colleges and village halls. You can usually find these on your local council's website.

Choosing a course

You can apply a number of filters to your course shortlist in order to identify the best one for you, as follows:

- Check which institutions will accept your grades.
- See which locations you prefer (or can afford).
- See which courses most closely match your academic/professional objectives. Read the prospectus and contact the appropriate admissions tutors to find out.
- Check each course's reputation: look them up on the website of the Research Assessment Exercise (RAE) (www.rae.ac.uk/results), which will be replaced by the Research Excellence Framework in 2014 (check on www.vitae.ac.uk). You could also ask for direction from research staff in your own department.
- Ascertain each course's employment prospects: speak to the admissions tutors and relevant supervisors to find out where past graduates have ended up.
- If you're planning on undertaking a PhD, check out each of the departments and supervisors. For example, visit them and see how supportive they're likely to be; compare each department and supervisor's enrolments over the last five years with the number of doctorates they have awarded (to assess their success rates); see which supervisors have had supervisor training and find out how long each supervisor is prepared to spend with you.

Self-assessment: Which course is for you?

Do a little research and identify three dream postgraduate courses of any kind.

The courses	Where they are?
• ______________________	• ______________________
• ______________________	• ______________________
• ______________________	• ______________________

Now that you've identified some really attractive courses, ask yourself if you should sign up for one of them. Will it help your career? Is this the right time in your life? Will you have to compromise because you don't have the grades or the money?

Funding

Postgraduate qualifications are funded differently from undergraduate study. The bad news is that the Student Loan Company will not generally fund postgraduate study, so you'll have to personally bear a greater burden of the costs and, of course, you'll also have to support yourself. However, the full picture is extremely varied depending on what you study and where. If you are considering a certain type of course, you should start by contacting your favoured course providers to see what funding is available. The more common sources of finance are listed below.

The Bank of Mum and Dad

Well – if they've paid your way so far, they may well go one step further just to get you out of their hair. Of course, you may also be able to contribute your own savings.

Institutional funding

Research Councils provide funding to university departments for a number of research and taught programmes. Institutions also offer a number of scholarships, research assistantships and teaching assistantships, where they pay your fees and provide you with a salary for undertaking specific duties. If you cannot gain access to these funds at the outset of your course, don't worry too much because you'll probably have a good chance of picking up some sort of salary as the years go by. Opportunities are advertised on www.jobs.ac.uk and www.postgraduatestudentships.co.uk. You should also contact the department where you want to study.

Bursaries and grants

These may be available for vocational courses such as social work and a range of healthcare courses. Check with the relevant professional group responsible for applications in your chosen field; some of these are shown above in the 'Vocational courses' section and on the companion website. A number of universities themselves also offer grants to students in certain situations, such as those with no family history of HE. Universities in the United States typically have a number of grants you can access as an international student. Contact the institutions themselves to see what's on offer.

Charities and trusts

A number of charitable organisations will support your study: for example, the Royal National Institute for the Blind has funds available for blind students. However, charities can usually only give you a few hundred pounds at most. You can find relevant grant providers at www.fundingeducation.co.uk and www.scholarship-search.org.uk.

Employer-funded study

Training budgets are usually quite tight nowadays, but if you can make a good argument as to why further study will improve your performance, you will probably get your employer to stump up some of the funds.

Professional and career development loans

If all other avenues fail, you could also apply for a Professional and Career Development Loan. These are commercial bank loans that can be used to assist with work-related learning. The interest is paid while you're studying, but afterwards you will still have to pay the loans back on full commercial terms. You can find out about these loans on www.direct.gov.uk.

Applying

Depending on the course, you need to apply either directly to the institution or to a central clearing house. Applications often open very early (up to 11 months in advance) and places can fill up quickly, so you need to be on the ball. Therefore, you should clearly ascertain where, how and when you need to apply at least a year before the course starts. If you don't have this amount of time, you can look for late opportunities or get some experience and apply for the following year's intake. Some courses will still be open right up to the starting date (or even beyond) – but you have to ask yourself why they are so unpopular!

Personal statement

As with your undergraduate application, you will probably be asked to complete a statement to back up your application. Here, you should clearly and systematically address what's required. For example, you may be asked to outline why you want to take up the particular course and what you can offer, or outline your relevant skills and experience. If no specific request is made and you are simply asked to write a personal statement, outline your skills, knowledge and commitment (why you want to study the course) and prove each through your relevant academic/professional experience. This will demonstrate to course providers that you will succeed on the course.

For example, the following personal statement is for a taught Masters course on 'Politics in the USA'.

Address the specific attributes required and stick to the word limit

Please outline your relevant skills, commitment and knowledge (500 words)

Introduce your statement – not yourself

Thank you for discussing this stimulating course when I visited you last month. I particularly enjoyed sharing everyone's enthusiasm and genuine love for the subject. In the following paragraphs I have systematically addressed why I have the specific skills, commitment and knowledge to succeed and add value to your department.

Relate each personal statement to the specific skills required in each different application

My relevant skills are an ability to conduct in-depth qualitative and quantitative social science research, good written communication, teamwork, flexibility and focus. I recently demonstrated these attributes by gaining 73% in my undergraduate dissertation where I juxtaposed the hope and promise presented by President Kennedy's inauguration with the compromise that marked his tenure. To fully explore this subject I was able to draw from hard copy and online resources both in the UK and the USA and direct testimony from a number of influential US politicians and journalists such as Senator Alan Dixon and Bob Woodward.

Outline *how* you demonstrate each of the skills required and give specific examples of when you have demonstrated them

My writing style is positive and accurate and I clearly convey complicated theories and concepts through short sentences and focused paragraphs. I have demonstrated these skills in a number of essays during my undergraduate study and as editor of my university's student newspaper. In teams, I can be relied on to listen to colleagues and encourage them to succeed: for example, when I worked closely with three colleagues in the Enterprise Society at university to win the National Student Enterprise Award. My flexibility and focus are best demonstrated by my ability to maintain high grades at university whilst balancing a range of technical jobs and outside interests such as website development and writing historical articles for several publications.

My commitment to this course is demonstrated in four key ways:

Use bullet points, but don't overdo them

- My passion for the subject.
- My longstanding interest and proactive drive to study US politics during my secondary and tertiary education.
- My recent visit to the department where I discussed the programme with Professor Tim Loghley and Doctor Franks.
- My clarity over the specific modules I will choose, i.e. Nationalism, The Senate and The Recent Presidents.

Show that you have researched the course

Use a simple structure including a straightforward introduction, paragraphs for each of your attributes and a summary

Having studied US politics during my A levels, degree and in my spare time, my relevant knowledge is extensive. For example, I understand the federal political system, the checks and balances on the power of the President, and the drivers of parties and factions such as the Democrats, the Tea Party and the Grand Old Party.

In summary, I have the research and communication skills to succeed on this course as well as a burning ambition and the appropriate knowledge. I look forward to hearing from you soon. Please feel free to contact me by phone or email if you have any questions.

Making the most of the course

Making plans

Whatever your motives for taking up further study, you should continually assess whether you're still getting the most out of it. For example, ask yourself if you're working hard enough, enjoying yourself, studying your favourite aspects of the subject and meeting interesting people.

Whether or not your career is uppermost in your mind at this moment, the course will soon come to an end and you'll have to move on, so you should carefully plan for this eventuality. One way to do this is to pretend that you're actually finishing tomorrow, figure out where you would like to be going and set specific goals so you can gradually get there. For example, if you want to be a teacher, you could quickly ascertain where you want to work, the skills you need to develop, when you should apply, how to put together effective applications and with whom you could network.

You should start planning as soon as possible because important dates often occur early on in your study. For example, if you sign up for a Masters and you then want to apply for a graduate training programme, you'll need to apply as soon as you start!

Networking

One of the hidden benefits of further study is the opportunity to meet interesting people. The contacts you make during your further study are at least as likely to open doors as what you have learnt, especially if you want to go into academia or a related industry. Make sure you take advantage of this chance to network, whether it's for career reasons or just to chat to people you admire. You can do this by:

- Asking for their help in your research.
- Asking your tutors to introduce you to interesting contacts.

- Getting involved in the wider activities of your department.
- Getting involved in the wider research community allied to your subject.
- Meeting employers who visit your department and university.

Finding out more

In this guide

- Planning your journey – Chapter 3.
- Promoting yourself effectively – Chapter 9.
- Tip-top application forms – Chapter 11.

On the companion website

Further examples of personal statements for postgraduate study.

On the web

You can find number of useful links on the companion website to dedicated postgraduate portals such as those provided by Kent University, the Open University and Prospects.

What to do next

- Consider whether further study fits your career strategy and, if so, choose a course which meets your objectives.
- Fit your study plans as seamlessly as possible into your general career journey: make sure it dovetails with your efforts to find experience and new networks.

Summary

- Further qualifications do not automatically enhance your career prospects.
- People have numerous motivations for considering further study, from avoiding the real world to gaining specific vocational qualifications. It's worth identifying your motives and seriously considering whether it's for you.
- There are a number of options including taught Masters, vocational courses, Masters by Research, PhDs, MBAs and short courses.
- Courses are listed on a number of online databases.
- Choose your course carefully by making sure it is well regarded and will deliver your specific objectives.
- Funding is often difficult, but you may be able to get scholarships, bursaries and assistantships as well as commercial loans.
- In your applications, design effective personal statements that address the specific attributes required.
- Make the most of your time on the course by planning carefully, monitoring your progress and building contacts.

Chapter

7

Taking time out

"Time is the wisest counsellor of all." *Pericles*

Contents

What you will gain from this chapter:

- **Decision making:** The confidence to choose appropriate 'time out' activities.
- **Opportunity awareness:** The vision to see a wide range of options.
- **Transition learning:** An appreciation of how to make the most your time out and promote what you've learnt.
- **Self-awareness:** The ability to identify why you want to take time out and reflect on what you learn on your journey.

Finding perspective

Time out can be another useful stepping stone on your way into a career because it can help you see all your options and give you some perspective at what can be such a confusing time. This chapter shows you how to make the most of your time away and outlines a range of possible activities.

Making the most of the experience

A good general guide would be to plan ahead, keep track of how things are going, look out for new opportunities and make sure you return at the right time to kick-start your career. For example, if you decide to apply for a graduate training programme or further study on your return, you probably need to be in the country from October onwards with plenty of time on your hands.

In more specific terms, it can help to clarify why you want to get away and to plan your trip accordingly. Various motives are discussed in the table below; see which ones relate to you.

Your reasons for taking time out	How you can make the most of the experience
You just need to rest and have some fun!	What a pure and noble motive – and you deserve it! If this sounds like you, don't just pick the first idea that comes along, ask yourself what you'd really love to do and look for appropriate opportunities, even if it's just sitting on a beach for two months! In terms of your career, you could take stock of what you actually enjoy during your break: it might be quite revealing. For example, you could find out if you prefer being alone or with friends, organised or haphazard, active or passive, and so on. In this way, your time out will help you appreciate more about what makes you tick; appropriate careers will then start to stand out.
You want to get away from things so you come up with some career ideas	While you're away, keep your eyes open and chat to people about what they're going to do when they get back. Many of the people you'll be interacting with will be in the same position as you and you may find they have some incisive observations (especially in front of a campfire with a cask of wine!).
You've planned your next steps in life but want a break	In this situation, the first thing to do is to make sure you get back in time to set yourself up properly for your next step. However, you could also find ways to develop the skills and contacts you'll need upon your return and look for opportunities to develop them. See the quote below from Jenny Archielle.
You want to get some useful experience	Figure out the sort of experience you want and look for relevant opportunities. You don't need to restrict your search to organised gap year opportunities; you could do your own research and contact people yourself before you leave. For example, see the quote below from Grace Lander. When you promote your experience to employers, make sure you stress your initiative in making it happen as this will help you stand out.
You can't find any decent work and are sick of doing nothing	If you're in a rut then it can be a great idea to completely change your lifestyle so you can view your problems from a new angle and see new solutions. However, make sure you use this energy when you return to your previous life (if you return) and don't just fall back to the same old ways.

"Working in retail is fulfilling but full-on. Once you start you are on a treadmill to greater things but there's no chance to get off, so enjoy yourself and travel before you start so you can focus on your job when you eventually get going."
Jenny Archielle, Graduate working in retail

"As part of my degree in Wildlife Conservation with Zoo Biology I was given the opportunity to spend a year in industry. I decided to pursue a perfect placement somewhere interesting. I chose three months in Key West, Florida and six months in Anchorage, Alaska (USA). By finding something for myself, I could really tailor what I got up to. In both Key West and Alaska I lived onsite at an animal rehabilitation centre which was a lot of responsibility!

The best part of tailoring something for yourself is choosing what you want to do and how you want to do it. Just make sure you agree terms with your employer in writing so you get as much out of your trip as possible. Due to USA visa requirements I couldn't be paid for my work, so saving up enough to fund the internships was a challenge. The upside is that when you offer yourself up to work for free people really appreciate the work you're doing and it looks great on your CV.

The most valuable experience I gained was the time spent learning veterinary procedures and techniques with the team in Alaska. Getting that sort of experience, even as a volunteer in the UK, is next to impossible. It was a fantastic opportunity to get really involved helping with surgical procedures and after-care. Public educational presentations in Alaska gave me the opportunity to work with live eagles, owls and other birds. While the public speaking practice was great, I was also trained in bird handling, a unique skill on my CV! Liaising with the public in both locations and educating large groups about wildlife and nature has given me the confidence to apply for jobs in wildlife education, a passion which was seeded during my placement."
Grace Lander, Recent graduate (1st class)

Now try it for yourself in the following self-assessment.

Self-assessment: Your time out

Identify two things you want to gain from your time away and suggest how you can make them happen.

What you want to gain	How you could make it happen
•	•
•	•

Where to go and what to do

You can go nowhere, anywhere or everywhere. Some backpackers visit a specific region whilst others get a round-the-world ticket and head off in search of adventure. The choice is yours. Some common destinations are France, Italy, Asia, Australia, the USA and Canada.

You can also do anything you want during your time away (if you can find the money). For example, you could learn French in New Caledonia, help children in Bogotá or teach English in Laos. What would you love to do?

Self-assessment: Your dream time out activities

Some typical time out activities are shown below. Identify three dream options of your own.

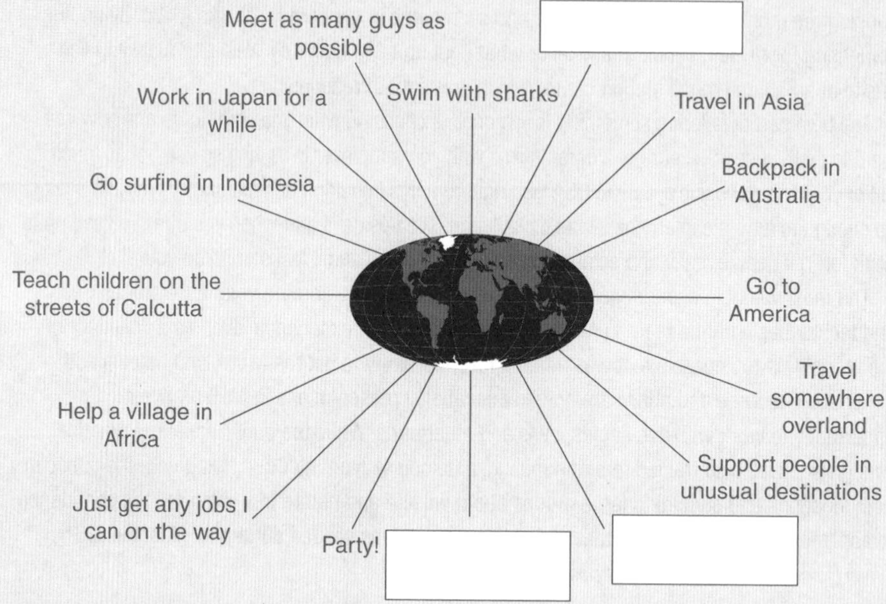

Options at home

Getting more experience

Find out about voluntary and paid experiences in the UK in Chapter 4.

Developing your hobbies

Many of us develop strong interests as we grow up but can never devote enough time to them because we're caught up in the rat race. This is your chance to cast off your shackles and focus on yourself for a while. Who knows – you may even find a really fulfilling career or a business idea. For example, you could learn French by working in a café in the French Riviera, develop your Taekwondo skills at an internationally acclaimed school or learn to fly a plane. Any one of these activities could lead to thousands of fulfilling roles.

Looking after relatives

Having relied on support from your family and friends to get through your degree, you may want to give something back. For example, you could look after your sister's infants whilst she looks for work, or care for your ailing grandfather. Carers can get an allowance from the government for their effort and this could be your chance to cement your family's future. Find out more at www.carers.org.

Going down the pub

It's quite natural to let your hair down once you've finally got your degree and you certainly deserve a rest, but be careful that your time out from the rat race isn't just an excuse to totally 'Turn on, tune in, drop out'.[1] If you're not happy with any of the careers you've considered, get out there and find one that gets you excited (see Chapter 2).

Options abroad

Overseas adventures are very popular because of the opportunity to travel, see the world and get some employment experience. You have the option to travel independently and organise your own activities or sign up for an organised 'gap year' programme. The advantages of organising your own journey are that you can be the master of your own trip and identify unique activities and destinations. The key benefit of signing up for an organised programme is that many of the administrative details will be sorted out for you so you don't need to worry about a thing.

Employers usually look favourably on applicants who have taken time out, especially if they've made the best of their time away and developed some key employability skills, such as a sense of responsibility, an ability to communicate and the capacity to manage their own affairs.

Part of the attraction of this journey is that there are an infinite number of things to do and places to see. Some of the more common destinations and activities are outlined below.

Teaching English

English is easily the world's dominant second language. Therefore, if you have good spelling and grammar, you could use your mother tongue to find some interesting work. If you're looking for casual work or voluntary opportunities, you can just approach overseas English language schools before you travel or once you've landed, but you will have much more chance of success if you take a formal TEFL qualification (teaching English as a foreign language) and sign a contract (for a year or two) before you leave.

TEFL qualifications come in all shapes and sizes, but most schools around the world will expect you to have a postgraduate certificate incorporating 120 hours of study and practice. Many British TEFL students take the Certificate of English Language Teaching to Adults (CELTA) awarded by Cambridge ESOL (see www.cambridgeesol.org) or the Certificate in Teaching English to Speakers of Other Languages (Cert. TESOL) awarded by Trinity College London (see www.trinitycollege.co.uk). These qualifications can be studied online or at numerous venues throughout the country and overseas.

Common teaching destinations include China, Japan, South Korea, Brazil and numerous countries in Europe. The following websites will give you a good idea of what you're in for:

- Cactus TEFL: www.cactustefl.com – Everything from information and advice to jobs and a useful blog.
- Esl Base Teach English: www.eslbase.com – Good all-round guide with a useful glossary of terms.
- University of Kent Careers and Employability Service: www.kent.ac.uk/careers/tefl.htm – Extensive list of useful resources.
- Japan Exchange & Teaching Programme: www.jet-uk.org – Long-term teaching positions in Japan.

Harvesting/agricultural work

Everything you eat is produced somewhere and someone has to grow it, pick it and send it on its way. Therefore, at any one time, there are a great number of temporary agricultural jobs on offer. For example, in Australia, some sort of fruit or vegetable is harvested every month of the year, such as capsicums (peppers), lychees, tomatoes, melons and mangoes. This is backbreaking work but you can usually camp out and have plenty of fun while you're doing it.

If you have other farming skills you could also pick up more professional work on a farm or ranch. For example, if you can ride a horse, maybe you could become a cowboy/jackaroo! Any research you do before you leave will be time well spent and it will probably be worth contacting individual farmers and orchard growers. These websites are useful:

- Lonely Planet's blog: www.lonelyplanet.com/thorntree/index.jspa.
- Official guide to fruit picking in Australia: http://jobsearch.gov.au/harvesttrail/.
- Calendar of fruit picking jobs in Australia: www.fruitpicking.org/fruit-picking-essentials/crops-calendar.
- Picking Jobs: www.pickingjobs.com – Fruit-picking jobs across the world.

Volunteering

> "Whilst backpacking in northern Thailand many years ago I bumped into some volunteer workers in a hostel. They were performing a number of supporting tasks in a refugee centre on the Thai–Myanmar border. I asked if I could come along and help. They agreed and I spent the next two months teaching English to enthusiastic children. It was a wonderful experience and later gave me the motivation to become a primary school teacher.
>
> I'm so glad I got involved, not least because the experience eventually gave me an idea of what to do in life!"
>
> *Steve Rook, author of this guide*

There are millions of charities across the globe. You just need to find one that matches your interests and offer your services. You can either do this in advance or turn up unannounced. One simple way to find opportunities is just to Google what you want to do and where – for example, a simple search for "Calcutta charities" comes up with 43,400,000 results including the following:

- Calcutta Hope: www.calcuttahope.org.
- Mother Teresa of Calcutta Center: www.motherteresa.org.

- Calcutta Rescue: www.calcuttarescue.org.
- Calcutta Children Charity: www.calcuttachildren.org.

Here are some other useful links:

- Charity Choice: www.charitychoice.co.uk – Database of UK charities in different sectors.
- Wikipedia: http://en.wikipedia.org/wiki/Main_Page – Search for "worldwide list of charities"
- VSO: www.vso.org.uk.
- The British Council's European Volunteer Service: www.britishcouncil.org/youthinaction.
- UNICEF: www.unicef.org.uk.
- Lattitude Global Volunteering: www.lattitude.org.uk.
- Volunteer Abroad: www.volunteerabroad.com – Worldwide experiences.
- Volunteer South America: www.volunteersouthamerica.net – Opportunities in South America.
- Oyster Worldwide: www.oysterworldwide.com – Paid and voluntary worldwide placements.
- Working Abroad: www.workingabroad.com – Find organisations that match your needs.
- Ecoteer: www.ecoteer.com – International opportunities offering food and board.

Nannying/au pairing

Look after wealthy people and their children either in the UK or overseas and get paid for the privilege. Also, play your cards right and you might even get to live in the family mansion! Being an au pair is a more general household role whilst nannies are typically more professional child-minders who often have good references and relevant qualifications such as a level three diploma in home-based childcare. Find work by contacting agencies that have vacancies where you want to work (either here in the UK or overseas). The website for the Association of Nanny Agencies provides advice on training and finding work at www.anauk.org. These are a few of the agencies in the UK and the USA:

- Gap 360: www.gap360.com/work-au-pair-america.
- Royal Nannies: www.royalnannies.co.uk.
- UK Nannies and Au Pairs: www.uknanniesandaupairs.com.
- Nanny Job: www.nannyjob.co.uk.
- Au Pair in America: www.aupairinamerica.com.
- America's Nannies: www.americasnannies.com.

Gap year placements/projects

A massive industry has grown up in recent years offering all sorts of exotic trips and placements across the globe, usually to help disadvantaged groups in some way. For example, you could help build a school in Gambia or look after some tropical reefs in the Caribbean. These packages are usually quite expensive but they deliver some amazing projects so, if you have the money, they're certainly worth considering. However, as with all business transactions, it's up to you to make sure everything's above board. For example, you should check out whether the projects you're considering will actually help the local groups they propose to serve (many don't) or indeed whether they will deliver the experiences you're expecting. Try to dig deeper than the shiny marketing documents by researching the firm online, seeing how long they've been in business, discussing them with relevant professional organisations and chatting to previous customers. Some popular organisations are listed below:

- Raleigh International: www.raleighinternational.org.
- Year Out Group: www.yearoutgroup.org.
- Personal Overseas Development: www.podvolunteer.org.
- i to i Volunteering: www.i-to-i.com.
- Worldwide Volunteering: www.wwv.org.uk.
- The Gapyear Company: www.gapyear.com.
- Real Gap Experience: www.realgap.co.uk.

Working at theme parks/resorts

Theme parks and resorts rely on students and new graduates to keep the doors open. There are usually numerous roles open to hardworking individuals, ranging from cleaning chalets and washing dishes to entertaining clients and running activities for children. Typical jobs can be found by contacting resorts directly or on websites such as the following:

- Resort work: www.resortwork.co.uk.
- Resort jobs: www.resortjobs.co.uk.

Helping out at events

If watching the tangerine and aubergine 'games makers' at the London 2012 Olympics inspired you, why not follow suit? Major music, sporting and cultural events regularly occur across the globe and many of them rely on temporary and volunteer workers. This is a great chance to take part in a vibrant activity closely linked to your personal interests and meet lots of like-minded people. Major sporting events include the Summer and Winter Olympics and the football and rugby world cups. Music events include the Roskilde Festival in Denmark and the Big Day Out in Australia. The best way forward here is to look at the websites running the events that interest you well in advance and see what they've got to offer. Some useful sites listing European festivals and events are shown below:

- E Festivals: www.efestivals.co.uk/info/working.shtml.
- EVENT JOBS: www.event-jobs.net.
- PAAM: www.paamapplication.co.uk/blog/2011/03/10/how-to-work-at-music-festivals-and-who-to-contact.
- BugBog: www.bugbog.com/festivals/european_festivals.html.

Summer camps

This is where you look after children or disabled people who are on holiday, especially in the USA. This work involves a range of roles from cleaning and cooking to teaching, counselling and running activities. In return you are typically given accommodation and a small wage. The following organisations offer a number of programmes around the globe:

- BUNAC: www.bunac.org.
- CCUSA: www.ccusa.com.
- Camp America: www.campamerica.co.uk.
- Lourdes volunteers: www.lourdesvolunteers.org.

Anything and everything

A large number of backpackers just get any work they can to pay their rent. For example, a quick survey of gap year travellers in a Sydney hostel in late 2012 reveals that the following roles were being undertaken:

- Bicycle courier
- Waitress
- Bar tender
- Bouncer
- Office temp.
- Lifeguard
- Shop assistant
- Telesales
- Driver
- Mechanic
- Marketing assistant
- Accountant
- Teacher

Finding work

There are three basic ways to find opportunities during your time out – these are outlined below.

Putting out feelers

If you're travelling, one effective way to get work is to contact people at your destination before you leave and discuss any roles that may be available. For example, if you're an experienced theatrical props-maker, why not contact theatres in the towns you'll be visiting and chat about any upcoming productions? Then you can visit your new contacts when you arrive and hopefully they'll throw some work your way.

Preparing your way

If you're a particularly organised traveller you may find it too daunting to look for work once you get to your destination. Therefore, sort out as many opportunities as you can before you leave. For example, you could sign up for a summer camp or a gap year project. The advantages of this approach are that you can carefully plan a rewarding experience and you'll be safe because you'll be working with like-minded people under the auspices of a reliable organisation. The downside is that you may not enjoy the project you've organised and have no time to try anything else. Therefore, it may be best to find a balance. Design an itinerary with specific planned activities but also leave enough time to go with the flow.

On the ground

A large number of backpackers haphazardly look for work once they arrive at their destination. Luckily, employers are often attracted to this supply of cheap labour and opportunities abound. You can often find work by:

- Asking at local hostels.
- Asking fellow backpackers.
- Looking at backpacker websites and magazines.
- Buying local papers.
- Scanning shop windows.
- Using social networks.
- Registering with local job agencies.

Where to stay

- If you're going on an organised trip either in the UK or overseas, rudimentary accommodation will probably already be organised. Otherwise, you'll probably have to stay in a rented flat, backpacker's hostel, hotel or tent.
- Hostels are a great place to stay and meet people, but you'll probably have to share a dormitory with three or four other people who snore and have a strange fascination for plastic bags at three o clock in the morning! Some hostels are party central, others are filled with workers who want to get to bed early, and official Youth Hostels are often quiet and clean, so choose your accommodation carefully.

Visas

Backpackers bring much-needed revenue so you can usually get into most countries fairly easily. However, each embassy and consulate will have its own unique rules and procedures, so it's often better to get your visas sorted out before you leave home (although this is not always possible). Agencies such as Trailfinders (www.trailfinders.com) will get visas for you for a fee but it's easy enough to organise them yourself. Working visa information on some popular regions and countries is shown below.

Europe

UK citizens can freely work in any European Economic Area country, which includes:

- Austria
- Belgium
- Bulgaria
- Cyprus
- Czech Republic
- Denmark
- Estonia
- Finland
- France
- Germany
- Greece
- Holland
- Hungary
- Iceland
- Ireland
- Italy
- Latvia
- Liechtenstein
- Lithuania
- Luxembourg
- Malta
- Norway
- Poland
- Portugal
- Romania
- Slovakia
- Slovenia
- Spain
- Sweden

Australia

British travellers who are under 30 years of age can work for up to a year in Australia. See www.immi.gov.au/visitors/working-holiday/417

New Zealand

British travellers who are under 30 years of age can work for up to 23 months in New Zealand. See www.immigration.govt.nz

Canada

British travellers who are under 35 years of age can work for up to a year in Canada via the International Experience Program, but get in early in autumn because places are limited! See www.canadainternational.gc.ca

The USA

You can work under a range of visas including the J1 (Exchange) visa which allow you to take up temporary work when you've just finished your degree in roles such as any casual work, camp counselling or internships. However, you must sign up for the visa through a recognised sponsor such as BUNAC, CCUSA or CIEE. A list of sponsors can be found at http://j1visa.state.gov/participants/how-to-apply/sponsor-search; why not contact them and see what help they can provide?

Promoting what you've learnt

When you're ready to move on in your career, you'll have to demonstrate the skills you've gained during your time out to employers and/or course providers. You should do this by identifying the skills required in the job or the course you're going for and outlining how you performed them during your time away. See Chapters 9–16 for more details.

Many backpackers come back thinking they've learnt nothing more than how to drink, party and sleep on a beach, but when you reflect on what you've done you'll see that you also developed some useful life skills. For example, if an employer requires an ability to work in teams you could prove this through your part in projects such as building a new school in the developing world.

Finding out more

In this guide

- Planning your journey – Chapter 3.
- Experience and internships – Chapter 4.

On the companion website

Examples of how you can sell your time out experience in applications and interviews.

On the web

A wide range of links are listed throughout this chapter, and you may also want to look at the up-to-date links on the companion website to organisations such as Prospects and various gap year organisations.

What to do next

If this chapter whets your appetite and you want to take some time out, see how you can fit a gap year into your future plans. You might decide to head off straight away for a few months, or get qualified and then head for the airport. Be careful, though, and consider these three things which may stop you from travelling as you get older:

- A reduced willingness to put up with bed bugs.
- A job and career you can't leave.
- A family.

Summary

- Taking time out from the career planning process can give you perspective on what you could do next.
- There are an infinite number of options both at home and abroad including developing your hobbies, looking after relatives, teaching English, harvesting, volunteering, nannying, gap year projects, working at resorts and events, summer camps and any other jobs you can get.
- You can look for jobs and other opportunities before you leave or once you're on the ground.
- Accommodation will usually be organised for you on gap year projects but most backpackers stay at hostels.
- Make the most of your trip by clarifying your objectives and assessing your progress.
- Promote what you've done when you apply for jobs or courses by relating your experiences to the skills required.

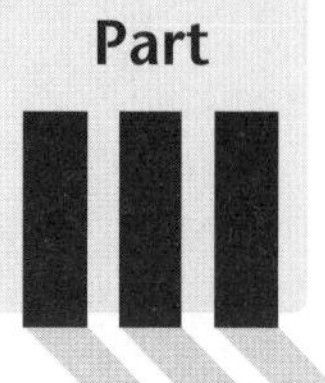

Part III

GETTING A JOB

Now you've chosen a career and planned your journey it's time to look for a job. Graduate vacancies come in all shapes and sizes, and this section shows you how to find them and effectively promote yourself as the right person for the role.

Chapter

8

Searching for graduate jobs

"You become a champion by fighting one more round. When things are tough, you fight one more round." *James J. Corbett*

Contents

What you will gain from this chapter:

- **Decision making:** The ability to focus on appropriate vacancy sources.
- **Opportunity awareness:** An awareness of where you can find interesting jobs, especially those in your chosen sector.
- **Transition learning:** The ability to take control of the job search process.
- **Self-awareness:** The wherewithal to reflect on your current job search strategies and alter your approach as necessary.

What are graduate jobs?

In the 'good old days', graduates went into a narrow band of clearly defined, skilled roles in areas such as medicine, banking and law. Nowadays, however, things have changed. Today's graduates can no longer expect to just fall into fulfilling graduate jobs as soon as they leave university, and many have to take a more meandering career journey. The good news is that degree holders still tend to earn far more than non-graduates over their lifetimes whatever career route they follow.

Consequently, a 'graduate job' can now mean almost anything, from a highly prized position to any job at all that might lead to better things. This chapter outlines the full range of employment options for graduates in the modern recruitment market.

Graduate training programmes

> "The qualities we look for in our trainees include common sense, a sharp intellect, independent thought, judgement and a good sense of humour. To thrive here, you will also need enthusiasm, commitment, a willingness to accept responsibility and the ability to get on well with others. Our work is intellectually demanding so the minimum standard we look for in our applicants is three very strong A-levels (or equivalent) and either a good 2:1 or a 1st in your first degree. The international nature of our practice means that our trainees have the opportunity to work abroad and although proficiency in a foreign language is a bonus, it is not a requirement.
>
> Our trainees come from a range of universities: it is the quality of the candidate, not your university, which is important to us. A law degree is not essential – approximately half of our trainees have not studied law at university.
>
> All future trainees must study the LPC at BPP Law School in Holborn, London. Those who have not studied law will also be required to study the Graduate Diploma in Law at BPP."
>
> *Graduate Recruiters, Slaughter and May*

Many of the larger graduate employers recruit graduates into organised training programmes. These schemes are very popular because they provide a secure route into work, good prospects and a relatively high salary. They are offered in a range of sectors but are especially prevalent in traditional professions and finance or business management roles such as accountancy, law, banking, investment banking and management consultancy.

Graduate training programmes are widely advertised and typically offered to candidates with excellent potential, as demonstrated by good grades, relevant skills and a burning commitment to succeed. They are available throughout the year and positions tend to start the following summer once students have graduated. However, you'll find that vacancies usually peak over the winter months from September to February. Therefore, if you're still studying, you need to be ready to apply as soon you start your final year. If you left university in the last two or three years then you are also usually still welcome to apply, especially if you have made the most of your time since graduating.

Application procedures for these positions are understandably long and convoluted and only the most appropriate candidates are hired. New recruits are trained in every aspect of the business for a year or two and then given specialist management/technical roles. Nowadays, even though they are attractively presented on campus and beyond, they only constitute a small proportion of total graduate opportunities, because:

- Many sectors, such as publishing and community work, do not generally favour this method of selection.
- Small and medium-sized firms tend to recruit candidates with particular skills directly into specific roles.

Two recent examples of graduate training programmes are as follows:

- Ernst & Young: www.ey.com/uk/careers – 900 vacancies in accounting, consulting, finance and IT, salary withheld, minimum of a 2.1/300 UCAS points, year-round recruitment but early applications advised (advertised in October).
- Unilever: www.unilever.co.uk/graduates – 70 vacancies in engineering, finance, human resources, IT, manufacturing, marketing, research and development and sales, £28,500, minimum requirement of a 2.2/300 UCAS points, relevant degree required for some roles, year-round recruitment but early applications advised (advertised in October).

Other graduate jobs

> “We are not a massive organisation and most people have never heard of us, but we hire graduates every year into a range of exciting roles. Therefore, we get less applications and recruitment is carried out on a more personal basis whereby we look for proactive people who have gone out of their way to find a fulfilling role.
>
> The number one recommendation I would make for graduate job hunters would be to take a step back and look for opportunities across the industry where you want to work, including SMEs, not just the obvious companies who have recognisable brands.”
>
> *Mark Hanrahan, Business Development Director, Nomenca Limited*

Many larger employers and the majority of small and medium-sized firms do not run graduate training programmes but instead recruit people with specific skills as and when they're required. Vacancies that call for new graduates often fall into two categories, sales roles and junior skilled positions, for which your degree will be good preparation.

Sales roles

These positions tend to have a high turnover and the work is usually based on commission: i.e. you get paid according to how much you sell. Sales can be a cut-throat business, but if you have the gift of the gab it might be for you. If you choose this path, make sure you nail the employer down about how much you'll be paid before you start. You should also check out the firm on forums such as those provided at www.thestudentroom.co.uk. Two recent examples of sales positions that have called for graduates are shown below:

- Trainee/Graduate Recruitment Consultant. Salary: £20,000–£21,000 per annum + bonus and benefits. After following the training programme and on achieving specific targets and you will be promoted to a Recruitment Consultant.
- Graduate Sales Executive. Competitive salary structure and commission plan. We are looking for individuals of a graduate calibre with the right attitude, drive and determination to succeed in a demanding sales role.

Junior-level positions

Entry-level graduate roles are very attractive because they will probably give you the chance to develop your skills and experience in a supportive professional environment. Therefore vacancies of this type can be very competitive and are ironically usually secured by the most experienced applicants. Consequently, so-called 'entry-level' positions are often actually the second or third step in a graduate's career journey.

Two examples are shown below:

- Trainee Graduate Process Engineer. Salary unspecified. As a Graduate Process Engineer you will be required to implement several projects and manage/supervise contractors.
- Graduate PPC Marketing Analyst. Salary – up to £17,000 per annum. This is an exciting role for a graduate with excellent analytical skills and an interest in search marketing.

Non-graduate jobs

Of course, numerous jobs are also offered every year that do not require a university education. These jobs are often menial, and you may wonder why you should even consider them when you've earned a degree. However, you shouldn't turn up your nose at them, because they will give you the opportunity to:

- Pay your bills and take the pressure off your career search.
- Get used to the work environment (and getting up in the morning).
- Network with key contacts (especially if you can find work in the sector you want to enter).
- Talk your way into a more substantial role.
- Gain the skills and experience you need.
- Enhance your CV and job applications by focusing on the more professional and relevant tasks you perform (even if you only undertake them one per cent of the time!).
- Keep your mum happy.

Two recent examples of non-graduate vacancies that may turn out to be the first step towards a fulfilling career are shown below:

- Health Care Assistant required for a Domiciliary Care Department. Successful applicants will have a minimum of six months experience as a Health Care Assistant. £7–£10 per hour.
- Support Services Adviser. Due to continued growth, the Support Services Advisers will assist the existing Support Services Team in taking incoming calls to the help desk. Salary: £7 per hour.

The scenic route

As outlined throughout this guide, you shouldn't panic if you can't find a fulfilling permanent job straight after university because there is still another well-trodden career path. This winding journey involves gradually enhancing the skills and experience you gained at university through activities such as networking, volunteering, training, temporary employment and internships.

Many graduates who follow this path find themselves in rewarding careers almost by accident, whilst others develop their skills and confidence to such an extent that they are then ready to apply for graduate training contracts or other graduate vacancies.

Where you'll find vacancies

Graduate vacancies in the UK are advertised on a massive patchwork of websites, social networks, directories, agencies and campus events. Major employers tend to annually advertise their posts on numerous high-profile platforms but small and medium-sized firms usually recruit graduates as and when they are required through limited channels such as job agencies and their personal networks.

Many of the more common seedbeds of graduate jobs are outlined below. Use them to identify specific sources of vacancies in your chosen sector and look for some interesting vacancies.

Graduate career websites

These sites provide general careers advice and advertise graduate vacancies at major recruiters in both the public and private sectors. The online databases are usually set up so you can look for jobs in specific industries and/or regions, and you can sign up to receive email alerts when relevant vacancies are posted. Many of the more popular websites, and the recruiters they promote, are highly visible on campus because they have the money to promote themselves effectively and produce shiny brochures and posters. However, you should always remember that they tend to focus on the needs of larger recruiters in a narrow range of sectors.

Four of the most popular general graduate careers advice websites that advertise UK vacancies in a wide range of sectors are shown below:

- Graduate Prospects: www.prospects.ac.uk – A highly respected and comprehensive website because of its links to the Association of Graduate Careers Advisory Services.
- Milkround: www.milkround.com – Student-friendly site with focused advice and useful forums.
- TARGETjobs: www.targetjobs.co.uk – Comprehensive website with tips on applying to specific employers.
- Graduate-jobs.com: www.graduate-jobs.com – Narrower range of jobs but some good forums and blogs and links to graduate vacancy websites.

Have a look at these websites to complete the following exercise.

Self-assessment: Your favourite graduate career websites

Identify your favourite two graduate career websites and list a current vacancy on each that looks interesting.

Your favourite graduate career websites	Some attractive vacancies currently on offer
•	•
•	•

University careers centres

Careers services advertise local and national graduate vacancies. Many of them automatically link you to the vacancies advertised on the Prospects website but they also tend to promote specific vacancies for their students and graduates that are not generally released. They may also be able to point you towards vacancies they've heard about through the grapevine.

Most careers centres will see their own graduates and you may also be able to get help from the careers centres at other universities, although some institutions may charge you for this service. You can find contact details for all the nation's centres on the AGCAS website at www.agcas.org.uk.

Visit your local careers centre and see how they can help you in your job search, plus enter some interesting current vacancies they are currently advertising.

Self-assessment: How your careers centre can help

Find your local university careers service and list two interesting jobs they have on offer.

Details of your local careers service	Two vacancies currently on offer
	•
	•

Graduate directories

Before websites ever existed the major recruiters promoted their vacancies in hard-copy directories. Surprisingly, these catalogues have largely survived the Internet age because they also provide good, up-to-date careers information and advice. They tend to arrive in university careers services from October onwards each year and you can usually pick them up for free. Some directories list graduate jobs in general whilst others focus on specific sectors. A few of the more common publications are listed below (as you can see, most of them are also available online).

- *The Times*, Top 100 Graduate Employers: Popular UK graduate employers and their roles (also available at www.Top100GraduateEmployers.com).
- Real Prospects Directory: Graduate Prospects' own directory with an extensive list of large graduate employers and their specific vacancies.
- TARGETjobs GET Directory: Similar guide to the Real Prospects directory (available at http://viewer.zmags.com/publication/1351c0ac#/1351c0ac/1).
- TARGETjobs (see www.targetjobs.co.uk/careers-products): Jobs in finance, construction, quantity surveying and civil engineering, engineering, IT, law, management consulting and property.
- Inside Careers (www.insidecareers.co.uk): Jobs in human resources, IT, logistics and transport, management, management accountancy and consultancy, marketing and sales, purchasing and supply, actuaries, banking, securities and investments, chartered accountancy, chartered tax advice, insurance, pensions, chemical, civil, mechanical, structural and electrical and electronic engineering, and chartered patent attorneys.
- Chambers Student 2012: The student's guide to becoming a lawyer (www.chambersstudent.co.uk).

Self-assessment: Using graduate job directories

Identify the two most useful graduate job directories in your chosen sector and list two of the interesting jobs that are listed.

Your favourite graduate directories	Two interesting jobs on offer
•	•
•	•

Professional organisations

Professional organisations are another good source of industry-specific information and vacancies plus they can also provide excellent networking opportunities. For example, the Royal Society of Chemistry at www.rsc.org offers a dedicated careers advisory service, links to jobs through *Chemistry World* and opportunities to rub shoulders with professionals in the field. You can find a full list of the professional organisations in each sector on the companion website.

Self-assessment: Useful professional organisations

Identify the two most useful professional organisations in your chosen sector and list two specific ways they can help you find a job.

Two useful professional organisations in your chosen sector	How they can help you find a job
•	•
•	•

Recruitment agencies

There are numerous job agencies across the UK, from multinationals to independent outfits on the high street. They tend to promote vacancies in specific sectors and contracts that last from a day to a lifetime. On the whole, agencies look for workers with specific employment experience and skills (such as being able to type more than 50 words per minute) so you'll usually need more than just a degree to get a job. Therefore, your first step might be to develop your skills within less skilled or voluntary experience.

Be careful when you sign up for agencies. Don't pay a registration fee, make sure their websites are regularly updated and, above all, remember that although they may promise you the earth – they often don't deliver! Regularly keep in contact with those that you join and, if no work is forthcoming, move on. You can find a full list of agencies in the UK on the website of the Recruitment and Employment Confederation (www.rec.uk.com). Local papers also usually list local agencies and your careers service will probably be able to recommend the best organisations in your area. Some popular national graduate recruitment agencies are provided below:

- The Graduate Recruitment Bureau: www.grb.uk.com.
- TheGraduate: www.thegraduate.co.uk.
- Gradplus: www.gradplus.com.
- Reed Graduates: www.reed.co.uk/graduate.
- Total Jobs: www.totaljobs.com/graduate – Jobs in all business areas, particularly finance, IT, sales and administration.
- Brampton Stafford Recruitment: www.brampton-recruitment-4-graduate-jobs.co.uk – Particularly interested in science, technology, engineering, maths, languages and IT graduates.

- RecruitmentRevolution.com: www.recruitmentrevolution.com.
- UKGraduateCareers: www.ukgraduatecareers.net.
- Meta-Morphose: www.meta-morphose.co.uk – Business to business roles.
- Matchtech: www.matchtech.com – technical roles.

Individual organisations

Many organisations don't advertise their vacancies but rely on people to contact them directly. You can find such employers through relevant professional organisations (see the companion website) or through your Internet browser by typing terms like 'publishers in London' or 'UK banks'. You can then target the specific organisations by:

- Contacting individual employees and asking for help (see Chapter 5).
- Asking your existing contacts if they can put you in touch with them.
- Attending events where you might be able to rub shoulders.
- Joining relevant groups on social networks.
- Sending speculative applications.
- Looking for casual roles at the organisations and moving up the hierarchy.
- Camping out on their doorstep and asking for a chance (don't get arrested!).

Working overseas

There are thousands of overseas graduate jobs that are open to UK graduates. The key questions you should ask yourself when looking for jobs overseas are:

- Are you allowed to work in that country? (If you're British you can freely work anywhere in the European Economic Area – see Chapter 7).
- What are the administrative procedures you have to go through to work in your chosen country?
- Do you need to speak the language? And can you?
- How do recruitment procedures differ?

You can look at the following websites:

- Prospects Working Abroad: www.prospects.ac.uk/working_abroad.htm.
- Going Global: www.goinglobal.com – International graduate advice and jobs.
- Graduate Jobs in Europe: http://graduatejobsineurope.com – Excellent information and advice for graduates seeking work.

Other

Jobs can be found anywhere and everywhere so keep your eyes and ears open. For example, your local paper may well advertise some posts, your contacts might know someone who needs help, or you might overhear someone in a pub who's just got a great contract. Don't be afraid to offer your services!

If at first you don't succeed

If you find yourself unemployed and lost when you finish your student days, make sure you take care of yourself. The last thing you should do is give up and sit at home watching

Doctors. Getting into your career is about reflection, hard work and perseverance, so you need to continually refocus your approach and improve your applications until you get to your destination. Consider the following strategies.

- Reassess what you have to offer and identify possible new roles or paths.
- Get used to taking control in other areas of your life so it becomes second nature.
- Get busy with any activities at all so you can develop your skills, get ideas and stay positive.
- Ask for help from everyone you can think of, such as careers advisers, your mum and dad, your brother and your friends.
- Consider going back to university or night school for a further course.
- Have a break and recharge your batteries.
- Set up your own business (see Part IV of this guide).

Self-assessment: Your plan B

If you're having trouble getting into your career, what could you do to get back on track?

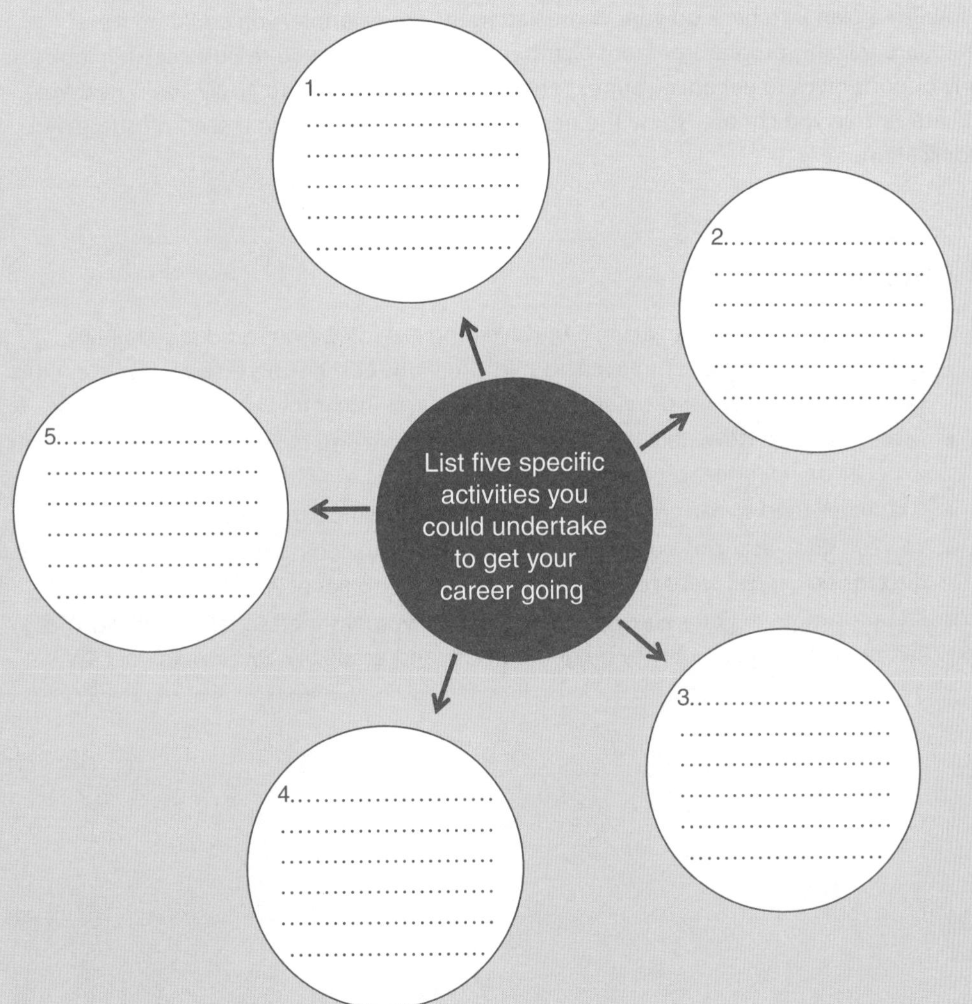

Finding out more

In this guide

- Planning your journey – Chapter 3.
- Experience and internships – Chapter 4.

On the companion website

- Details of professional organisations in specific sectors.
- Case studies of students and graduates who have turned their careers around.

On the web

- www.prospects.ac.uk – Read about the job market in your chosen sector.
- www.nottingham.ac.uk/careers – Look up 'Types of jobs' for useful links in a wide range of industries.

What to do next

Establish a plan B to back up your chosen strategy. For example, you could go for a graduate training programme from October to March, but if you're unsuccessful, look for any opportunities to enhance your experience and skills in time to apply again next year. Whatever role you choose, study the next chapters to make sure you send off successful applications.

Summary

- Graduates start their careers in a massive range of roles, from graduate training programmes at major employers to part-time jobs at the supermarket, but every job will help you gradually develop your skills and get into a fulfilling role.
- Most graduates now start their careers on a meandering path involving employment experience, volunteering and networking.
- Graduates tend to earn more than non-graduates whatever route they take.
- You can find vacancies on a wide range of sources including graduate job directories, careers websites, careers services and job agencies.
- If you struggle to get your career going, don't worry as it often takes a while. You can re-energise your journey by getting busy and gradually developing your CV.

Chapter

9

Promoting yourself effectively

"All the world's a stage." *William Shakespeare*

Contents

What you will gain from this chapter:

- **Decision making:** The ability to focus on appropriate attributes for each separate application.
- **Transition learning:** An awareness of the need to target applications and present yourself effectively.
- **Self-awareness:** A deeper appreciation of how you demonstrate the necessary attributes required in specific vacancies.

Putting your best foot forward

The job application process is about quality, not quantity:

- Every time you apply for a new job, you need to carefully identify the specific attributes required and positively prove you have them.
- First impressions count so it's absolutely essential that you engage the reader, spell everything correctly and use appropriate grammar.

This takes time and effort but you'll be rewarded.

This chapter shows you how to promote yourself effectively with these two considerations in mind. The following chapters extend this understanding to specific application tools such as CVs, applications and interviews.

What employers are after

> "Here at KPMG in addition to your academic qualifications we look at nine key Behavioural Capabilities. These are the skills and behaviours which you will need to demonstrate to be successful at KPMG. These are the same capabilities that all KPMG employees need to demonstrate across the globe. This includes assessing whether a candidate is enthusiastic about a career at KPMG, whether the person builds relationships internally and externally and works collaboratively to achieve success. KPMG is a high performing culture and we are looking for candidates who show self-awareness, are forward thinking, curious and creative. A positive approach to self-development and awareness of the external marketplace are also extremely important. KPMG staff are continually growing and developing and our future depends on nurturing great individual talent and providing an environment where people can flourish personally and professionally."
>
> *Blair England, Graduate Marketing Officer, KPMG*

> "What do we look for? Well, we're looking for people who have excelled academically, high-flyers, people who stand out from their peers. You will be willing to try new things and put yourself out of your comfort zone. You need to have strong drive to address challenges you'll face.
>
> There is a lot to learn and just as you've mastered a role it's normally time to begin the next challenge. You'll need to be a quick and eager learner with a passion to really own projects and drive them forwards. With the variation of categories, departments and locations to explore you will need to be adaptable and be flexible to uncover it all.
>
> Key ingredients are self-motivation, energy and drive; you will be responsible for 'real projects' and 'real responsibility' from day one."
>
> *Graduate Recruiters, Kraft*

Skills, commitment and knowledge

For employers, the modern recruitment process is quite straightforward – they simply want to find the best people for the job based on its unique requirements. Therefore, they systematically identify candidates by assessing everyone against clear and objective selection criteria. Selection criteria are usually based on the three elements of success in any field – your skills, commitment and knowledge. This is shown below.

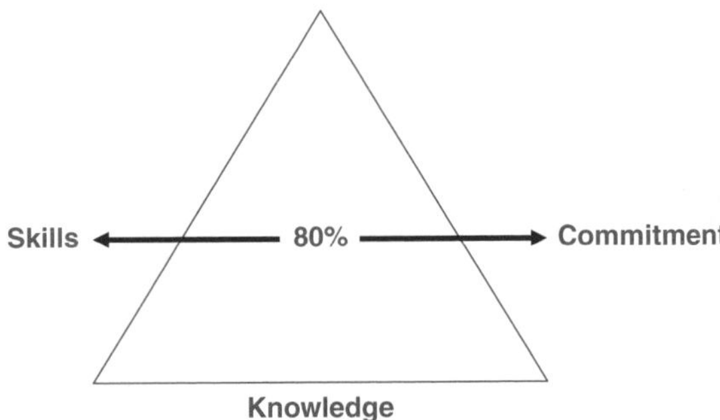

Employers seek a wide range of skills including:

- *Personal qualities*, such as the ability to turn up on time and be reliable.
- *Advanced transferrable skills*, such as teamwork and commercial awareness.
- *Technical competencies* relevant to the specific job, such as the ability to cook if you want to be a chef.

Find out more about the key skills required by modern-day employers in Chapter 3.

Commitment is about your genuine interest in the specific career, organisation and vacancy. This is absolutely vital to employers because they are looking for passionate candidates who are able to proactively take control of their own careers and make a difference.

Knowledge is clearly related to your potential success in the recruitment process but, as shown in the diagram above, it is not as important as your skills and commitment. This is because, if you have the ability to do a job and you want to do it, then you'll soon learn what's required. Nonetheless, many employers still call for a relevant degree or a particular technical understanding, such as computer-aided design.

Experience

Some employers focus heavily on your experience and don't necessarily mention your other key attributes. This could be for several reasons including the following:

- They assume that, if you've done the job before, then you'll probably be able to do it again.
- They want you to take the initiative and relate your experience to the skills, commitment and knowledge required.
- They just want to limit the amount of applications they receive!

Proving your skills

It is harder to prove your skills than it sounds, but it gets easier with practice. This is because it's not sufficient to just list various examples of where and when you have demonstrated the competencies required by employers. You also need to outline your specific strengths, i.e.:

- *How* you perform the skill to a high level.
- *When and where* you have performed the skill well (provide a specific example).

For example, you could describe your teamwork and Photoshop skills as follows:

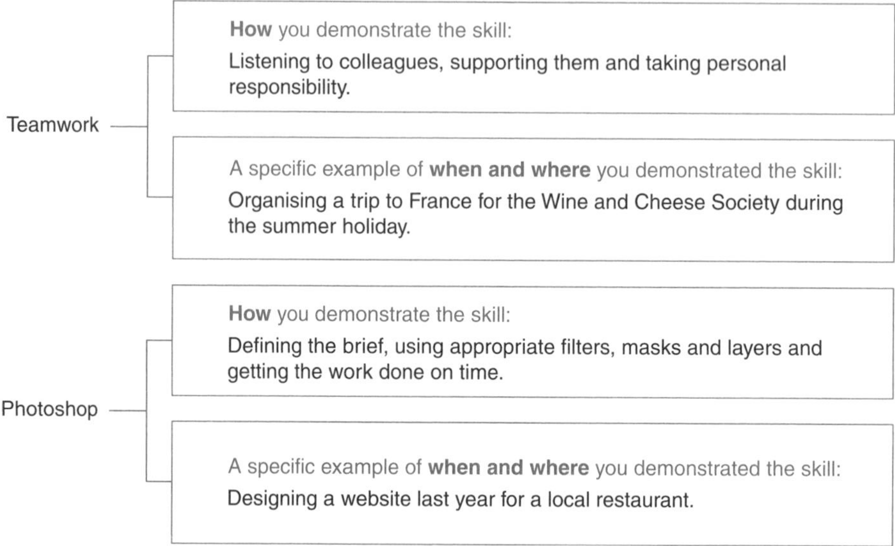

Now you've seen how it's done, try it for yourself. In the exercise below, describe how and when you have performed two of the skills required in your chosen career.

Self-assessment: Demonstrating your skills

Prove you have a technical and a transferable skill required in your chosen career.

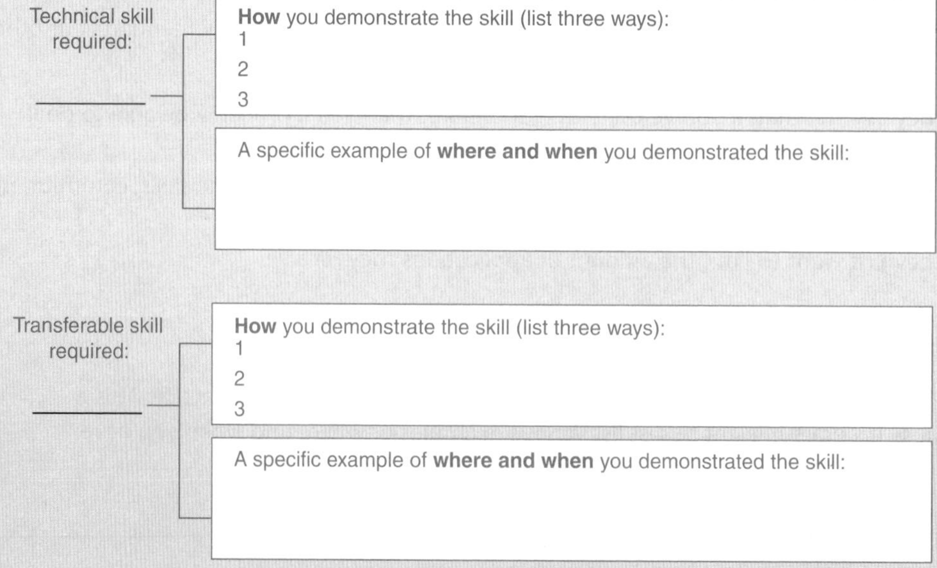

Take your time to practise proving your skills in this way because it's crucial to your chances of success and, once you know what you're doing, you'll never forget.

Proving your commitment

Of course, skills alone do not prove your potential; you also need the necessary commitment, i.e. the desire to succeed. You can do this by demonstrating that you know what the job entails and you have a genuine passion for what you'll be doing. Use the following four-step process.

1 Research the job

Research the role, sector and specific vacancy using the following sources:

- Graduate career websites such as www.targetjobs.co.uk.
- The websites of professional organisations (see the companion website).
- Organisations' individual websites.
- Contacts at the organisations themselves, such as the recruitment manager.
- Contacts who know about the sector you want to enter.
- Forums on websites such as www.thestudentroom.co.uk.
- Social networking sites and groups.
- News organisations such as www.bbc.co.uk and www.guardian.co.uk.
- Employers at careers events.
- Other students and graduates who are applying to the same organisation.

2 Demonstrate why you want the job

Clearly outline what attracts you to the particular industry, organisation and role. This demonstrates that you've done your research and reflected on why you are suitable.

3 Show how you've targeted that specific role

Demonstrate how you've actively gone about targeting the specific role for which you're applying, and how your experience has confirmed that you have chosen the right path. For example, you should clearly relate your degree and your previous employment experience to the role.

4 Plan how you will develop your career over the next five years if you get the job

Here you can impress employers by demonstrating that you're looking for more than a job, i.e. you're interested in forming a mutually beneficial long-term partnership (see Chapter 16).

Proving your knowledge

You can prove your knowledge by:

- Learning the key concepts, methods and data.
- Outlining exactly where you picked up the necessary knowledge (e.g. during a particular module at university or as part of your role at work).
- Describing what you know and how it relates to each specific vacancy.

For example, if you need to know which inorganic compounds are produced when decomposing tissue oxidises, you could state that you studied this process in detail during your biochemistry final-year module and outline your specific understanding in relation to the role.

If your degree is obviously relevant then you can directly relate what you've learnt in it to the job description. If your degree is not clearly linked to the role, you need to tease out the relevant skills and knowledge you gained. For example, if you have a degree in English and you want to be a probation officer, you could emphasise your ability to communicate and quickly research complicated text.

Proving your experience

If employers ask for experience, but no other attributes, it's up you to outline what you've done and relate it to the requisite skills, commitment and knowledge. For example, if an advert simply states that an organisation needs a barman with six months' experience, list your relevant positions and relate them to the qualities you will need in that specific organisation, such as ability to pull a pint or make cocktails.

Targeting specific jobs

You can use a wide range of resources to research what's required in specific roles. Some of these are listed below.

Job adverts

Adverts generally include the key attributes required in a vacancy. Selection criteria are usually clearly stated but some may be hidden. For example, the following attributes are required in advert below:

- *Skills*: An outgoing personality, the ability to pick things up quickly and competence with C# or VB.net, SQL Server or Oracle and web technologies.
- *Commitment*: A passion for IT, a strong desire to learn new technologies and a commitment to developing your skills and career.
- *Knowledge*: C#SQL .Net, SQL Server, Oracle knowledge and an IT degree.

Trainee Software Developers

Big-Box software developers are looking for recent graduates with IT-related degrees coupled with C#SQL.Net knowledge. You will have a real passion for IT and a strong desire to learn new technologies. You will have an outgoing personality and an ability to pick things up quickly. This is a great opportunity for a graduate to secure a position with a company that is committed to developing your skills and your career. Skills required: C# or VB.net, SQL Server or Oracle knowledge and web technologies.

Personal specifications

Most graduate employers provide formal personal specifications. These include job descriptions that outline the specific tasks involved in the role and selection criteria, which are the formal benchmarks used to assess applicants.

An example job description and selection criteria are provided in the activity below. See if you can identify all the skills, commitment and knowledge required (the answers are provided below).

Self-assessment: Untangling personal specifications

Identify the skills, commitment and knowledge required in the following teaching position.

Job description and personal specification **Maths Teacher**
We can offer you: • The opportunity to work in an outstanding school. • Well-motivated children. • The full support of a professional team of staff. • The benefits of working in an innovative and forward-thinking school. • Professional development to support you in your career. • An attractive rural location in semi-rural Cheshire. **Are you someone who:** • Is an inspirational and passionate teacher of maths? • Has a desire to further improve a strong faculty? • Wants to make a real difference to the lives of young people? • Is passionate and committed to continually improve? • Is able to teach the full range of age and ability across KS3, GCSE and A level?

Answers:

- *Skills*: Outstanding teaching, being able to motivate children and support colleagues plus being an inspirational and passionate teacher with the capacity to teach the full range of ages and ability.
- *Commitment*: Being forward thinking, committed to professional development, happy to live in a rural community, a desire to improve the faculty and make a real difference to young people's lives, committed to professional development (again) and high standards.
- *Knowledge*: Maths curriculum across KS3, GCSE and A level.

Direct contact

Sometimes, you can find out a lot by just contacting employers and asking for an informal chat. This will give you the opportunity to ask about any aspects of the job that are not obvious in the advert or the job description, for example:

- The key skills they're seeking.
- How your experience will help you fit in.
- Where you'll be based.
- Any professional training you will be able to undertake.

This approach will help you target your applications more effectively and impress employers but, before you contact anyone, make sure you've done your research and know what you're talking about! You may also want to thank the employer for their help in your cover letters, as this will remind them of your previous conversations.

Some quick English revision

Spelling

Employers (or their computer programs) specifically look for spelling mistakes in applications. For your part, there's no excuse for any spelling mistakes because you can check your work with your word processor's spell-check facility and a dictionary (e.g. www.dictionary.cambridge.org/dictionary/british). However, when using a spell-check program make sure of the following:

- You don't correct the word to something completely different. For example, if you spell 'connection' incorrectly your computer may automatically change it to 'confection'.
- The language on your computer is set to English UK not English US (you can do this in Word by clicking on Tools>Language>English UK).

Dictionaries are especially useful when you want to check which version of a word to use when two or more words sound the same but have different meanings depending on how they're spelt (homophones). For example: *Where/we're/were*; *its/it's*; *there/their/they're*; *dear/deer*; and *practice/practise*. Finally, make sure you spell everyone's names correctly!

Punctuation and grammar

It should go without saying, but you need to write sentences that make sense! Advice on four common problem areas is shown below:

- **Commas**: Use when you want to list items, join two phrases together, avoid repeating words and mark off weak interruptions of sentences.
- **Capital letters**: Use in the following instances...
  - The first word of a sentence.
  - The first word of a direct quotation which is a sentence.
  - The first word, and each significant word, of a title (e.g. the Bible).
  - The name of a day or a month (e.g. Monday).
  - The name of a language (e.g. English).
  - A word expressing a connection with a place (e.g. British).
  - The name of a nationality or an ethnic group (e.g. Jews).
  - A proper name (e.g. Huddersfield).
  - The name of a historical period (e.g. Elizabethan).
  - The name of a holiday (e.g. Christmas).
  - A significant religious term (e.g. Passover).
  - A brand name (e.g. Palgrave).
  - The pronoun 'I'.
- **Apostrophes**: Use when you want to indicate possession or combine two words (e.g. shortening *do not* into *don't*).
- **Tenses**: Use the tense appropriate to the situation and stick to it!

Style

English is a wonderfully flexible language that can be used in an infinite number of ways. For example, academics use convoluted sentences and long words whilst texters avoid vowels and use as few words as possible. Job applications also have their own unique style that takes a bit of getting used to. Some pointers to remember are:

- Write formally and avoid colloquial phrases.
- Avoid contractions such as 'don't' or 'can't'.
- Use short sentences and short paragraphs.
- Use simple words.
- Use positive action words such as those listed below.
- Avoid phrases like 'I think...' and 'I believe...' as they indicate doubt.

Positive action words

Positive words leave a positive impression, especially if you back up any claims. For example, consider the impression created by each of the following three statements and stick to the third style in your applications.

- I am good at communicating. (Boring!)
- I am an effective and enthusiastic communicator. (More dynamic, but shallow)
- I demonstrate effective and enthusiastic communication skills by carefully listening to clients and diligently adjusting my message to meet their needs. (Skills are outlined in a positive, upbeat style)

Some examples of positive adjectives and adverbs are shown below:

Ability
Accomplished
Actively
Adaptable
Advanced
Ambitious
Analysed
Analytical
Approachable
Aptitude

Calculate
Capacity
Careful
Caring
Clearly
Collegiate
Committed
Composed
Comprehensive
Conduct
Confident
Coordinate
Create

Decisive
Dedicate
Demonstrate
Dependable
Design
Determined
Develop
Diligent
Discipline
Discover
Dynamic

Eager
Effectively
Efficient
Encourage
Energetic
Enquiring
Enterprising
Enthusiastic
Evaluate
Excel
Experienced

Flexible
Focused
Fresh
Friendly

Generate
Goals
Guide

Happily
Hardworking
Help
Highly
Honest

Implemented
Independently
Influence
Initiative
Innovative
Inspire
Interested
Intuitive

Judgement

Keen
Knowledgeable

Launched
Leadership
Logical

Maintain
Manage
Mature
Motivated

Negotiate
Nurture

Objective
Observe
Open
Opportunity

Plan
Praise

Relentless
Reveal

Sustain

Tenacious

Wise

Structure and format

There are a number of things you can do to make sure your applications stand out and look attractive, as follows:

- Use a consistent style and headings.
- Make sure the key points stand out and are easily identifiable from a quick scan.
- Use good quality white paper and black ink from a good printer.
- Consider spacing your lines by at least a factor of 1.5.
- Use basic bullet points.
- Type in an easily readable 'sans serif' font such as Arial or Verdana, make sure the size of your text is easy to read and avoid italics or using bold words in the middle of sentences.
- Leave enough white space on each page so the reader isn't daunted by how much she has to read (more text isn't necessarily better). You can do this by maintaining sufficient margins.
- Perfectly align the text using the tabs (see below).

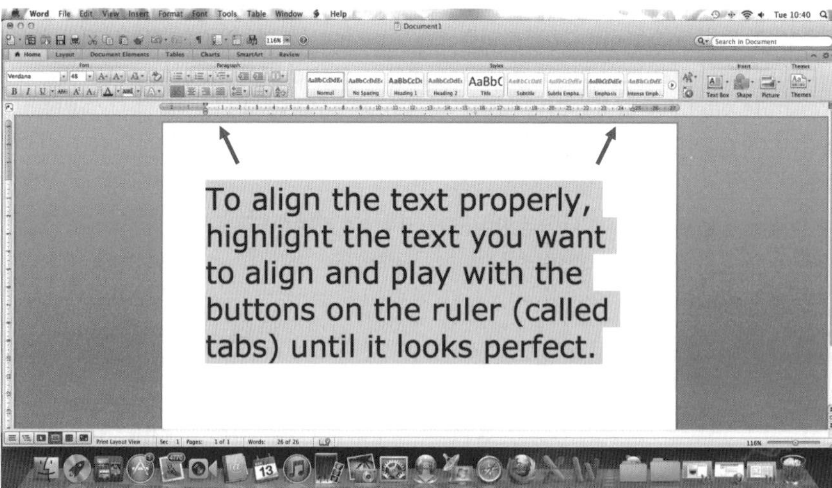

Updating your work

Always make sure your applications are up to date and focused on the specific vacancy in hand. Don't just cut and paste previous applications without updating what you've written. For example, you won't get a job at Sky TV if you send them a copy of a previous BBC application where you outlined why you want to work for a public service broadcaster!

Drafting and checking

You should expect to make several drafts of your application before sending it off, as you will probably have to refocus it several times and correct numerous mistakes. Use the following guidelines:

- Allow your creativity to flourish and write your applications freely without worrying about any errors; then edit them later.

- When you've finished, make sure you've addressed all the attributes required.
- Once you've edited your applications get someone else, such as a careers adviser, to check them. You won't notice many of your own errors because you're so familiar with what you've written.

If you have a disability

If you have a disability that hinders your capacity to upload your applications, such as dyslexia, get some help from the relevant university service. You should also consider asking the employer to take your disability into account or to provide an alternative application procedure.

You have to declare your disability if it will affect your ability to execute the role, but not if it won't affect your performance. On the whole, larger recruiters will do whatever they can to ensure you are given the same opportunity as other candidates but small and medium-sized firms may be less conscientious. Organisations that carry what's called a 'two ticks' symbol will definitely interview disabled candidates who meet the minimum qualifications for the role. Find out more about this scheme on the companion website.

Finding out more

In this guide

- Planning your journey – Chapter 3.
- Targeting your CV – Chapter 10.
- Tip-top application forms – Chapter 11.
- Cover letters that open doors – Chapter 12.
- Impressing at interviews – Chapter 13.

On the companion website

- Further vacancy adverts and job descriptions broken down to reveal their requisite skills, commitment and knowledge.
- Further demonstrations of how you could prove the more common transferable and technical skills required by employers.

On the web

Find up-to-date links on promoting yourself effectively via the companion website, including resources on assessing job descriptions, demonstrating your skills and using effective English.

What to do next

- If you're confident that you have all the attributes required in the jobs you're chasing, keep on applying and identify how you can promote yourself more effectively. The next chapters provide practical guidelines on constructing good CVs, application forms and cover letters.

- If you're not sure whether you have the requisite attributes to break into your chosen career, keep on looking for ways to develop those specific attributes, such as lower-skilled jobs or voluntary positions. See Chapters 3 to 7.
- Try not to discard your dream career too easily. There are probably thousands of people doing the job you want to enter, so why shouldn't you? Nothing worth having ever comes easily.
- Whether or not you're confident with your written English, get help before you send off your work. Also, take your time over your first attempts; you'll soon speed up as you get more experienced.

Summary

- In order to put together successful applications you need to prove that you have the specific attributes required and therefore you have to take the time to research what they are.
- Employers typically look for skills, commitment, knowledge and experience.
- You can research jobs by analysing job adverts, job descriptions/personal specifications, contacting the organisations and through various other channels.
- You can prove your skills by elucidating how you demonstrate the skill to a high level and providing a specific example.
- You can prove your commitment by showing an understanding of the role, the organisation and the industry and linking them to your interests.
- Knowledge is usually less important than skills and commitment but it helps to understand the jargon and technical information that will be required in each role.
- Good spelling, grammar and punctuation are absolutely crucial to your chances of kick-starting your career.
- Create a good first impression by structuring your work attractively.
- Use positive words and sentences.
- Tailor every new application to the specific post and update your experiences and attributes.
- Carefully check your applications for spelling/grammar mistakes and make sure they look attractive.

Chapter 10

Targeting your CV

"I have no skills at the moment but I hope to develop them at your firm."
Extract from a genuine CV!

Contents

What you will gain from this chapter:

- **Decision making:** The ability to target your CV appropriately.
- **Transition learning:** The ability to promote yourself effectively.
- **Self-awareness:** The capacity to link your personal abilities to the requirements of specific jobs.

What is a CV?

CVs are your shop-window advertising, giving you a wonderful opportunity to quickly and effectively promote what you have to offer. This chapter shows you how to construct impressive marketing documents that will help you advertise your attributes, secure interviews, and hopefully get a job!

Four example CVs are provided later in this chapter and four more are shown on the companion website.

What is a good CV?

> In both job-hunting and recruiting, I have learned the importance of tailoring each job application. When recruiting, it is immediately obvious when someone has sent a generic application, which has probably been sent to 50 other employers. This gives the impression that the job hunter wants any job rather than the role in question. This kind of application, which is very easy to do in an era of email/online applications, will rarely get you an interview, never mind a job.
>
> In my experience as a job hunter, applying for fewer jobs, but tailoring each application to the specific role and employer in question, is a far better approach. Doing this results in a greater number of interviews than the scattergun approach of applying for anything and everything with the same CV and letter.
>
> Another somewhat linked point is about attention to detail. Always check you are referring to the right person, job title and organisation. It may seem obvious, but as an MEP I have received job applications where the letter was addressed to another MEP from a different political group! I have also received job applications where the role referred to is incorrect, probably a result of amending another application. When I worked in a consultancy firm with a female MD, we sometimes received applications addressed to 'Mr X', indicating that the person had not bothered to visit our website, which included a message from the MD along with her name and photo. This may sound harsh, but applications with such basic errors end up in the bin.
>
> *Rebecca Taylor, MEP for Yorkshire and the Humber*

About 80 per cent of CVs are quickly discarded within seconds, 10 per cent are dismissed after further consideration, and the remainder are considered for interview. This statistic can sound quite sobering but it's actually good news to anyone who is prepared to put in the work and produce high quality applications, because good CVs get results! Therefore, if you spend 30 hours on three CVs you will probably get further than if you spend the same amount of time on 30!

Poor CVs

Poor CVs tend to be long random lists of people's skills and experience that are unrelated to the vacancy on offer. These documents are typically discarded in a matter of seconds because recruiters can immediately see that the skills they require are not proven. The majority of poor CVs also have numerous spelling mistakes and are poorly formatted. You can see a typical example later in the chapter, labelled Example CV1.

CVs – The good, the bad and the ugly

Average CVs

Average CVs at least relate the person's experience to their skills, but not the specific attributes required in the role. They tend to outline as many skills and experiences as possible in the hope that some of them will hit the mark. Of course, it's a one in a million shot that these 'catch all' CVs end up covering the specific skills required by any particular employer, so they also tend to be quickly discarded. Example CV2 later in the chapter is a typical average CV.

Good CVs

Good CVs (Example CVs 3 & 4 plus the CVs on the companion website) are effective marketing tools that contain the following elements:

- They are tailored to the specific attributes required in a specific role. For example, if you're applying for a job in a pub, then you'll probably need to demonstrate that you can change a barrel of beer and deal with drunk people on a Friday night, but these skills should probably be avoided if you're applying to the Civil Service! (Even if they'd probably be quite useful.)
- Previous experience and education are clearly linked to the specific skills, commitment and knowledge required.
- Relevant skills are outlined in full (see Chapter 9).

When to use a CV

CVs can be used in the following circumstances:

- When you meet an employer or contact.
- When organisations ask for one.
- If organisations give you the choice to send one with your application forms.
- If you're making speculative applications.

Rules and conventions

There are no rules to CVs, but there are several conventions which are very important because employers will quickly dismiss CVs that don't follow an easily recognisable pattern. This has become especially important in the Internet age because recruiters are increasingly scanning text for important information rather than conscientiously reading through them from start to finish.

These are the key rules to follow:

- Use two pages unless:
  - you have been otherwise advised;
  - you are applying for academic roles, in which case you can use three;
  - you are applying for business roles such as management consultancy where one page will do;
  - you are applying for a role overseas where other guidelines prevail (see www.prospects.ac.uk/country_profiles.htm).
- Make sure your headings are clear and well highlighted.
- Put key information at the top of each page.
- List everything in reverse-chronological order, i.e. the most recent events first.
- Use your name as the main heading and don't bother writing 'Curriculum Vitae'.
- Make sure your key attributes stand out at first glance.
- Make sure dates are easy to see and that there are no gaps.

What to include

The distinct advantage of CVs over other job applications is that you can stress your strengths and obscure your weaknesses. For example, if you got poor A level grades, you could consider leaving them out. Also, you don't have to stick to the common headings if you can tailor yours more appropriately. For example, your education section could be headed 'Qualifications', 'Education and Qualifications', or 'Undergraduate study'/'Postgraduate study'.

Usual sections

Most CVs will have the sections listed below. Look at the example CVs in the following pages and those on the companion website to see how they look in practice.

Personal details

Include your name, email address, phone numbers, how you can be contacted at any relevant social networks, and your address. If you live somewhere different in the holidays or you're going to move when you graduate then state clearly when you will be at each address, as in Examples CV3 and CV4. Create a professional voicemail reply message and email address incorporating your name (sexychops@hitmail.com won't really give a good first impression – hopefully!). As a rule, do not include information relating to your age, sex, nationality, marital status or health. You might want to put all your contact details at the top of your CV, as in many of the example CVs provided, or just put your key contact information at the top and your full address nearer the end, as in Example CV6 on the website, thus freeing up some valuable advertising space at the top of your document.

Education

In this section you should record the names of each institution you attended since secondary school: the towns, dates, qualifications and grades (especially if they're good). If you studied overseas you should also include the name of the country and the UK grade equivalent, which you can find at www.naric.org.uk (your university's careers office should have the password).

Once you've listed the course details, briefly relate your qualifications to the attributes required in the specific vacancy. If you're going for a job that's closely related to your degree, as in Example CV3, you should relate your key modules to some of the technical skills mentioned in the job description. If the vacancy is unrelated to the job you're seeking, as in Example CV4, then you could link your studies to your relevant transferable skills. Allow more space for recent and relevant studies. For example, you could devote one line of your CV to your GCSEs, two for your A Levels and five for your degree. Most students and new graduates promote their education above their employment experience on their CVs because their degrees are their main selling point.

Employment experience

Using the same format as your education section, outline the names of each organisation, where they are, when you worked there and what you did. Remember – all experience counts whether it's paid or unpaid. Outline your duties and responsibilities that are most relevant to the job you're seeking, even if they weren't your major tasks, as in Example CV3. Finally, relate what you've done to two or three of the specific skills required.

People use a wide range of headings in this section and often break it up into separate headings to suit their personal situation. For example, if you have a great deal of experience, but most of your relevant work history is quite old, you could make it more noticeable by splitting your employment experience into two sections entitled 'Relevant Experience' and 'Additional Experience', as in Example CV6.

If you're struggling to come up with any experience to put in this section, you really need to get out there and get a job or some voluntary experience. In the meantime, you could list anything you've done on your degree or your spare time that could loosely be described as work.

Interests

Relate your hobbies and pastimes to the job you're seeking and the skills required. This is usually a good section to focus on transferable skills such as communication, teamwork and organisation.

Referees

If you're still studying, or you recently graduated, provide the contact details for a professional referee (a current or recent employer) and an academic referee (a tutor or your personal tutor). If you graduated a while ago, list two professional referees. If you have a good reason for not including the details of your referees – for example, you don't want your boss to know you're looking for another job – you can just write 'References available upon request'. Make sure you get permission from your referees before including their details on your CV and keep in touch with them about the work you're seeking. Include all contact details including phone numbers and email addresses.

Optional sections

As previously stated, you can create any sections you want in your CVs, especially if they increase your chances of finding a job. Here are some options.

Personal profile/Career objective

CVs are increasingly prefaced with a personal profile and/or career objective, usually placed just below the personal details section. Such summaries can be a good way of highlighting your abilities and experience but they are often verbose and self-indulgent. If you do decide to include a profile and/or career objective then focus on your personal qualities, experience, skills, and personal strengths. Also, make specific, substantiated claims, frame it in the third person (don't refer to yourself as 'I' or 'my'), and use positive 'action' words. See Examples CV3 and CV4.

Skills

If you want to highlight your relevant skills, one option is to outline them in a specific section, following the skills-based CV format rather than the chronological/traditional style. This is a good way to bring your skills to the fore but if you do this, you should avoid mentioning them in other areas of your document as this could create confusion. See the guide on different CV formats below.

Additional skills

This is a good section to have if you've already covered all the important skills that are required but have some extra competencies that will help you stand out, such as an ability to speak languages or a driving licence. See Example CV5 on the website.

Achievements (also called Awards or Prizes)

This is the section for all you over-achievers who have impressive accomplishments to promote, such as scholarships, professional accolades and/or business triumphs. See Example CV3.

Other popular headings

'Research', 'Publications', Positions of responsibility', 'Personal attributes', 'Qualifications'.

The two main CV formats

Employers are accustomed to seeing two main types of CV – chronological/traditional and skills-based. These are described below. Unfortunately, graduates often assume that chronological CVs focus on experience, whereas skills-based CVs emphasise your key attributes. This is not true. Traditional and skills-based CVs should both highlight your key experiences in order to prove that you have the requisite skills, commitment and knowledge; they are just structured differently.

Chronological/traditional CV

As shown below (and in Examples CV3 and CV5 on the website), this type of CV directly links your education, work experience and interests to your relevant skills. It is a particularly effective CV format if you have a great deal of relevant work history because it highlights your experience.

The usual structure of a chronological/traditional CV:

Name

Personal details

Outline your contact details

Education

Outline what you've studied and use your education to prove you have some of the skills required

Employment history

List the jobs you've done and use your experience to prove you have a few more of the skills required

Page 1

Interests

Outline your pastimes and hobbies and, again, relate them to the requisite skills

Referees

Provide the contact details for two referees

Page 2

Skills-based CV

Skills-based CVs outline your relevant education, employment experience and interests in one section and collate your skills together under an additional heading. The skills section should therefore have examples from every walk of your life, especially your time at work. This type of CV is especially useful if your employment experience isn't particularly relevant but you have all the attributes required. See Examples CV4 below and CV6 (on the website).

The usual structure of a skills-based CV:

Name

Personal details

Outline your contact details

Education

Outline what you've studied

Employment history

List the jobs you've done

Interests

Outline your pastimes and hobbies

Page 1

Skills Profile

Prove you have the 7/8 skills required in each vacancy using examples from each walk of your life

-
-
-
-
-
-

Referees

Provide the contact details for two referees

Page 2

Alternative CV styles

One-page CVs

As shown alongside and in Example CV7 (on the website), one-page CVs usually resemble skills-based documents but all the information is squeezed into one side of A4. Therefore you have to be very brief, focusing on your most relevant education, employment experience and three or four skills.

This one-page résumé, popular in North America, is quickly becoming the norm in a range of finance-related industries such as management consulting, investment banking and even corporate law. Most of these industries have application forms for students and graduates so this issue rarely arises but, if this is your area of interest, you should certainly have a one-page CV for networking purposes.

Name

Personal details

Contact details

Education

Your studies

Employment history

The jobs you've done

Skills

Focus on your key abilities

Interests

Referees

Contact details for two referees

The usual structure of a one-page CV

Academic CVs

CVs for academic posts (as shown below and in Example CV8 on the website) usually contain a third page. The first two sheets follow the pattern of the traditional or skills-based CV shown above. The third page is an appendix of your research/teaching achievements such as an academic abstract, publications and conferences/courses attended.

Academics tend to prefer more formal CVs in the traditional format and you should be very careful to highlight your relevant attributes and experience. It's very important to have a good understanding of the research/teaching involved in the post before you apply.

The usual structure of an academic CV:

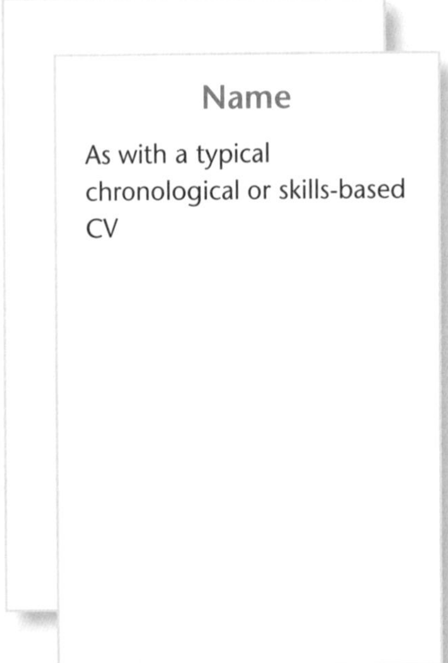

Pages 1 & 2

An appendix comprising a list of your research/teaching experience

Page 3

Digital CVs

Most CVs nowadays are viewed online, so students and graduates in creative industries have the opportunity to produce attractive web-based documents that show off their skills and a portfolio of their work. These digital documents typically have a basic level of data that can be printed out, and hotlinks to other information and artwork and video/audio tracks. Various links to digital and social network CVs can be found on the companion website.

Putting your CV together

Now you know what CVs are, you can quickly put one together using the five-stage process outlined below. Look at the example CVs to see the different ways of doing it.

1. Research the post and identify the attributes required (see Chapter 9).

↓

2. Choose the CV format that best suits your application for the particular role.

↓

3. Creatively think of headings that best demonstrate your specific attributes.

↓

4. Choose the best experience to prove each skill.

↓

5. Put pen to paper.

↓

Example CVs

Four example CVs are provided over the next few pages and four more are shown on the companion website, as follows:

Example CV1 – a poor CV
Example CV2 – an average chronological CV
Example CV3 – a good chronological/traditional CV
Example CV4 – a good skills-based CV

On the following pages

Example CV5 – a second good chronological/traditional CV
Example CV6 – a second good skills-based CV
Example CV7 – a good one-page CV
Example CV8 – the format for an academic CV

On the companion website

Brief job details and personal specifications are provided for each example so that you can see how well (or badly) they have been targeted at the particular vacancy. You should also note:

- The first seven CVs are from the same fictitious person so you can clearly see how they have been targeted and adapted to focus on different jobs.
- The first three CVs are for the same job so you can see a gradual improvement.

Example CV1 – a poor CV

The CV below is allegedly targeted at the publishing role listed alongside but, as you can see, it represents almost everything that could (and does) go wrong with modern CVs.

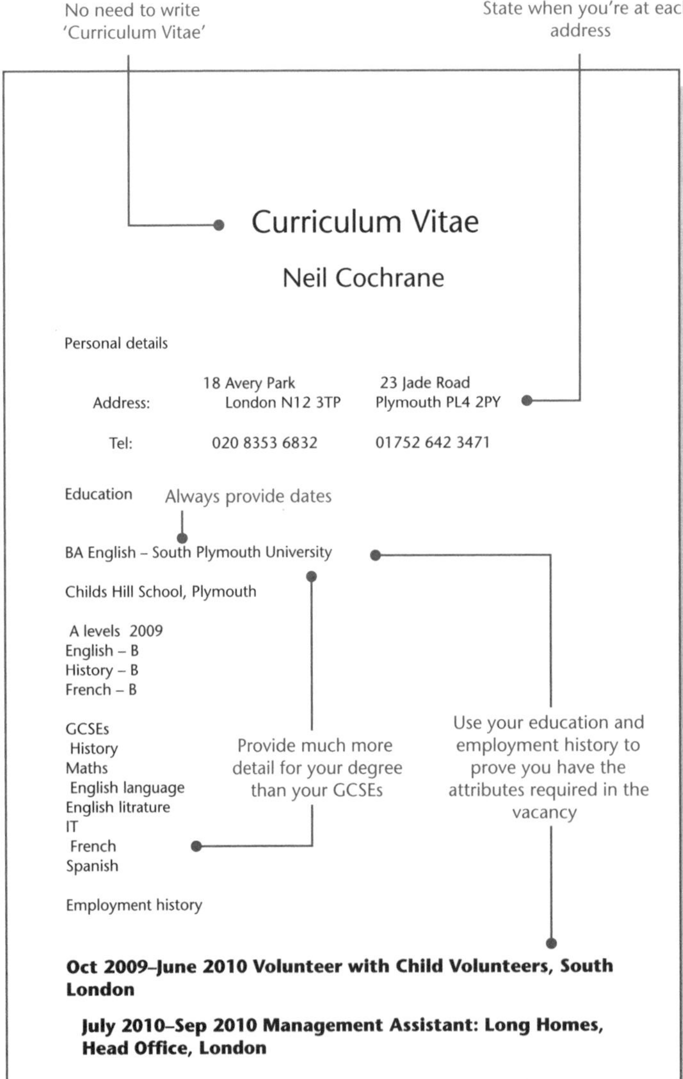

Job description (For CVs 1–3)

Graduate Media Publishing Assistant

You will assist with all aspects of content development for books, journals and digital publications.

Key duties:

- Day-to-day development of content, including liaison with authors and editors
- Scheduling, i.e. chasing authors, editors and other contracted services
- Assisting editors in a fast-paced environment
- Supervising interns and volunteers when required

Experience/skills required:

- Experience of managing freelance editorial and production work
- A relevant degree
- An interest in media, especially films
- Quick, accurate and effective editing skills
- Excellent English skills and a second language
- Good communication skills
- An ability to build relationships with a wide range of people
- Good IT skills, including knowledge of Adobe InDesign and Photoshop

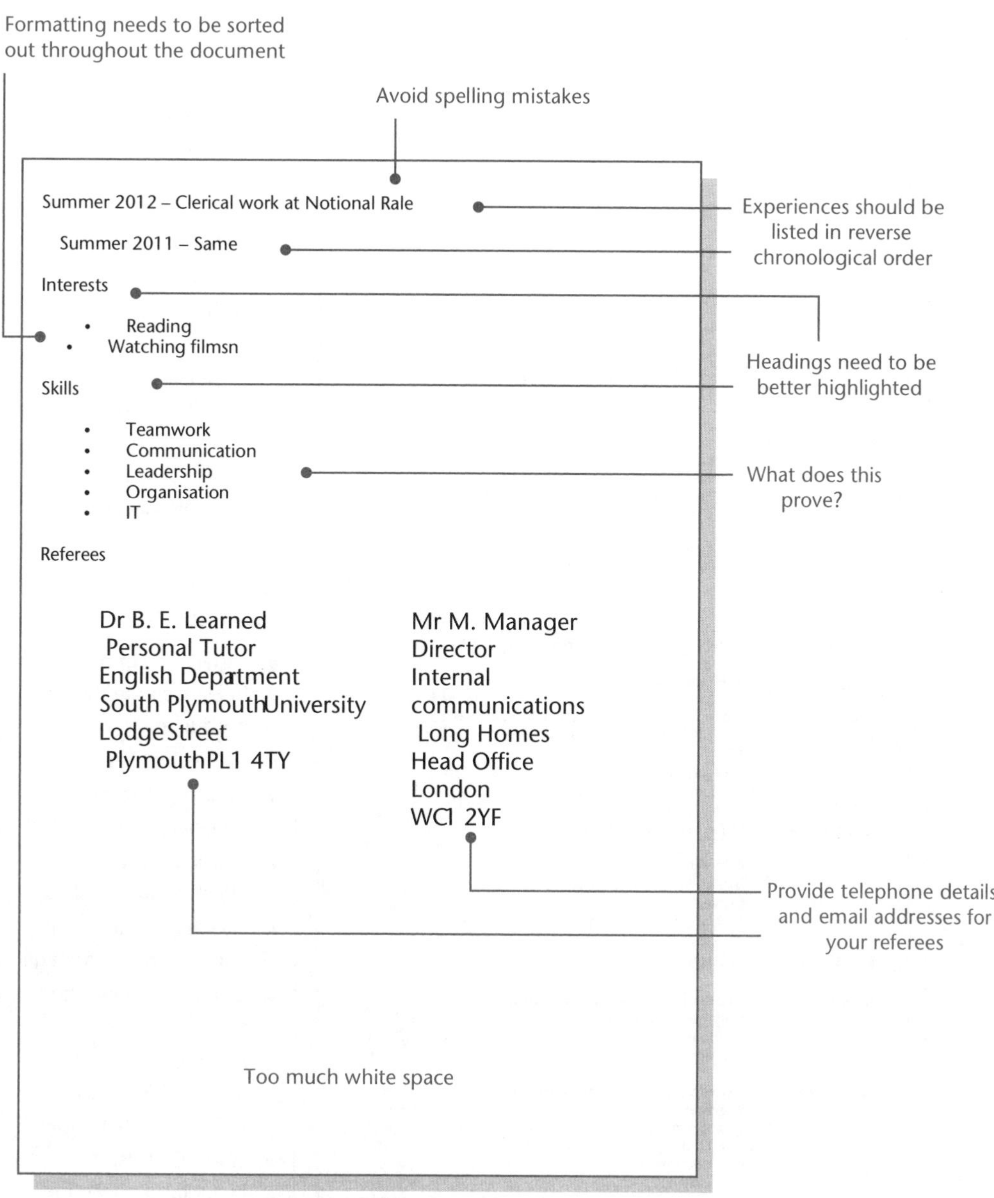

Formatting needs to be sorted out throughout the document
Avoid spelling mistakes
Summer 2012 – Clerical work at Notional Rale
Summer 2011 – Same
Interests
Reading
Watching filmsn
Skills
Teamwork
Communication
Leadership
Organisation
IT
Referees
Dr B. E. Learned
Personal Tutor
English Department
South PlymouthUniversity
Lodge Street
PlymouthPL1 4TY
Mr M. Manager
Director
Internal
communications
Long Homes
Head Office
London
WC1 2YF
Experiences should be listed in reverse chronological order
Headings need to be better highlighted
What does this prove?
Provide telephone details and email addresses for your referees
Too much white space
Page 2

Example CV2 – an average chronological CV

The CV below is formatted appropriately and everything is spelt correctly. It also makes a better job of outlining the person's experiences and relating them to skills required in the workplace. However, no attempt has been made to relate the person's experience to the specific attributes required.

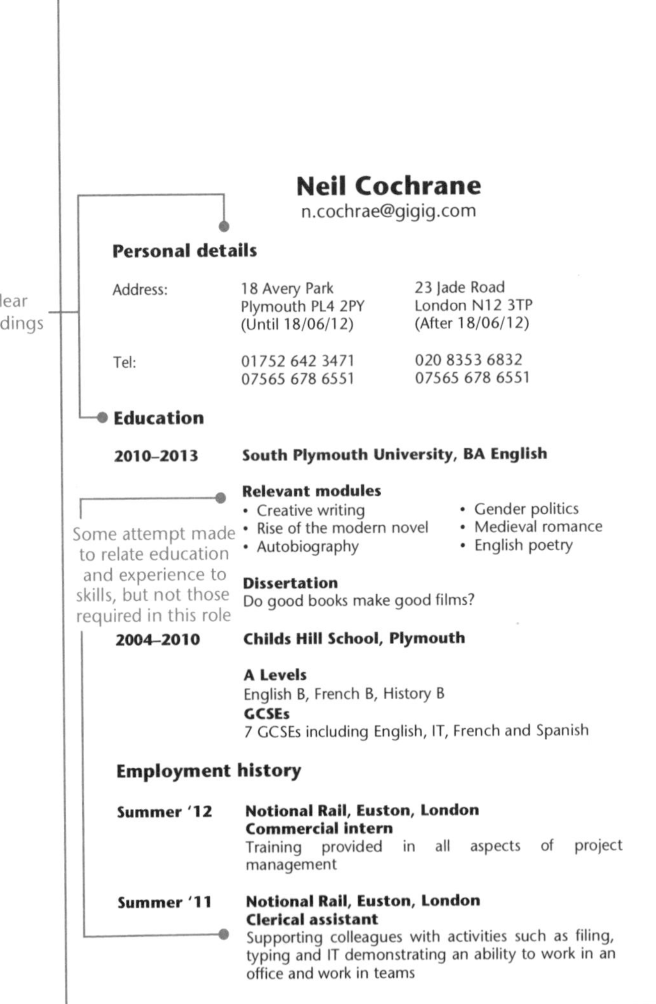

Neil Cochrane
n.cochrae@gigig.com

Personal details

Address:	18 Avery Park Plymouth PL4 2PY (Until 18/06/12)	23 Jade Road London N12 3TP (After 18/06/12)
Tel:	01752 642 3471 07565 678 6551	020 8353 6832 07565 678 6551

Education

2010–2013 **South Plymouth University, BA English**

Relevant modules
- Creative writing
- Rise of the modern novel
- Autobiography
- Gender politics
- Medieval romance
- English poetry

Dissertation
Do good books make good films?

2004–2010 **Childs Hill School, Plymouth**

A Levels
English B, French B, History B
GCSEs
7 GCSEs including English, IT, French and Spanish

Employment history

Summer '12 **Notional Rail, Euston, London**
Commercial intern
Training provided in all aspects of project management

Summer '11 **Notional Rail, Euston, London**
Clerical assistant
Supporting colleagues with activities such as filing, typing and IT demonstrating an ability to work in an office and work in teams

Page 1

Job description (For CVs 1–3)

Graduate Media Publishing Assistant

You will assist with all aspects of content development for books, journals and digital publications.

Key duties:

- Day-to-day development of content, including liaison with authors and editors
- Scheduling, i.e. chasing authors, editors and other contracted services
- Assisting editors in a fast-paced environment
- Supervising interns and volunteers when required

Experience/skills required:

- Experience of managing freelance editorial and production work
- A relevant degree
- An interest in media, especially films
- Quick, accurate and effective editing skills
- Excellent English skills and a second language
- Good communication skills
- An ability to build relationships with a wide range of people
- Good IT skills, including knowledge of Adobe InDesign and Photoshop

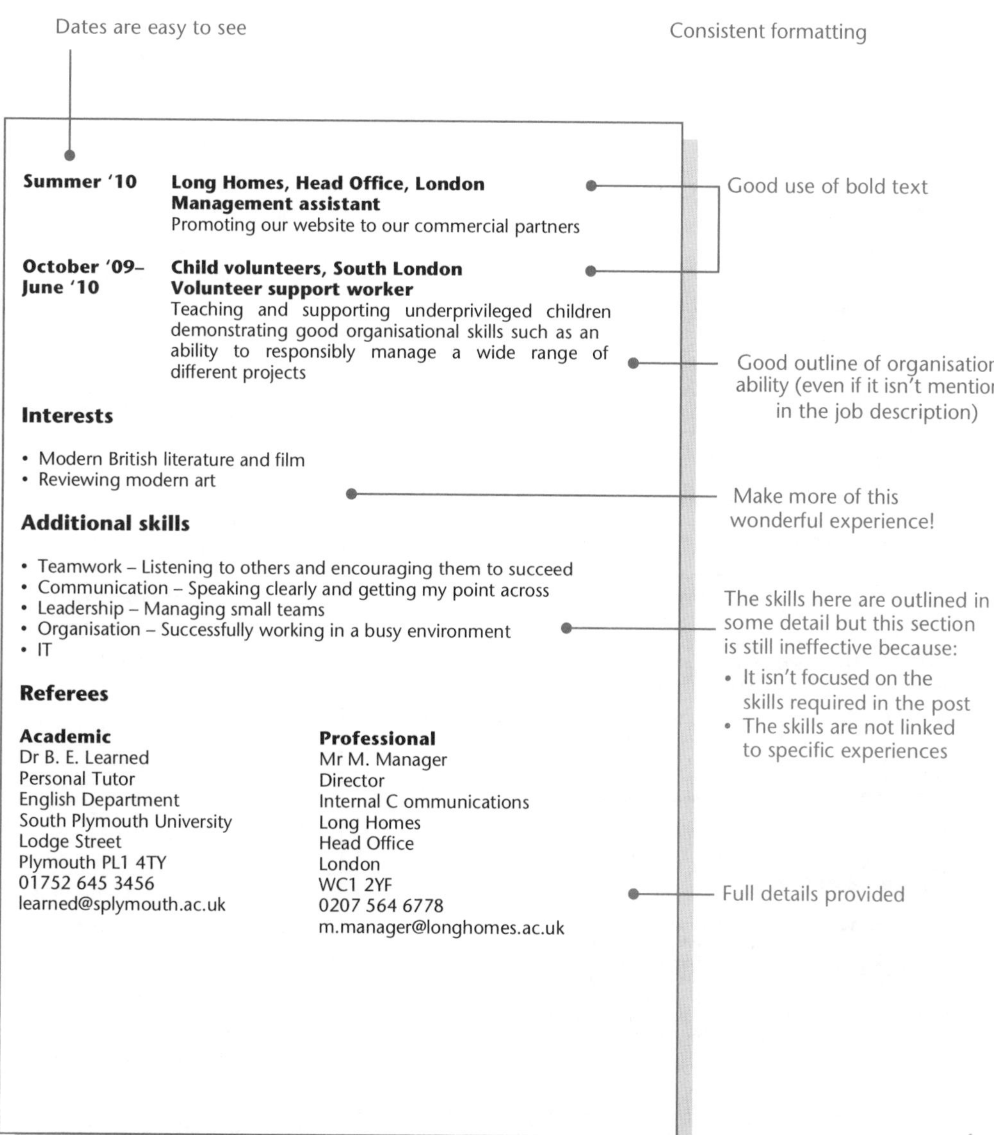
Dates are easy to see
Consistent formatting
Summer '10
Long Homes, Head Office, London
Management assistant
Promoting our website to our commercial partners
October '09–
June '10
Child volunteers, South London
Volunteer support worker
Teaching and supporting underprivileged children demonstrating good organisational skills such as an ability to responsibly manage a wide range of different projects
Good use of bold text
Good outline of organisationa
ability (even if it isn't mention
in the job description)
Interests
• Modern British literature and film
• Reviewing modern art
Make more of this
wonderful experience!
Additional skills
• Teamwork – Listening to others and encouraging them to succeed
• Communication – Speaking clearly and getting my point across
• Leadership – Managing small teams
• Organisation – Successfully working in a busy environment
• IT
The skills here are outlined in some detail but this section is still ineffective because:
• It isn't focused on the skills required in the post
• The skills are not linked to specific experiences
Referees
Academic
Dr B. E. Learned
Personal Tutor
English Department
South Plymouth University
Lodge Street
Plymouth PL1 4TY
01752 645 3456
learned@splymouth.ac.uk
Professional
Mr M. Manager
Director
Internal C ommunications
Long Homes
Head Office
London
WC1 2YF
0207 564 6778
m.manager@longhomes.ac.uk
Full details provided
Page 2

Example CV3 – a good chronological/traditional CV

The CV below stands out. The formatting is uniform and clear, everything is spelt correctly and the content is unmistakably targeted at the specific attributes required in the job. The skills are also proven with reference to specific experiences.

Key contact details clearly presented

Profile is written in the third person, i.e. without using the pronouns 'I' or 'me'

Neil Cochrane

07565 678 6551 n.cochrane@gigig.com

Personal profile

Dedicated English graduate with a strong interest in the film industry, substantial editorial and production experience, qualifications in French and Spanish and relevant IT skills.

Personal profile sums up specific skills, interest and experience relevant to the role

Personal details

Address:	18 Avery Park Plymouth PL4 2PY (Until 18/06/12)	London N12 3TP (After 18/06/12)
Tel:	01752 642 3471	020 8353 6832

Education

2010–2013 **South Plymouth University, BA English, 2.1**

A highly relevant degree focusing on the contemporary use of English in modern media

Relevant modules

- Creative writing
- The rise of the modern novel
- English poetry
- Autobiography

Dissertation: 'Do good books make good films?' A 5000-word report linking contemporary literature to ersatz American screenplays.

Demonstrated a clear and accessible critical style and a deep understanding of good written communication in a wide range of contexts.

Degree is effectively linked to the specific role

2004–2010 **Childs Hill School, Plymouth**

A Levels: English B, French B, History B
GCSEs: 7 including English, IT, French and Spanish

Employment history

Summer '12 **Notional Rail, Euston , London**
Commercial editorial intern

- Developed and edited content for the firm's annual report in a high-pressure environment.
- Successfully liaised with a wide range of colleagues and managed freelancers by building strong relationships and keeping in touch.

Try to get your key experience on the front page

Page 1

Don't let the contents of the last entry on the first page spread onto the second

Job description (For CVs 1–3)

Graduate Media Publishing Assistant

You will assist with all aspects of content development for books, journals and digital publications.

Key duties:

- Day-to-day development of content, including liaison with authors and editors
- Scheduling, i.e. chasing authors, editors and other contracted services
- Assisting editors in a fast-paced environment
- Supervising interns and volunteers when required

Experience/skills required:

- Experience of managing freelance editorial and production work
- A relevant degree
- An interest in media, especially films
- Quick, accurate and effective editing skills
- Excellent English skills and a second language
- Good communication skills
- An ability to build relationships with a wide range of people
- Good IT skills, including knowledge of Adobe InDesign and Photoshop

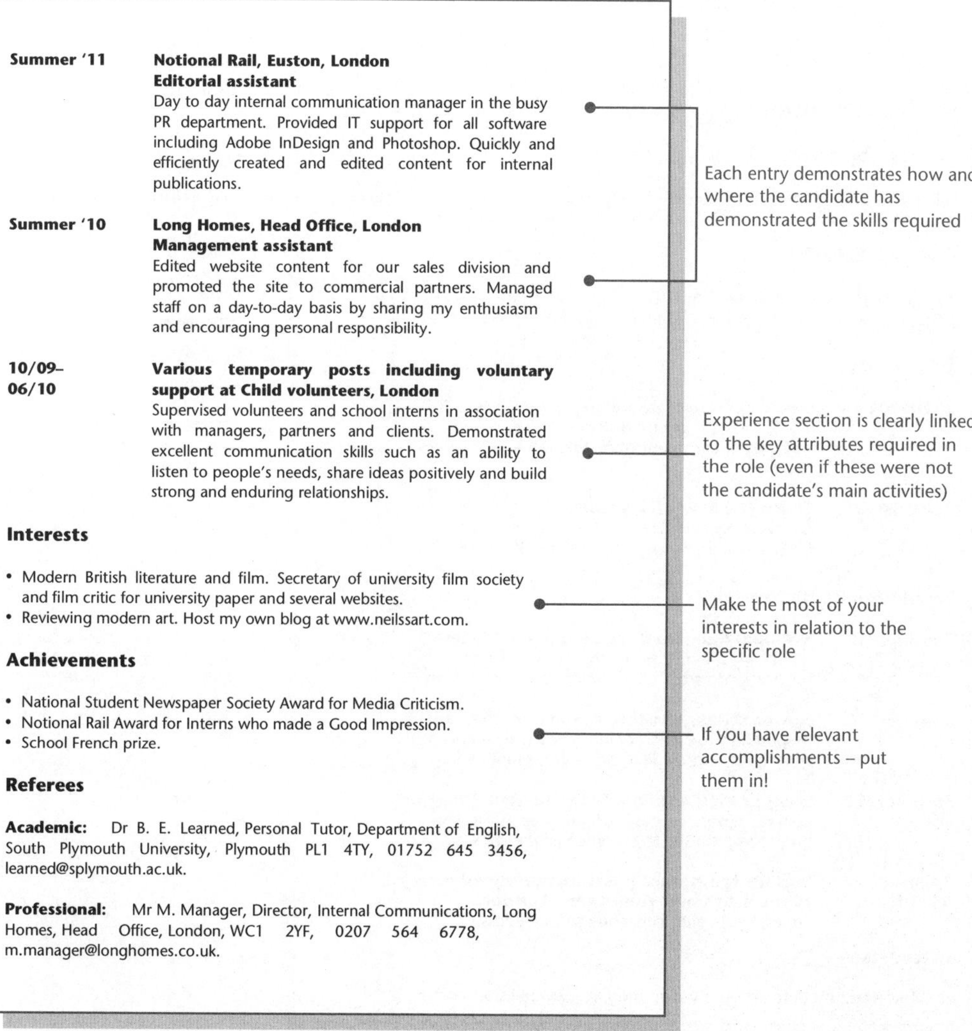

Summer '11 **Notional Rail, Euston, London**
Editorial assistant
Day to day internal communication manager in the busy PR department. Provided IT support for all software including Adobe InDesign and Photoshop. Quickly and efficiently created and edited content for internal publications.

Summer '10 **Long Homes, Head Office, London**
Management assistant
Edited website content for our sales division and promoted the site to commercial partners. Managed staff on a day-to-day basis by sharing my enthusiasm and encouraging personal responsibility.

10/09–06/10 **Various temporary posts including voluntary support at Child volunteers, London**
Supervised volunteers and school interns in association with managers, partners and clients. Demonstrated excellent communication skills such as an ability to listen to people's needs, share ideas positively and build strong and enduring relationships.

Interests

- Modern British literature and film. Secretary of university film society and film critic for university paper and several websites.
- Reviewing modern art. Host my own blog at www.neilssart.com.

Achievements

- National Student Newspaper Society Award for Media Criticism.
- Notional Rail Award for Interns who made a Good Impression.
- School French prize.

Referees

Academic: Dr B. E. Learned, Personal Tutor, Department of English, South Plymouth University, Plymouth PL1 4TY, 01752 645 3456, learned@splymouth.ac.uk.

Professional: Mr M. Manager, Director, Internal Communications, Long Homes, Head Office, London, WC1 2YF, 0207 564 6778, m.manager@longhomes.co.uk.

Page 2

Example CV4 – a good skills-based CV

This CV separates the candidate's experience from his skills because his degree and employment are not clearly related to the vacancy. This allows the candidate to show how he has demonstrated the required skills in all aspects of his life. The other advantage of this format is that recruiters can easily check off your relevant skills.

Job description

Graduate Trainee (retail)

We are looking for graduates from any degree discipline with the following attributes:

Skills:

- Good customer service
- Communication (written and spoken)
- Teamwork
- Liaison with colleagues
- Analysis
- IT
- Management
- Commercial awareness

Personal qualities:

- Adaptability
- Initiative
- Enthusiasm
- Creativity
- Hard-working

Career objective summarises the candidate's key attributes in the third person (without using 'I' or 'me').

Neil Cochrane n.cochrane@gigig.com, 07565 678 6551

Career objective

Diligent English graduate with excellent communication skills and business acumen looking for a stimulating team-based role at a leading UK retailer.

Contact details

18 Avery Park, Plymouth, PL4 2PY, 01572 642 3471 (until June 2012)
23 Jade Road, London N12 3TP, 020 8353 6832 (after June 2012)

Education

2010–2013 **South Plymouth University, BA English, 2.1**
A professionally oriented degree focussing on written and spoken communication in a range of modern contexts.

2004–2010 **Childs Hill School, Plymouth**
A Levels: English B, French B, History B
GCSEs: 7 including English, IT, French and Spanish

Employment history

Summer '12 **Notional Rail, London, Commercial intern**
Managing the distribution of internal communication publications across the company's sixteen offices.

Summer '11 **Notional Rail, London, Customer Assistant**
Responding to customer enquiries and liaising with colleagues to provide appropriate solutions.

Summer '10 **Long Homes, London, Management Assistant**
Editing website content for our sales division and promoting the site to commercial partners.

10/09–06/10 **Various temporary posts including voluntary support at Child volunteers, London**
Supervising volunteers and school interns.

Interests

- Reviewing modern art on my own blog at www.neilssart.com.

Page 1

Briefly link your education and employment experience to the job but outline your skills in detail on the second page

The list of skills should be copied directly from the job description, but some can be amalgamated into one heading so there are 7/8 titles in total.

Make sure the headings stand out

Specific experiences should be taken from every walk of life, but primarily from your employment experience

Skills profile

Customer service/Commercial awareness: Strong ability to increase sales by listening to customer needs and responding quickly and effectively as demonstrated by excellent feedback from customers and managers at Notional Rail and Long Homes.

Written communication: My English language degree and communication experience in a number of professional contexts have given me excellent spelling/grammar and an ability to tailor messages for different media and audiences.

Spoken communication: A clear spoken voice and the patience to listen give me an instant facility to get my message across and digest the views of others. For example, by building a consensus between the diverse range of interested parties during my internship at Notional Rail.

Teamwork/Liaison with colleagues: Able to actively listen to colleagues, support them and roll my sleeves up and make a meaningful contribution. For example, by persuading hesitant internal contacts to use our website during my time at Long Homes.

IT: Happy to use a wide range of software including Word, Excel, PowerPoint and Access to interpret data and make formal presentations. Demonstrated my ability during my editing work at Notional Rail, my analysis of sales figures at Long Homes and my personal art blog.

Management: Throughout my employment experience I have effectively led people by sharing my enthusiasm and providing consistent support. For example, during my time at Child Volunteers where I was able to inspire new recruits and give them the confidence to succeed.

Adaptability/Initiative/Creativity: Always happy to brainstorm new solutions. For example, by introducing selected advertising at Notional Rail to ensure the continued success of our internal communication.

Enthusiasm/Hard-working: Clearly demonstrated by my invitation from Notional Rail to complete an internship this year, after my previous successes at the firm.

Referees

Academic: Dr B. E. Learned, Personal Tutor, S. Plymouth University, Plymouth PL1 4TY, 01752 645 3456, learned@splymouth.ac.uk.
Professional: Mr M. Manager, Director, Internal Communications, Long Homes, London, WC1 2YF, 0207 564 6778, m.manager@lhomes.co.uk.

Page 2

As far as possible, specifically outline **how** you demonstrate each skill

Three or four lines are enough for each skill

Chapter 10

CV checklist

Finally, before sending off your CV make sure it looks good from the employer's perspective, i.e. that it quickly and clearly proves you have the qualities they need. You want them to scan the document and quickly exclaim, 'Wow – he's perfect!' Here are ten questions you can ask yourself before buying a stamp or pressing 'Send':

- ☐ Have I targeted my CV at the specific skills and experience required?
- ☐ Have I demonstrated how I've shown each skill (rather than just listed them)?
- ☐ Have I used appropriate headings?
- ☐ Have I used positive action words and keywords from the personal specification?
- ☐ Have I highlighted the main points?
- ☐ Are the dates easy to see?
- ☐ Have I checked the spelling and grammar?
- ☐ Is it attractive and easy to read?
- ☐ Are my CV, and the various sections, short and to the point?
- ☐ Have I whetted the reader's appetite?

The two-minute test

One way to make sure you've targeted your CV appropriately is to ask a friend to look at it for one minute and tell you what skills the organisation requires in that specific role. If they identify the correct skills then you know that you've targeted things appropriately and are on the right track.

Finding out more

In this guide

- Planning your journey – Chapter 3.
- Tip-top application forms – Chapter 11.

On the companion website

- An example digital CV.
- Example CVs 5 – 8.
- Example social network CVs.
- Example CVs aimed at specific sectors.
- Further examples of how you could demonstrate some more common transferrable and technical skills required by employers.

On the web

There are numerous example CVs on the Internet, but beware, many of them are sub-standard. Some reliable websites are listed on the companion website including those provided by Kent and Oxford Universities.

What to do next

Take stock. If you are still struggling to produce an impressive and persuasive CV, don't worry – it takes time. Reread this chapter and revise how each of the example CVs was constructed in relation to the specific job description. Also – get some help from a qualified and experienced university careers adviser (if you've already left university, contact your local university careers service or the one where you studied and ask what help they can provide).

If you are confident that you are constructing effective CVs but are still having no success, look for any job where you can develop your skills and experience, even if it's only stocking supermarket shelves or a voluntary role. Research the sector in greater depth and keep looking for organisations to approach. Finally, get out there and network to get your foot in the door (see Chapter 5). Don't give up without giving things a good try – it's often the graduates who persevere and keep on improving their strategy who finally succeed.

Summary

- CVs are marketing tools to prove you have the specific skills required by employers.
- Most CVs received by employers are poor or distinctly average, therefore it doesn't take much work on your part to improve your sales document and stand out from the crowd.
- Poor CVs tend to be long, boring lists of people's experiences. Good CVs use experience to clearly and quickly prove that a candidate has the skills required.
- You should include your education, work experience and any other sections that best suit what you have to offer.
- The two main types of CV are chronological (traditional) and skills-based. Both styles should prove that you have the skills required in a vacancy but they are compiled differently.
- Before putting pen to paper, take the time to improve your understanding of what makes a good CV and ensure that your document represents you effectively.
- Carefully check your CV before sending it out.

Chapter

11

Tip-top application forms

"So – inoculation I have all the experience you require." *Extract from a genuine application form!*

"You should take about 15–20 hours over each application because it's more about quality than quantity. Copy the questions into Word and think about them for a few days before answering them – Also, double check your spelling!"

Alex Popa, Recent graduate

"There are a variety of competencies that we shortlist candidates against:

- problem solving
- achieving results
- communicating and influencing
- leadership
- drive and motivation
- building relationships

We recommend that you demonstrate these competencies in your personal achievements in order to reach the interview stage. It is a requirement that every candidate for the graduate scheme has a 2:1 or above in any degree discipline. Candidates also have to complete psychometric tests including numerical and verbal reasoning before being invited to interview.

We do look for candidates who have experiences outside of academia; however, these do not have to be in the charity sector. Many candidates who apply have a personal experience of cancer and therefore the charity is close to their hearts."

Graduate Recruiters, Cancer Research UK

Contents

What you will gain from this chapter:

- **Decision making:** The objectivity to focus on appropriate skills.
- **Transition learning:** The capacity and confidence to promote yourself effectively.
- **Self-awareness:** The practical facility to link your abilities to the requirements of specific jobs.

Why employers use application forms

Employers use application forms because CVs are too vague. They hope that forms will force candidates to uniformly answer specific questions and promote particular skills. However, just like CVs, most completed application forms fall well short of the mark. This chapter shows you how to successfully complete application forms and stand out from the crowd.

Questions about you (your personal details)

Make sure you give your home and term-time address (if they are different) plus the dates you'll be at each, and make sure you have a professional-looking email address.

Questions about what you know (your education/qualifications)

Highlight the most relevant aspects of your studies. For example, if the recruiter asks you to include the individual units that make up your degree, list the most relevant ones first. If you haven't achieved the UCAS points or degree level required, don't just send the form off and hope for the best because it will probably be discarded. Contact the organisation, give them a good reason why your grades weren't as good as you hoped and ask them to look at your application anyway.

Questions about what you've done (your work history)

This section gives you a great opportunity to demonstrate that your work history is relevant to the role you're seeking. Here are some tips:

- Try to link your previous roles to the job you're seeking; be creative but don't lie. For example, if you're going for a job as a trainee accountant you could describe a vaguely relevant previous job as 'Accounts Assistant'.
- Outline your most relevant tasks and achievements in previous roles, even if they were only a minor part of the job.
- Use positive words (see Chapter 9) and stress your individual responsibilities.

For example, the following work history section of an application form has been targeted at the specific personal specification. The links are circled.

Example personal specification for a job in retail

Job description: Retail Trainee

Selection criteria:

Personal qualities	*Skills*
• Adaptability	• Good customer service
• Initiative	• Communication
• Enthusiasm	• Teamwork and management
• Creativity	• Liaison with colleagues
• Commercial awareness	• Analysis

Relating your work history to the job requirements

Job title	**Responsibilities**
Retail supervisor *(This job actually involved a wide range of mundane tasks in a car plant including the odd supervision of new staff.)*	• Managed new recruits • Liaised with customers, colleagues and managers to analyse promotions • Ensured standards of customer care • Contributed to 10% increase in sales by introducing a creative new stock rotation policy

Questions about your skills

Why skills are important

Employers ask questions about the skills they require because they want to make sure you focus on your relevant abilities. Unfortunately, however, most students and graduates find this section very difficult because they are not used to describing their own abilities in such an overt and objective way.

Your answers

The good news is that there is a well-established process for breaking these skills-based questions down and answering them effectively, as follows:

1 Clarify the question

Break each question down into its constituent parts. This will enable you to tackle one section at a time and mirror the structure of the question in your answer. Look at the example below and try it yourself in the self-assessment exercise.

Describe a challenging project you have managed. Outline your objective, how you planned for success, what you did, how you overcame any problems and how you measured your success. (200 words)

This question is asking you to:

(a) Describe a challenging project you have managed.
(b) Outline your objective.
(c) Outline how you planned for success.
(d) Outline what you did.

(e) Outline how you overcame any problems.

(f) Outline how you measured your success.

Self-assessment: Dissecting skills-based questions

Break the following question down into its constituent parts. The answers are provided below.

Describe a team situation where you influenced others. Outline the circumstances, how you persuaded your colleagues to adopt your approach, how you overcame any disagreements and what you achieved.

(a)

(b)

(c)

(d)

(e)

Answers: (a) Describe a team situation where you have had to influence others. (b) Outline the circumstance. (c) Outline how you persuaded your colleagues to adopt your approach. (d) Outline how you overcame any disagreements. (e) Outline what you achieved.

2 Ask yourself – Why are they asking me that?

Before answering each question, research the role and figure out exactly why the employer has focused on that particular skill. For example, teamwork questions are common because the wrong person could severely upset the existing group dynamics in an organisation and cause untold problems.

3 Answer the question

Address the sub-questions in the same order they are asked. Answer any sections related to the situation and the task very briefly so you can focus on how you performed the skill to a high level. At this stage, don't worry too much about your spelling and grammar or the word limit – just let your creative juices flow. Here are some useful guidelines:

- Use short, punchy sentences.
- Devote a paragraph to each of the question's sub-sections.
- Add keywords from your research into the organisation/role and positive words.
- Avoid comments that imply uncertainty like 'I think I can…' /'I believe I am…'
- Stress your own role, and what you achieved, i.e. use the word 'I' not 'we'.
- Use recent and relevant examples from every walk of life.
- Include the key text from the questions in your answers, as shown below:

Describe a team situation where you influenced others. Outline the circumstances, how you persuaded your colleagues to adopt your approach, how you overcame any disagreements and what you achieved.

You could start each paragraph in your answer as follows:

- 'A team situation where …'
- 'The circumstances were …'
- 'I persuaded my colleagues by …'

- 'A disagreement I faced was...I overcame this by ...'
- 'I achieved ...'

4 Edit your answer

Adjust your grammar and spelling, the tone of your answer and its length.

Some good and bad examples of answers

Question 1: *Describe a challenging project you have recently managed. Outline your objective, how you planned for success, what you did, how you overcame any problems and how you measured your success.* (200 words)

Too much focus on the situation and task

Bad spelling/ grammar

Poor answer: While I was In my second year at uni I had to plan how to raise money for a new set of gym eqipment for our Karate club I tried hard with Gill Hunter and Jane Barber and Brian Heddon and James and we tried hard to think of ways to raise cash and we met once a weak in the common broom at the top of the Grounds bilding down by the river. We had to figure out who would want to give us some monee and how to get it out of them Brian had a few ideas and so did Jane so we tried it and asked lots of people and came up with a plan and pretty soon we got some monee and our parents came through in the end with the rest.

Focus on your personal actions, i.e. what 'I' did not what 'we' did.

This answer doesn't fully answer the question

The full quota of words is not used

There are insufficient paragraphs

Good answer: I recently managed a challenging fund-raising initiative for my university's karate cub. My objective was to raise £2000 for new gym equipment.

Brief , clear outline of situation and task

Positive words create a positive image

I effectively planned the task by brainstorming ideas with colleagues, asking for help from experienced contacts and writing a specific proposal including contingency plans.

After exhaustively considering all our options I decided on a dual strategy of chasing corporate sponsorship and launching an eye-catching event involving leading UK athletes and local celebrities.

The answer clearly answers the question

This answer stresses the candidate's personal actions

Unfortunately, a significant problem soon emerged. It became clear that, whereas the corporate sponsorship activities were immediately bearing fruit, the event was taking up far too much time. At first I just worked harder but, after discussing things with colleagues and professional event managers, I decided to scale things back and focus on the sponsorship side of things. I was careful to share my reasoning with colleagues and get their complete support before moving on.

The answer contains exactly 200 words

Each paragraph systematically addresses a sub-section in the question

I measured our success by counting the money we had raised and assessing how I could improve my project management skills. I made £2100 and built good relationships with new commercial partners and decided that, in the future, I would more carefully link activities to the available resources, particularly time!

A positive ending

Question 2: *Describe a team situation where you influenced others. Outline the circumstances, how you persuaded your colleagues to adopt your approach, how you overcame any disagreements and what you achieved.* (200 words)

This answer doesn't answer the question; it just lists various teams the candidate has been in

Poor answer: I love working with other people. I've worked in numerous teams throughout my time at school and university. At school I was in the rugby team and the hockey team. At university I also played rugby and really got involved with social activities on campus. I get on with people easily because I'm quite outgoing and I think I can be fun. In my job at McDonalds it's really busy and teamwork is essential. I helped my dad out last year in his quest to balloon from the east coat of England to the west. We had great fun. In our rugby team we regularly get together to discuss things and improve our play but so far we still haven't won a game! So, in conclusion I am a popular fellow and am welcomed into teams with open arms.

The full quota of words is not used

The answer is rambling, for example, rugby is mentioned early on and again in the last section – these comments should be connected

There are insufficient paragraphs

Good answer: I greatly enjoy sharing my ideas with teammates and working collaboratively. For example, I recently influenced colleagues in my Art History Society to develop a new interactive website that would hopefully increase our membership.

I persuaded colleagues to engage with this project by outlining the financial ramifications of decreasing student numbers, sharing good practice from another society and personally building a consensus for change. This involved listening to my colleagues' concerns, making compromises and supporting them with their pet projects.

The applicant clearly outlines how he persuaded his colleagues and solved the disagreement

One key disagreement I faced was over the amount of work required when we all had busy lives. I solved this dilemma by making it clear that I understood that time was short and promised to assiduously look for a solution. I established a twenty-minute brainstorming session to come up with some creative ideas and asked everyone I knew for help. Through my open and positive attitude I encouraged colleagues to get involved in the problem solving process and our least enthusiastic member eventually came up with the answer.

Each paragraph systematically addresses a sub-section in the question

Using funds from a university work-experience initiative we hired an IT student to write the website over the summer holidays. The finished product was amazing and we tripled our membership in the following year.

A positive ending

The STAR method of proving your skills

Sometimes employers break the habit of a lifetime and ask relatively straightforward questions about your skills, allowing you to structure your answers as you wish. In this situation you can promote how and when you have demonstrated the requisite skill using the STAR method outlined below. As you can see from the diagram, STAR is a mnemonic that demonstrates an effective way to prove a skill by describing the following:

The STAR method of proving your skills

- **A situation where you have used the skill:** Provide brief details of an example where you've effectively demonstrated the skill required (use 10% of the words allowed). Brevity is essential because your answer should focus more on what you did than where and when.
- **The task you faced:** Briefly paint a picture of what you had to do. Again, use just enough words to establish the context of your example (up to 10% of your allocated word limit).
- **The actions you took:** This should be the main element of your answer (70% of the word limit) because employers need to quickly identify how you demonstrated the requisite skills to a high level. State explicitly how you performed the attributes required using terms that are clearly transferable. For example, to prove your organisation skills in a project you could clearly highlight how you planned ahead, set specific targets, assessed your progress, made changes where required, and measured your success.
- **A positive result:** You will always leave a good impression if you quantify your success. For example, the good answer below states that 'the children's grades rose by 17%'.

The two-minute test

In order to practise reflecting on your skills using the STAR approach, think of some of your greatest achievements in life (personal or professional), identify the key skills you used and consider how you demonstrated them so effectively.

An example answer using the STAR method is shown below. You also will see later in the book how this method can also be used to construct personal statements and answer difficult interview questions.

Question: *Give an example of a time when you have had the opportunity to demonstrate effective problem-solving skills.* (100 words)

Needs more detail about what the problem was and how it was solved

Poor answer: My job as sales co-ordinator involved making decisions about which of the team was to work in which area, and what to do if appointments were cancelled. As a retail assistant in charge of a department I had constantly to solve problems as they arose. As an English Teacher in Hungary I had to decide on the progress of the pupils and how to stimulate their learning.

Only one example is required, not three!

Brief outline of situation and task

Good answer using the STAR method: I demonstrated problem-solving skills as an English Teacher in Hungary. My problem was controlling the students and stimulating them to learn.

Action: Explicit outline of how the skill was performed to a high level

I improved matters by asking students, colleagues and parents for help, researching teaching strategies and designing stimulating activities. I found out that the last teacher had not followed typical Hungarian protocol, for example she had given the children unfamiliar freedoms without the necessary discipline. With this knowledge, I set up a far more rigid and firm environment and established a new, interesting curriculum.

The rest of the summer was a wonderful experience and the children's grades rose by 17%.

Result: Short and positive

Questions about your commitment

Application forms also tend to ask questions about what attracts you to the particular career, industry, organisation and/or role. Two such questions are shown below, along with a breakdown of what's required.

- *What attracts you to our firm and this graduate pathway?*
- *Why are you interested in training to become a chartered accountant at our firm?*

Read these questions carefully as it's not always obvious what's required. For example, the second question above actually has two questions wrapped up in one, i.e. Why are you interested in becoming a chartered accountant? And why are you interested in training at that specific firm?

In order to answer these questions you need to show that you know what's involved in the route you've chosen, it conforms to your interests and aspirations and your experience has confirmed your decision (see Chapter 9 for more detail).

Some good and bad examples

Question 1: *What attracts you to our firm and this graduate pathway?* (200 words)

Vague PR speak which doesn't look genuine

Poor answer: I have always wanted to work at your firm because you are a dynamic organisation that is ambitious and dedicated to its customers and committed to the future of engineering. I have always wanted to work for you ever since I was at school.

This answer should outline what attracts you to them, not your skills

I have the degree you require and the skills such as CAD and teamwork, organisation and teamwork. I have gained some useful experience during my holidays at Old England Engineering and Jet3 Design in Sunderland. I also have other work experience and have got involved in many activities at university such as rock climbing and media production. You are the first company I am applying to.

Rambling and irrelevant

Good answer: I am attracted to PWK for two key reasons. Firstly, the extensive training programme, recently acclaimed by CarIndustry.com, will provide me with valuable expertise in my chosen speciality, and secondly, I am keen to learn my trade at a firm renowned for producing popular cars at the cutting edge of technology, such as the Panther 2.1 GS.

Starting your answers using text from the questions makes them easier to follow

My passion for working at PWK was recently confirmed during my placement at Jet3 Design in Durham where I contributed to PWK's new Greyhound Electronic Brake Force Distribution System. During this project I was lucky enough to visit your assembly plant and get a first-hand view of your internationally renowned research facility.

I have chosen the Electrical and Electronic Engineering Development Graduate Pathway because I am greatly excited by recent technology advancements in the field of digital motor electronics within the auto industry which lead to enhanced performance and greater safety. For example, recently in my degree, I have been designing application specific integrated circuits that provide intuitive driver information systems such as a GPS chip which enables a motorist to drive more economically in different traffic conditions.

Be specific about what attracts you to the role, sector or organisation

Show your knowledge of the organisation and specialisation

Question 2: *Why are you interested in training to become a chartered accountant at our firm?* (150 words)

What?

Poor answer: I want to be a chartered accountant because I love numbers and have studied maths and accounting at school and university. This is a challenging career which I feel I have what it takes because I have always gained good grades and enjoy what I am doing. My father is a chartered accountant. Audit and tax. Sometimes I consider other careers but they are too demanding because I just like numbers. I don't enjoy the more social aspects of some roles but I can be relied upon to get numbers right. My mother is in a different career but she enjoys it. Accountants are meant to be boring but what's wrong with that!

Short and focused

This question has two parts

Good answer: I am passionate about becoming a chartered accountant in public practice because I enjoy managing financial systems and budgets; undertaking audits; liaising with clients and providing financial, tax and transaction advice.

Show how your experience confirmed your decision

I confirmed this career interest during my employment experience last year at GWD. During my time there I gradually developed the technical skills to assist trainee accountants in every aspect of their role and communicated with a wide range of clients. I greatly enjoyed the busy environment and the excitement of supporting a diverse range of businesses.

I am interested in training at Coopers because you initially offer a wide range of work opportunities. This will enable me to confidently choose my specialism once I am part qualified. I am also attracted to your expert training because it is carefully integrated into students' monthly schedules so I will always be able to link my study to my daily activities.

Show you've done your research

The two-minute test

To test your genuine interest in a vacancy, pretend you're on the phone to your mum and outline what specifically attracts you to a particular vacancy in less than 30 seconds.

Personal statements

Employers often give you the chance to demonstrate your relevant competencies in a single, persuasive account called a personal statement. This is your chance to prove that you are the right person for the job.

You will usually be asked to outline qualities such as your relevant knowledge, education/qualifications, skills, commitment and experience, but sometimes you'll just get a vague request such as 'Please provide a statement in support of your application.' Whatever you are asked, the key to completing these statements is to clearly and systematically demonstrate that you have the specific criteria required. If no specification is provided, it's up to you to research what qualities the recruiter is looking for and prove you have them – find out how to do this in Chapter 9. If no word limit is provided then one or two pages will usually suffice.

Structuring your answer

In order to make it easy for employers to follow your statement and identify the key information, follow these guidelines:

- Include an introduction and conclusion. The introduction should outline what you're going to cover in your statement and the conclusion should tie everything together and provide a positive ending.
- Divide the text into short separate paragraphs for each point.
- Use headings if they help you highlight your key attributes.

Some examples

Example: *Please provide a personal statement to back up your application.* (The personal specification is shown opposite)

Poor answer

No introduction or conclusion

I have had a burning passion to help youngsters in trouble ever since my parents divorced when I was thirteen and I had to move across the world to a new school without any friends.

The qualifications should be linked to the role

I have a degree in psychology and am currently studying for a Level Two Certificate in Youth Work Practice.

No outline of HOW skills were performed to a high level

Much of the content is relevant but it doesn't mirror the structure of the personal specification

I also have all the skills you require. I communicate effectively with young people by listening to their needs, encouraging them and setting clear boundaries. I have an enhanced criminal records bureau check and have been working with young people for many years without any issues arising. I have continually maintained high standards by remaining vigilant and always taking careful precautions such as never touching children or meeting them without other people around. I recently demonstrated my capacity to persevere during a residential summer school at Bath University with a group of fifty school students connected to our youth club.

What did you learn from this experience?

I have extensive experience of helping young people. At school I volunteered as a play leader for younger children at our local youth club. At university I provided guidance for young students on our special phone-in service and helped out at Bath Youth where I helped large groups of young people in residential care.

Clear introduction of what's included in the personal statement

Good answer

In the following paragraphs I have systematically addressed the qualifications, experience, skills and special factors outlined in the personal specification.

Headings taken directly from the personal specification

Qualifications: A psychology degree has given me an understanding of human behaviour and the interpersonal and facilitation skills needed to provide practical help for young people. I am currently studying for a Level Two Certificate in Youth Work Practice at Bath Youth where I have specialised in building rapport with large groups.

Previous experience of leading young people: I have extensive experience of helping young people. At school I volunteered as a play leader for younger children at our local youth club. At university I provided guidance for young students on our special phone-in service and helped out at Bath Youth where I supported large groups of young people in residential care. My experience has taught me the importance of building rapport, setting firm boundaries and working hard!

Relate your experience to the skills required in the post

Knowledge of the voluntary sector: My training and experience have given me a sound understanding of the scope and work of the voluntary sector in modernising public services in our 'Big Society'. On a more personal note, I also appreciate the current funding limitations, increased workload and fundamental need to be ever committed and dedicated.

Committed to personal development and learning: I have demonstrated my commitment to personal improvement in three key ways:

- My extensive voluntary employment experience.
- My choice of a relevant degree.
- My decision to start my youth work certificate whilst still at university.

Bullet points can break up text, but avoid them if you're filling the form in online

I plan to extend my qualifications once I have started training and look forward to working with colleagues and managers to enhance my skills.

Personal Specification Trainee Youth Worker

Qualifications and experience

- Level 2 Qualification in Youth Work (attained/ working towards)
- Previous experience of leading young people
- Knowledge of the voluntary sector

Skills and abilities

- Commitment to personal development and learning
- Strong verbal communication skills and ability to build rapport with a large group of young people
- Ability to set professional boundaries
- Ability to persevere

Special factors

- Enthusiasm/ commitment for working with young people

Strong verbal communication skills and ability to build a rapport with a large group of young people: I communicate effectively with young people by listening to their needs, encouraging them and setting clear boundaries. For example, I recently managed a successful trip to a local theatre for our youth centre by letting the students choose the play, giving them an incentive if they followed the plot (a trip backstage) and establishing firm but fair procedures for when individuals misbehaved.

Use examples to prove your skills but also outline how you demonstrate the skills to a high level

Throughout my career I have built a strong rapport with people from all walks of life and empathy for the objectives of colleagues and young people. I treat people with kindness and respect and therefore receive the same in return.

Ability to set professional boundaries with young people: I fully appreciate the great responsibility we have to ensure the safety of the young people under our care. I have an enhanced criminal records bureau check and have been working with young people for many years without any issues arising. I have continually maintained high standards by remaining vigilant and always taking careful precautions such as never touching children or meeting them without other people around.

Ability to persevere: I recently demonstrated my capacity to persevere during a residential summer school at Bath University with a group of fifty school students connected to our youth club. I was determined to share the great opportunities that university can offer but the young people seemed to be far more interested in each other than the activities on offer. I stuck with my plans and found creative ways to inspire the students and was really happy when our feedback showed that 70% of the group expressed an interest in signing up for a degree once they finished school.

A bit of your personal story can balance the formality of the rest of the statement

Enthusiasm/commitment for working with young people: I have had a burning passion to help youngsters in trouble ever since my parents divorced when I was thirteen and I had to move across the world to a new school without any friends. My enthusiasm was recently applauded in an article in our local newspaper as follows:

Short quotes can add colour to your statement

"Dave's enthusiasm for working with students always leaves them positive and energised."

I hope this statement convinces you that I can add value to your service and would cherish the opportunity to discuss the role more fully at interview.

Positive ending

Questions about your referees

Unless otherwise stated, you will normally have to provide details of an academic and professional referee. Preferably, your referees should be people who supervise you in some way and can therefore attest to your strengths and suitability for the role. Academic referees are usually key contacts in a faculty, people such as personal tutors or lecturers on a key module. Your professional referees should be a current or recent manager/supervisor at work. Get permission from your contacts before including them as referees and keep them up to date.

Online applications

Employers often ask candidates to complete their applications online. Sometimes, you will just be asked to complete a word-processed document but, nowadays, you will probably be presented with a bespoke online form, as shown below. Usually, the first thing you need to do is create a username and password so you can save what you've done at any time and come back to it later. You are usually allowed to return to your form as many times as you want and add to your answers or edit what you've already written. However, you should be careful not to leave your application until the last minute because, sometimes, the company's server will get overloaded and you could be locked out.

A typical online application form

Your application

Welcome back, John Doe

Work your way through the sections below. Before the closing date you can adjust the information as many times as you wish. Once you have marked each answer as complete, you will be able to submit your application.

Section	Status	Started	Last updated
Personal details	Completed	11/05/'13 07:36	13/05/'13 09:23
Current employment	Not started		
Education	Not started		
Personal statement	Not started		
Additional information	Not started		
Reference 1	Completed	11/05/'13 08:12	11/05/'13 08:12
Reference 2	Completed	11/05/'13 07:15	11/05/'13 07:15

Update these sections anytime by just clicking on the link

You can usually answer the questions in any order

There are some distinct advantages to online forms:

- You can save your work online and return to it anytime, anywhere.
- You don't have to find an envelope and buy a stamp.
- If you apply for more than one job at the same organisation, you won't have to repeatedly fill in your personal, employment, education and referee details.
- You can easily read through previous applications.

However, you should look out for the following mistakes:

- Online text generally contains more errors than the printed word because we are unaccustomed to assiduously checking online content.
- The spell-check facility used on the form may not be as robust as the one on your own word processor and may not reveal errors.

For these reasons, it usually makes sense to initially write your answers on your own word processor, print them out to check and finally, cut and paste them into the online form. However, once you have incorporated your text into the form, make sure your answers are still formatted as they should be and the word/character count is still within the permitted limit (different programs count words and characters in different ways).

Getting your work checked

Whether you're completing your form online or in hard copy, you'll soon lose all perspective and all the words will start to blend into each other to form a big blancmange! In this situation, when you read through your work your brain tends to automatically correct any mistakes because it knows what you meant to write. Therefore, you often don't notice the most glaring errors. For this reason, you really need someone else to check your work for spelling and grammar mistakes and also to ensure you've actually answered the question! You've paid your university careers service hundreds of pounds through your fees, so why not ask them?

Finding out more

In this guide

- Promoting yourself effectively – Chapter 9.

On the companion website

- Further example answers to tricky questions.
- Further personal statements.

On the web

There are numerous web resources on job applications. On the whole, it's probably better to look for advice on university websites or well-respected graduate career websites such as Prospects or TARGETjobs. Particularly useful sites are listed on the companion website.

What to do next

- Reflect on the applications you've already sent. Don't just check the spelling and grammar but make sure you have demonstrated all the attributes required, particularly the skills. Get a careers adviser to check what you've written and confirm you are effectively targeting the jobs you're going for.
- As with CVs, if you are confident with your applications but are still having no success, look for any job where you can develop your skills and experience, research the sector in greater depth, network and keep looking for new organisations to approach. Don't be tempted to cut corners and start sending less well-targeted applications.

Summary

- Employers use application forms in an attempt to standardise the application process and make it easier to fairly identify the best candidates.
- Relate your work history to the job you're going for.
- Answer questions about your skills by clarifying what's being asked, assessing why it is important, generating a response which effectively addresses what's required and editing your work.
- Use the STAR approach to answer straightforward skills-based questions whereby you describe a relevant example by briefly outlining the situation, task, action and result.
- Prove your commitment by showing that you know what's involved in the career/job you've chosen, that it conforms to your interests and aspirations and that your experience has confirmed your decision.
- Effective personal statements address the specific attributes required.
- Many graduate applications are now conducted online. These are often less well tailored than those completed on paper, so print out your answers and check them thoroughly.
- Always get your work checked by someone else.

Chapter 12

Cover letters that open doors

"I am applying to your firm because you have good benefits, sick leave and early retirement." *Extract from a genuine cover letter!*

Contents

What you will gain from this chapter:

- **Decision making:** The objectivity to choose your key attributes for each application.
- **Transition learning:** The ability to effectively highlight your attributes.
- **Self-awareness:** The ability to reflect on your own abilities.

What are cover letters?

Cover letters are short introductions to your application that should whet the reader's appetite and encourage them to delve deeper into your CV or application form. Therefore, they need to highlight your key attributes as outlined in depth throughout your application.

When to use cover letters

The default position is to include a cover letter with your application form or CV unless it is not possible or you have been otherwise advised. Send your cover letter as an attachment if you're applying by email.

What to include

Traditionally, cover letters were your chance to tailor your generic CVs or application forms to specific positions. However, when you've already targeted your main application documents, it can be difficult to know what to add. The answer is to highlight the key points in your application and establish your unique selling points.

Cover letters are, in effect, your elevator pitch, i.e. your chance to promote yourself to the recruitment manager in the time it would take for you to travel with him to his floor in an elevator.

Are you ready?

You can only target your cover letters effectively if you know what's involved in the specific vacancy and you have thought about the relevant qualities and experience you have to offer. Try the following two-minute test to see how ready you are to put together a formal cover letter.

The two-minute test – your elevator pitch

Quickly list your main qualities in relation to the specific job you're seeking. If this is easy then you're ready to target your cover letter. If it's a struggle, take a quick look through Chapter 9 before reading on.

Your relevant skills

- ____________________
- ____________________
- ____________________
- ____________________
- ____________________
- ____________________

Your relevant qualifications and knowledge:

- ____________________
- ____________________
- ____________________

Your relevant experience:

- ____________________
- ____________________
- ____________________

Formatting your letter

Use the following layout as a template for your letter:

Your name and address
Date

The full name of the person being addressed
Their position
Address

Dear Mr/Mrs/Ms ________,

RE: Name of position and reference number

Paragraph 1: Write a positive introduction outlining how you heard about the job and listing the documents you have enclosed.

Paragraph 2: Outline why you are interested in the role. Clearly demonstrate that you have researched what's involved in the job and have reflected on its suitability.

Paragraph 3/4: Highlight your key skills and experiences.

Paragraph 5: End positively, outlining when you will be available for interview.

Yours sincerely
Your signature
Your name

There are a few guidelines to follow in your cover letters:

- Use one page of A4 paper.
- Try to address your letter to a named person. If no name is provided, contact the organisation to ask who deals with recruitment. If no name can be found, you should address your letter to Dear Sir/Madam and sign it off 'Yours faithfully'.
- Use a formal, professional tone.

Speculative letters

Sometimes you may want to write to an organisation out of the blue offering your services; this is usually called a speculative application. These 'fishing' letters may be effective, especially if you have some outstanding qualities or experience, but nowadays they usually fall on deaf ears unless you have already established some form of initial contact and your letter is integral to your wider networking strategy. You can find out more about effective networking in Chapter 5.

Example cover letters

A poor cover letter

The following cover letter is designed to accompany CV3 in Chapter 10. The spelling and grammar are good but the letter is clearly too generic to get the employer excited. The job description and personal specification for the role are provided alongside.

Neil Cochrane
18 Avery Park
Plymouth
PL4 2PY
25/05/2013

John Hughes
Manager – digital production
Demand Publications
12 Huntingdon Lane
London, WC1 2AA

The contact details have clearly been cut and pasted into a generic template

Dear Mr Hughes

RE: Graduate Media Publishing Assistant, Ref. AT 234/34

Please find attached my CV for the above role which I recently noticed in a professional recruitment website.

I am interested in working for Demand publications because you are a well renowned firm in the sector.

My CV shows that I have all the qualities you require. As you can see, I have good communication, teamwork, organisation, problem solving and editorial skills as well as indepth commercial awareness.

I have a relevant degree and extensive experience where I have undertaken all the duties required in this role. I also speak French and Spanish.

I hope my CV convinces you of my suitability for the role and I look forward to discussing my application more fully at interview. Please do not hesitate to contact me if you have any questions.

Yours sincerely

Neil Cochrane

Neil Cochrane

Skills and experiences are not related to the specific job

Job description (For CV3, Chapter 10)

Graduate Media Publishing Assistant

You will assist with all aspects of content development for books, journals and digital publications.

Key duties:

- Day-to-day development of content, including liaison with authors and editors
- Scheduling, i.e. chasing authors, editors and other contracted services
- Assisting editors in a fast-paced environment
- Supervising interns and volunteers when required

Experience/skills required:

- Experience of managing freelance editorial and production work
- A relevant degree
- An interest in media, especially films
- Quick, accurate and effective editing skills
- Excellent English skills and a second language
- Good communication skills
- An ability to build relationships with a wide range of people
- Good IT skills, including knowledge of Adobe InDesign and Photoshop

A better cover letter

The following cover letter is again designed to accompany Example CV3 in Chapter 10. The job description and personal specification for the role are provided alongside.

Genuine interest is demonstrated by the reference to Digital World

Neil Cochrane
18 Avery Park
Plymouth
PL4 2PY
25/05/2013

John Hughes
Manager – digital production
Demand Publications
12 Huntingdon Lane
London
WC1 2AA

Introduction refers to previous contact with the employer – this will get you noticed

Dear Mr Hughes

RE: Graduate Media Publishing Assistant, Ref. AT 234/34

Thank you for discussing the above role last Thursday on the phone. I particularly enjoyed hearing you talk so positively about the exciting opportunities opening up in this sector. Please find attached my CV.

As I explained last week, this vacancy immediately sparked my interest because it represents a stimulating and fulfilling introduction to modern media publication in a firm that is renowned for creating new opportunities, as shown by your recent innovation award from Digital World.

My CV shows that I have all the qualities you require. In particular, I would like to draw your attention to my communication skills, ability to build rapport and capacity to undertake and manage freelance editorial and production work at a large multinational firm. Furthermore, I also speak French and Spanish.

My genuine interest in this sector is demonstrated by choice of a media-related English degree and extensive relevant experience. During my internships I also mastered all the duties required in this role. For example, I developed and edited a large number of public communication messages using software packages such as InDesign and Photoshop and constructively liaised with authors and colleagues across the organisation.

I hope my CV convinces you of my suitability for the role and I look forward to discussing my application more fully at interview. Please do not hesitate to contact me if you have any questions.

Yours sincerely

Neil Cochrane

Neil Cochrane

Relevant skills and experience are highlighted)

Job description (For CV3, Chapter 10)

Graduate Media Publishing Assistant

You will assist with all aspects of content development for books, journals and digital publications.

Key duties:

- Day-to-day development of content, including liaison with authors and editors
- Scheduling, i.e. chasing authors, editors and other contracted services
- Assisting editors in a fast-paced environment
- Supervising interns and volunteers when required

Experience/skills required:

- Experience of managing freelance editorial and production work
- A relevant degree
- An interest in media, especially films
- Quick, accurate and effective editing skills
- Excellent English skills and a second language
- Good communication skills
- An ability to build relationships with a wide range of people
- Good IT skills, including knowledge of Adobe InDesign and Photoshop

Chapter 12

Another good cover letter

The following cover letter is designed to accompany the retail-based Example CV4 in Chapter 10. The job description and personal specification for the role are provided alongside.

Neil Cochrane
18 Avery Park
Plymouth
PL4 2PY
25/05/2013

The candidate demonstrates genuine interest in this specific role by outlining what attracts him to the organisation's training programme

Jenny Jones
Trainee Manager
Johns and Spencers
32 Windmill Lane
London
W1 4YP

Dear Mrs Jones

RE: Graduate Trainee Role (Retail)

Please find attached my CV to support my application for the graduate trainee (retail) roles you recently advertised on plostacs.co.uk.

I am attracted to this vacancy because of the international regard Johns and Spencers has in terms of caring for its workforce and the inclusive and developmental nature of your nine-month training programme which provides practical experience from day one.

My CV shows that I have all the qualities you require. In particular, I would like to draw your attention to the customer service and communication skills I have demonstrated during my various commercial roles. I find it easy to build rapport with customers, colleagues and managers by showing respect, listening carefully and sharing my ideas positively. Furthermore, I will also add value to your organisation through my ability to speak French and Spanish.

The applicant outlines how he performs the key skills to a high level

My successful customer facing experience and wide interests are testament to my enthusiasm and creativity as well as my ability to work hard and balance my commitments. For example, I expanded my blog last June and brought in increased advertising revenue at exactly the same time as my exams.

A few examples back up your arguments

I hope my CV convinces you of my suitability for the role and I look forward to discussing my application more fully at interview. Please do not hesitate to contact me if you have any questions.

Yours sincerely

Neil Cochrane

Neil Cochrane

Job description (For CV4, Chapter 10)

Graduate Trainee (retail)

We are looking for graduates from any degree discipline with the following attributes:

Skills:

- Good customer service
- Communication (written and spoken)
- Teamwork
- Liaison with colleagues
- Analysis
- IT
- Management
- Commercial awareness

Personal qualities:

- Adaptability
- Initiative
- Enthusiasm
- Creativity
- Hard-working

A good speculative letter

The following cover letter is for a speculative application to a local bookshop, which may be successful as part of an overall networking strategy (see Chapter 5).

Jane Ford
34 Lister Street
Highgate
London
N6 2KL
25/05/2013

Helen Miles
Manager
Holford Books
64 Gratton Street
Highgate
London
N6 HGS

Dear Mrs Miles

Thank you for meeting me last week and discussing the opportunities and challenges of managing a bookshop in the twenty-first century. I am writing to ask if I can come back to work for you during your busy periods at the weekends and have therefore enclosed my CV.

If possible, your speculative applications should be part of a wider networking strategy

As you know, I plan to become a management consultant in the retail sector when I graduate in two years time, so I will benefit from any hands-on experience I can get.

As you can see from my CV I have all the qualities you require. In particular, I would like to draw your attention to the wide reading I have undertaken during my English A level and degree. I also have excellent customer service and communication skills which I developed during my previous retail roles at Shiver Sheds and RV McColl in Archway.

Outline your relevant skills and experience

I am particularly interested in continuing to work at Holford Books because I have greatly enjoyed the way you communicate your longstanding enthusiasm and commitment for your role even though you clearly work so hard.

I hope my CV convinces you of my suitability for the role. Either way, I wish you well over summer. Please do not hesitate to contact me if you have any questions.

Show your best wishes and genuine thanks for any help already given

Yours sincerely

Jane Ford

Jane Ford

Finding out more

In this guide

- Effective networking – Chapter 5.
- Promoting yourself effectively – Chapter 9.

On the companion website

Further cover letters for a range of different situations.

Chapter 12

On the web

There are numerous web resources on job applications. On the whole, it's probably better to look for advice on university websites or well-respected graduate career websites such as Prospects or TARGETjobs. The following sites are particularly useful:

- http://career-advice.monster.co.uk/ – Good short summary with extensive range of examples.
- www.kent.ac.uk/careers/ – Look for cover letter advice and examples.

What to do next

Apply to as many jobs as you can but don't get sloppy. Writing positive cover letters is a great way to remind yourself about your full range of skills and boost your self-esteem.

Summary

- Cover letters are your chance to briefly highlight your key attributes.
- You should outline why you are interested in the role being advertised and why they should be interested in you.
- Speculative letters should preferably be conducted as part of a wider networking strategy.

Chapter 13

Impressing at interviews

"I like to do all the talking myself. It saves time and prevents arguments." *Oscar Wilde*

"The key to impressing recruiters at interviews is to discuss things confidently and assuredly. By this stage in your application employers will know what you can offer academically and what experience you have. The interview is designed to see if they like you and whether or not you will impress your colleagues and clients (after all – they will be spending a lot of time in your company!).

You can enhance your self-confidence and your interview technique by getting involved in extra-curricular activities, getting help from your careers service and through lots of practice."

Declan Ramsay, Associate Assurance, Grant Thornton

Contents

What you will gain from this chapter:

- **Decision making:** The capacity to choose effective answers under pressure in interview situations.
- **Transition learning:** The ability to effectively portray your skills, commitment and knowledge.
- **Self-awareness:** The capacity to reflect on your interview persona and improve.

So, you have an interview

If you have secured an interview then give yourself a pat on the back – this is a major achievement. Employers would not go through all the hassle if they didn't think you were up to the job!

Getting interviews is good news even if you don't get the job, because you can practise your technique and make valuable contacts. Furthermore, if you can secure one interview then you'll probably get more.

Each new interview is unique so you cannot plan for every eventuality but there are many common practices and techniques for which you can prepare. This chapter takes you through the whole process from start to finish, so you will be able to confidently sell yourself in a range of different situations.

Why employers use interviews

Since the dawn of time employers have almost always interviewed the best candidates for vacant positions. This is because it's human nature to want to see what you're buying before handing over the cash. Recruiters also want to make sure they like you and you have the potential to quickly build rapport with colleagues, customers and managers.

What's in it for me?

For your part, it can help to view interviews as a conversation in which each party is seeking information. At a time of such high unemployment it is understandable if you are tempted to just listen and accept almost anything, but you owe it to yourself to ask sensible questions about the role and make sure it's right for you. This will also impress employers.

Types of interview

You can expect an interview for most jobs and graduate employers often make you sit through two! The four main types of interview you might face are outlined below. Advice on how to succeed is provided later in the chapter.

Telephone interviews

Nowadays, many initial one-to-one interviews for graduate roles are conducted on the phone. These interviews are usually quite short and general because the purpose is generally to sift out the least prepared candidates as quickly as possible.

One-to-one interviews

As the name suggests, this is a meeting where you will discuss your application with just one representative from the organisation. This is the more common type of interaction for casual and voluntary roles, employment experience opportunities and the initial interview for a graduate role (where you will usually meet someone from human resources or even an outside agency).

Group interviews

This is where you will be interviewed alongside other applicants. You will typically be asked to discuss a specific topic with your fellow candidates and the interviewers.

Panel interviews

Panel interviews typically include current employees, managers, clients and/or representatives from human resources (HR). This type of interview is usually undertaken towards the end of the recruitment process for more professional roles.

What employers want to know

As outlined in Chapter 11, the key attributes sought by employers are your skills, commitment and knowledge. Therefore, almost all the questions will focus on these elements. These key ingredients of success in an interview have been portrayed in the Venn diagram below because some questions will fall into more than one category. For example, a question such as 'Tell us about yourself' actually tests your skills, commitment *and* knowledge.

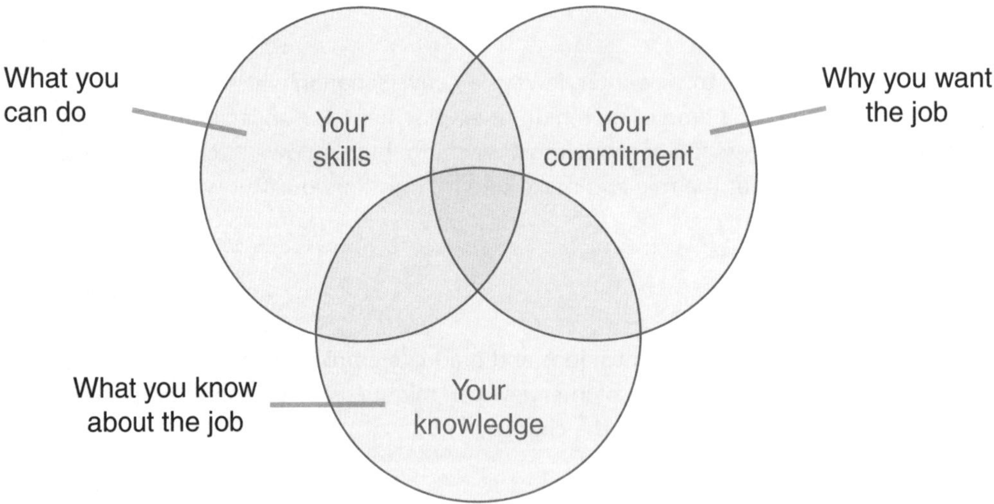

Providing effective answers

We all have nightmares about what we're going to be asked at interview, and this is quite understandable because there are just so many possible questions and lines of enquiry. One good way to prepare is to:

- Focus on what you have to offer rather than what they might ask. This way, you might not know all the specific questions but you will know the answers!
- Learn the most common answers by heart.

Your answers should be short and punchy but not flippant. Aim for about one and a half minutes and be positive – say what you want to say, don't repeat yourself and end on a positive note, so at least they know you've finished!

Skills-related questions

Questions about your skills form the heart of most graduate interviews.

Technical skills

Obviously every job will have its own unique technical requirements which cannot all be listed here, but questions about your technical skills will look something like this:

- Please tell us how you would go about translating a technical manual for a piece of equipment you do not understand. (For a translation job)
- How do you differentiate your teaching activities? (For a teaching role)

Transferable skills

These questions form the backbone of most graduate interviews because so many skills are transferable from one role to another. Several examples are provided below. As you can see, the questions do not always actually name the specific skill being tested and it's up to you to figure out what they're after.

Problem solving:

- Tell us about your problem-solving skills.
- Tell us about a time you solved a difficult problem.
- Imagine a valued client calls you for urgent help but you don't normally provide this service, what would you do?
- Do you think a problem shared is a problem halved in the workplace?

Teamwork:

- How do you work well in a team?
- Can you please give us an example of when you have had to use your teamwork skills to get a positive result.
- What would you do if one of your teammates refused to cooperate?
- Do you think teamwork gets the job done more efficiently?

Management/leadership:

- How do you manage other people?
- Give us an example of when you have been in charge of a group of people and you overcame a problem.
- What would you do if your team was getting sloppy?
- Do you think good leadership is based on respect?

Verbal communication:

- How do you communicate well with colleagues?
- Give us an example of when you have had to get a complicated message across to a colleague.
- How would you communicate with disgruntled customers?
- Do you think the secret of good communication is keeping quiet?

Organisation:

- How do you organise your day?
- Tell us when have had to manage a considerable workload.
- If you had a full workload and a manager asked you to complete another task at short notice, what would you do?
- What do you think is the secret to good organisation skills?

IT:

- Are you comfortable communicating through social media?
- Tell us about a time you have had to use customer relationship management software.
- If we asked you to design a new website, where would you start?
- How do you think web2 technologies and the social media affect us?

Commercial awareness:

- Do you understand our business?
- Give us an example of when you have had to minimise costs to make a profit.
- Imagine we asked you to identify some new markets for our product, where would you start?
- Do you think this industry has a future in the digital age?

Doing your homework

Answering skills-based questions is actually much easier than it sounds. You don't have to learn a million answers by rote because, whatever the question, your skills remain consistent. Therefore, as long as you know exactly how you perform your relevant skills and have some specific examples you should be able to immediately answer any relevant query. The trick is to:

(a) Use the resources listed in Chapter 11 to research the specific skills required in a particular vacancy.

(b) Briefly list three ways you perform each of the skills and a specific example. Index cards are very useful for this exercise.

Skill Required: Problem Solving

How I perform the skill:
- Identifying the issues
- Researching solutions
- Finding a well supported resolution

Example
- Illness last summer at SWPartners

(c) Practise wedging the skills and examples you've identified into a range of relevant questions. You can find example questions via the links at the end of this chapter but you can also put yourself in employers' shoes and just imagine what questions they will ask.

(d) Learn your answers to the most common skills-based questions in your chosen sector off by heart. For example, teamwork and communication are commonly required in most posts.

Skill Required: Written Communication

How I perform the skill:
- Target audience
- Adjust my style according to the topic
- Check spelling & grammar

For Example
- This long book I'm writing!

Skill Required: Team work

How I perform the skill
- Listening
- Encouraging
- Working hard on my task

Example
- Website in last job

Examples of how this strategy can be used are provided below for a transferable skill which is commonly requested (problem solving) and a technical skill required in a specific industry (translating technical documents).

Example 1 – Problem solving

Fitting your skill outline into typical questions:

- *Tell us about your problem-solving skills*

"I solve problems by calmly identifying the specific issues involved, widely researching possible solutions with the help from colleagues, and creating a well supported resolution.

This question is so basic it's easy to wedge in the information you have already prepared about your skill on your index card (and in your memory)

For example, during my internship at SW partners I realised that, due to illness, we would not have enough German speakers to translate two important documents by the agreed date.

Provide an example even if one is not expressly requested

I immediately looked into the problem and identified exactly how much work was still required and how long this would take. I discussed the problem with my most experienced colleagues and asked them to talk to their teams to see if we could find a solution.

Following this path I gained respect and support from colleagues across the business and two extra German translators were temporarily seconded to my department. Following this approach we got the work done on time but I also established a new company protocol for sharing resources."

Include a positive ending

Your skill outline:

Skill Required: Problem Solving

How I perform the skill:
- Identifying the issues
- Researching solutions
- Finding a well supported resolution

Example
- Illness last summer at SWPartners

- *Tell us about a time you solved a difficult problem*

Same answer as the previous example.

- *Imagine a valued client calls you for urgent help but you don't normally provide this service. What would you do?*

Sometimes, questions about specific skills don't actually name the attribute involved so it's up to you to identify the specific skill required (in this case, problem solving)

Here you just have to link the way you demonstrate your problem-solving skills (as written on your index card) to the example provided instead of the example you have prepared, as follows:

"I solve problems by calmly identifying the specific issues involved, widely researching possible solutions with the help from colleagues, and creating a well supported resolution.

In this scenario I would carefully identify exactly what the client required and the proposed deadline. I would then tell him that I would call him back in half an hour. In the meantime I would discuss the problem with my most experienced colleagues and ask them to talk to their teams to see what help we could provide. Finally, I would thrash out the best solution we could provide at such short notice.

Just relate your stated problem-solving skills to this scenario

Once we'd found the solution, I would ring the client back at the time stated and positively outline the help we could provide.

At a later time I would also re-contact the client to discuss the issues involved at greater leisure and see how our service level agreement could be adapted to everyone's benefit. In this way, I would not only help the client but also increase our custom."

Include a positive ending

- *Tell us about a time you solved a problem to deliver a satisfactory outcome*

You could answer this question exactly as you answered the first two questions listed above.

- *Do you think a problem shared is a problem halved in the workplace?*

This question easily fits your stock answer. All you have to do is include an introduction about your opinions on sharing problems and stress how you have done this in your example, as follows:

"I certainly think that problems become much easier to solve if you get help from others and you build a consensus.

I solve problems by calmly identifying the specific issues involved, widely researching possible solutions with the help from colleagues, and creating a well supported resolution.

Introduce your stock answer by relating it to your opinion

For example, during my internship at SW partners I realised that, due to illness, we would not have enough German speakers to translate two important documents by the agreed date.

Outline your example even if one is not expressly requested

I immediately looked into the problem and identified exactly how much work was still required and how long this would take. I discussed the problem with my most experienced colleagues and asked them to talk to their teams to see if we could find a solution.

Following this path I gained respect and support from colleagues across the business and two extra German translators were temporarily seconded to my department. By involving colleagues I got the work done on time but I also established a new protocol within the organisation for sharing resources."

Stress your group interaction and how this was beneficial

- *You have relatively little employment experience – there's no way you'll be up to solving complex problems here*

This is a challenging question designed to see how you can look after yourself under pressure. Try not to get too stressed or defensive – just calmly outline your stock answer, stressing the effectiveness of your problem-solving strategy:

Introduce your stock answer by stressing your ability to solve complex problems

"Being new to the role I will rely on the support of colleagues and managers but I have regularly demonstrated an ability to solve complex work-related problems by calmly identifying the specific issues involved, widely researching possible solutions with the help from colleagues, and creating a well supported resolution.

For example, during my internship at SW partners I faced a particularly difficult dilemma. I realised that, due to illness, we would not have enough German speakers to translate two important documents by the agreed date. I calmly looked into the problem and identified exactly how much work was still required and how long this would take. I discussed the problem strategically with my most experienced colleagues and asked them to talk to their teams to see if we could find a solution.

Following this path I gained respect and support from colleagues across the business and two extra German translators were temporarily seconded to my department. By involving colleagues I got the work done on time but I also established a new company profile for sharing resources."

Example 2 – Translating technical documents

Of course, very few of you will ever have to prove this specific skill but it is useful to read through this example to see how to answer specific technical questions related to the specific career you want to enter.

Your skill outline:

Skill Required: Translating technical documents

How I perform the skill:
- Refer to similar translations
- Use industry related glossaries
- Consult professionals

Example
- User manual for German record-player

Fitting your skill outline into typical questions:

- *Tell us about your translation skills in relation to technical documents*

This is a very straightforward question about a specific skill so you just need to outline your abilities and provide your example.

"In order to translate technical documents accurately I study similar translations, refer to industry-related glossaries and check my work with professionals in the field.

Again – this question is so basic it's easy to just outline the information you have already prepared about your skill on your index card

For example, I recently translated an instruction manual for a record player from German into English during my employment experience at FEA instruments. I started this project by reading through old manuals online and consulting specialist dictionaries until I had built up a lexicon of the terms I would require in both languages.

Just repeat your example

Once I had a reasonable understanding of the product I then drafted my first translation before correcting the spelling, syntax and grammar.

Finally, I asked for feedback from the firm's technical office in the UK and then forwarded my completed work on time to my client in Germany. It turned out that my contact in Germany actually spoke excellent English and praised me for my work."

Include a positive ending

- *Give us an example of a time when you have had to translate technical documents*

Same answer as the previous example.

- *Imagine I asked you to translate German documents from a totally unfamiliar industry. What would you do?*

This is a very similar question that just requires a small adjustment to your introduction along the following lines:

"Firstly, I would like to say that I have translated numerous unfamiliar documents throughout my studies and my employment experience at FEA Instruments.

In order to translate technical documents accurately I study similar translations, refer to industry-related glossaries and check my work with professionals in the field.

For example, I recently translated an instruction manual ..."

- *Surely you need an electronics degree to translate this stuff?*

Deny this criticism by calmly outlining your skills and referring to your stock example:

"Actually I can translate technical skills and have done so throughout my studies and my employment experience in my experience at FEA instruments.

In fact, I have found that it can be quite an advantage if I am unfamiliar with the relevant technical terms at the start of a project because I am not tempted to use the jargon or old-fashioned terms that experts tend to use.

Try to outline your relative strengths

In order to translate technical documents accurately I study similar translations, refer to industry-related glossaries and check my work with professionals in the field.

For example, I recently translated an instruction ..."

Carry on with your stock example

Try it yourself

Now you know how to answer these skills-related questions, try it yourself.

Self-assessment: Proving your skills

1. Fill in the virtual index card below about your personal teamwork skills.
2. Think of two questions employers in your sector could ask you about your teamwork skills and practise the answers using what you've written on the card.

Skill Required: Teamwork

How I perform the skill:

-
-
-

Example

The questions they could ask and your answers:

Question 1: ______________________

Your answer ______________________

____

Question 2: ______________________

Your answer ______________________

____

Commitment-based questions

What they want to know

Employers want to make sure you have the commitment to succeed as well as the skills. In short, they want to assure themselves that you're a serious candidate, i.e. you have carefully researched the vacancy and carefully confirmed that it's right for you. Some typical commitment-based questions are shown opposite.

- What do you think this job involves?
- Why do you want to work for us?
- What do you see as the main challenges in this role?
- Why have you chosen this career?
- What attracts you to this role?
- Did you enjoy your employment experience?
- How does this job fit in with your personal career plans?
- What are your salary requirements?
- What characteristics will the successful applicant need for this position?
- Why did you choose your specific degree?
- What subjects have you most enjoyed/least enjoyed studying and why?
- What motivates you and stimulates your interest?
- Where do you see your career going in the next five years?
- Can you think of any improvements to our products/services?
- You don't have much experience – are you sure you want to get into this career?

Doing your homework

This seems like a daunting array of questions, but you will be able to answer them all if you are able to articulate the following aspects of your application:

1. In-depth knowledge of the vacancy, role, organisation and industry.
2. How the vacancy matches your interests and aspirations.
3. The positive steps you've already taken to turn your career dreams into reality.
4. How your experience so far has confirmed your decision.
5. Where you want your career to go in the future.

Try this in the exercise provided alongside.

Self-assessment: Your career path

Link four key events in your life to the vacancy, role, organisation and sector you're targeting

Your main experiences since you were 18

Your experience/achievement:

____

How this experience prepared you for the job you're going for:

____

____

Your experience/achievement:

____

How this experience prepared you for the job you're going for:

____

____

Your experience/achievement:

____

How this experience prepared you for the job you're going for:

____

____

Your experience/achievement:

____

How this experience prepared you for the job you're going for:

____

____

Some examples

- *What do you think this vacancy involves?*

Describe what you'll be doing in the job but also demonstrate other evidence for your commitment such as features of the role itself that you find attractive, as follows:

"As far as I understand it the key functions are:

- *Translating a range of documents between English and German including technical manuals for electronic equipment.*
- *Translating French and Spanish when the need arises.*
- *Interpreting at live events.*
- *Liaising with customers to ensure high levels of service and increased business.*
- *Representing the firm at trade fairs and conferences.*

List the key duties from the personal specification

This is a really exciting role for me because Shaw's is known for its flexibility and determination to find new markets. Therefore, I believe that working at your firm will give me a chance to develop my skills on a wide range of projects in a number of different sectors."

Sell your commitment to the role by briefly outlining why you find the specific role so attractive

- *Why do you want to work for us?*

Cover the same issues in your answer but focus more on what attracts you to each particular organisation and vacancy.

"Shaw's attracts me for several reasons:

- *You are a leader in the field.*
- *You are known for your flexibility, for example your recent amalgamation of your translation and interpretation arms has allowed you to grow and react quicker to client needs.*
- *You work in a wide range of interesting markets.*
- *Your vision means that there will also be a wide range of exciting opportunities, for example, I notice that you have just been signed up by the Anglo-German army cadet force.*

Focus on what attracts you to the firm. Demonstrate that you have done your research and that you genuinely want to work for them

This job will also give me a great opportunity to use each of my languages and interpret as well as translate and will allow me to work in my favourite technical sector, as I have a strong interest in electronic equipment.

You could also use this opportunity to briefly outline what attracts you to the job

So, in summary, I am excited about working at Shaw's because the organisation matches my positive and ambitious outlook and the role is linked to my interests and aspirations."

A short, punchy ending

- *What do you see as the main challenges in this role?*

Define the main challenges you will face but also make it clear how you will overcome them.

- *Why have you chosen this career?*

Outline what attracts you to the career and the steps you've taken to make it happen/what attracts you to that specific vacancy.

- *What attracts you to this role?*

Same answer as above.

- *Did you enjoy your employment experience?*

Outline what you enjoyed about your experience but also show how it informed your career decision and your motivation to go for this particular job.

- *How does this job fit in with your personal career plans?*

Define the career steps you want to pursue now and in the future and clearly outline how this role fits in with your plans and ambitions.

- *What are your salary requirements?*

Demonstrate that you know the going rate but try to avoid giving a specific figure.

- *What characteristics will the successful applicant need for this position?*

State one or two of the elements listed on the job description and outline how you have overcome then during your previous experience.

- *Why did you choose your specific degree?*

Honestly outline why you chose your particular degree. Don't worry if you initially planned on going into a different career – everyone has a right to change their mind! Either way, you should also relate your degree to your current career plans by outlining the skills you've gained (technical and/or transferable).

Demonstrate how your choice of degree fits your long-term career plans and outline what you've learnt.

If this is not the case, state that you had different plans when you chose your degree but clearly state how your degree has actually prepared you for this specific role and vacancy.

Questions about your knowledge

These are straightforward questions about your technical understanding of specific work-related issues, for example:

- Translate the following sentence for me into German: 'Make sure you disconnect the equipment from the mains before unscrewing the cover.'
- What is thermal oxidation?
- What is a pseudomorph?

In order to prepare for these questions it's a good idea to develop a general understanding of the more common jargon, concepts and principles related to the job. Look through your old textbooks and scan some relevant professional websites. If you've only got half an hour, a quick look at Wikipedia should do the trick. Don't worry – these questions are less common than you may imagine because employers tend to value your skills and commitment above your knowledge.

Multifaceted questions

As the Venn diagram here shows, many questions are designed to test a combination of your commitment, skills and knowledge. Some examples are provided below along with advice on what you need to consider.

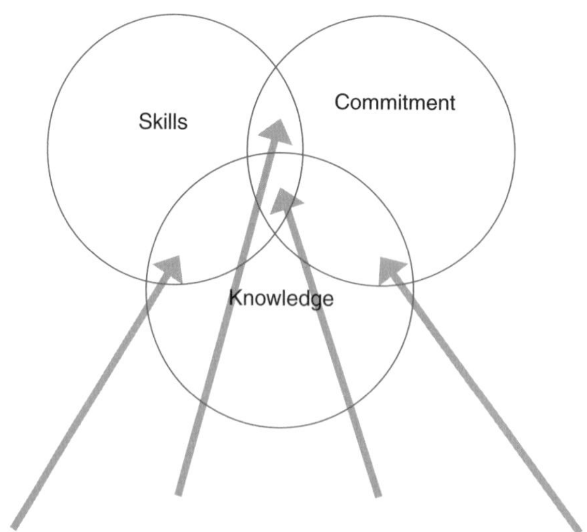

Multifaceted questions can cover aspects of your skills, commitment and knowledge all at once

Some examples

- *What are your unique selling points? / What have you got to offer? / Why should we hire you? / Tell us a little about yourself / How would others describe you? / Why should we choose you? / What are your strengths?*

Some form of this question is asked at the start of almost all interviews because it tests your all-round offering, i.e. your commitment, skills and knowledge. This is because you need to have researched the specific skills and knowledge required in the role before you can outline your proficiency in each of these areas.

Start by listing the top two or three skills and pieces of knowledge that are required in the role and then systematically prove you have them using the techniques already outlined earlier in this chapter.

For example (for a role as a Personal Assistant):

"My main selling points in relation to this role are my good all-round confidence with all Microsoft Office software, my ability to type at fifty words per minute and my capacity to liaise effectively with a wide range of people.

These are the key skills required in the role

For example, during my secretarial role at Withers last year I was able to support my manager at the last minute by developing an Excel spreadsheet and a PowerPoint presentation for a talk he was asked to undertake at short notice, which won us a large contract.

Provide an example which demonstrates each of the three skills you have highlighted

In this role I will quickly get to know my colleagues, managers and clients so I can become an effective cog in the system and help the department drum up trade."

Relate your skills to the vacancy

- *Tell us about your extra-curricular activities*

List what you do but focus on how your hobbies and interests demonstrate your commitment for the specific role and your skills/knowledge. For example, you could claim that your membership of the rugby club demonstrates your commitment to teaching P.E. as well as your teamwork and coaching skills.

- *How will your degree help you in this role?*

Outline the skills and knowledge you've gained that are especially relevant to this specific role and career.

- *What are your main achievements?*

State your main achievements which are relevant to the role and outline the skills and knowledge you gained.

- *What is your main weakness?*

Again, this is a very common question because it tests each of your attributes. One strategy for answering this question is to:

1 Outline a relatively unimportant weakness in relation to a skill that is not so relevant to the specific role.
2 State what you've done to address the skill.
3 Comment on how your actions have actually given you a relative strength in other areas which are relevant to the role.

For example (for someone going for a role as a teacher):

"During my degree I found that I sometimes had problems analysing complicated legal texts such as deeds of covenant. I addressed this problem by focusing on one section at any one time and taking notes. This technique has largely solved this problem but it also helps me advise students generally about how to effectively take notes and summarise information."

Off-the-wall questions

Sometimes employers bowl you a complete googly just to see how you react. These questions typically require you to find an abstract way to demonstrate your relevant attributes. For example:

- If you were an animal/biscuit, which one would you be?
- What was the last film you saw?
- If you were a premier league footballer, who would you be and why?

It's OK to take your time over these questions – after all, there's no way you could have prepared an answer beforehand! You should endeavour to provide an answer that demonstrates you have the skills, commitment and/or knowledge required in the role. An example is shown below:

- *If you were an animal which one would you be (for a job as a fire-fighter)?*

"I would be a wolf because they're brave, they like new challenges and work collaboratively.

State which animal you would choose to be and explain why

For example, I recently had to help a man who got stuck in a quarry after a heart attack in my voluntary role for Cumbria Mountain Rescue.

I had to work closely with expert colleagues to figure out a way to get the man out of the deep culvert and then had to carry him back to base over rough terrain for twelve miles.

Outline an example of where you have demonstrated these attributes

I was absolutely exhausted but so fulfilled that I had taken part in a team which had saved someone's life."

Pick an animal that you can relate to the qualities you would need in the specific vacancy

Quick case questions

These questions are usually asked in interviews for management consultancy roles and other similar positions. Four examples are shown below:

- How many red cars are there in Germany?
- If you grew Christmas trees, how would you increase your market share?
- How were Internet sales affected last week by the bad weather?
- How many table tennis balls are there in the UK?

These questions are designed to test your ability to investigate an issue and clearly communicate your thinking. Therefore your answers aren't as important as the parameters you set and your logical and accurate calculations. The other key to answering quick case questions is to also clearly explain your thinking at each stage of your working and make sure the interviewer is keeping up. If you get the chance, show your assumptions and calculations on paper or a flip chart. Follow this process:

- *Define the question.* For example, in the first example shown above about red cars in Germany, you could check whether the interviewer just means registered cars or whether you should also include those being manufactured, being stored for export or rusting away in scrap yards.
- *Estimate some reasonable parameters.* For example, in order to calculate the number of red cars in Germany you could establish the following numbers (having ascertained that only registered cars are to be counted):
  - The population of Germany is about 75 million.
  - Families have roughly 1.5 cars on average.
  - The average single person has about 0.75 of a car (some people don't drive but others have two cars or more).
  - About 50 million people live together as families and 25 million are single.
  - Each family comprises about 2.5 people (including children and one or two adults).
  - About 20% of cars are some shade of red.
- *Calculate the answer:*

$$\text{The number of families} = \frac{\text{50 million (total number of people in families)}}{\text{2.5 (average number of people in each family)}} = \text{20 million}$$

Number of cars in families = 1.5 x 20 million = 30 million
Number of cars with single people = 0.75 x 20 million = 15 million
Total number of cars = 30 million + 15 million = 45 million

Therefore, the total number of red cars in Germany is roughly $\frac{\text{45 million}}{5}$ = **9 million**

Prepare for these quick case questions by working through the three other examples shown above and explaining your working effectively to a friend.

You can find out more about this type of question at www.caseinterview.com.

Questions for them

At the end of most interviews you will be given the chance to ask your own questions. This is your chance to find out anything about the role you've yet to discover and impress

Chapter 13

the panel with your research. As a general guide, you should stick to one or two genuine questions you have about the job or the organisation which will clearly affect your specific role.

There's no harm in bringing four or five questions in with you on a card or a piece of paper, as this clearly shows that you are well prepared. In this way, you'll have spare questions if some of your queries have already been addressed.

For example, ask questions like:

(a) I have six hours of lectures each week during the semester; can I get shifts around these times? (For a casual role while you're studying)
(b) I notice that during my training I will be given the opportunity to work in a range of sectors of the business. Please could you outline what these are?
(c) Will I have access to a mentor and experienced colleagues when I start working there?
(d) Where do you see my career progressing over the next few years? (Give them some of their own medicine)

You should avoid overly grand questions about the organisation in general, as these will almost certainly not be germane to your application, or queries about insignificant details such as your salary or annual leave.

For example, avoid questions like:

(a) How much will I be paid?
(b) How long will my hours be?
(c) Do you have flexible work hours?
(d) I notice your company is the third biggest on the New York Stock Exchange. What plans do you have for expanding your interests in Europe?
(e) Over the last twenty years your organisation has expanded massively into North Eastern Europe. Will you be extending this approach now you have invested in Rotush Energy in Russia?

Looking good and sounding sharp

So far in this chapter we have focused on your answers to those difficult interview questions, but you should also make sure you speak clearly and use effective body language. In fact, as shown in the pie chart here, the way you look and sound are actually more crucial to your chances of success than what you say. This is because:

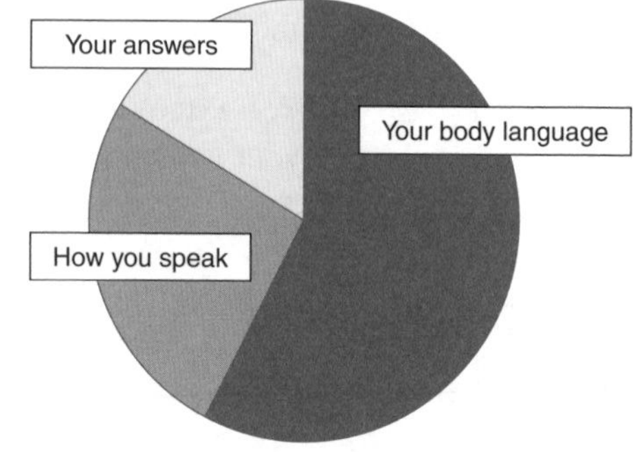

- Employers will have established your credentials through your application – they want to meet you in the flesh just to see if you'll fit in.
- Interviewers are heavily influenced by first impressions and these are often formed instantaneously.

Many candidates are so unaware of these aspects of performing well at interviews that they often get turned down for a whole host of jobs without ever realising that maybe they should just buy a new suit or shine their shoes!

Your body language

The way you present yourself is the most important element of interview success. In fact, psychologists tell us that candidates are usually chosen for jobs within seven seconds of walking through the door!

Obviously you can't completely change your body language overnight, but there are a number of things that most of us could do to present ourselves in a more positive light. Many of these are listed below but, before you look, see how many you can identify off the top of your head.

The two-minute test: Your body language

List some elements of good body language.

____

____

____

____

____

____

____

What you can do

- Dress appropriately. For most graduate roles this means a well-pressed suit and shiny shoes or a formal dress/skirt and blouse (especially if you're female). For some creative roles alternative attire may be advisable but, if you're not sure, ask the employer. As a general rule, if you can't decide which outfit to wear, choose the one that is more formal.
- Wash your hair and have your yearly bath, plus don't forget to brush your teeth and put on some deodorant and subtle/expensive perfume.
- Have a healthy dinner the night before and avoid any alcohol so you wake up fresh and ready.
- Get to the interview in good time so you are not stressed and hot under the collar.
- Smile and try not to scowl when you're concentrating. This tells the other animals you're friendly.
- Be friendly with everyone you meet, as you never know who'll be watching.
- Walk confidently (upright and purposefully).
- Try to remember the interviewers' names so you can address them personally. First names are usually appropriate nowadays.

- If you shake hands, do it with a bit of gusto – no one likes a limp handshake. You should practise this with your friends and family.
- Sit upright in your chair and don't fold your arms.
- Look at the interviewer when they ask each question and scan the panel during your answers.
- Show energy and enthusiasm.

Don't worry if you're a bit of a shrinking violet – most students and graduates find it difficult to present themselves confidently. One way to prepare yourself for interviews is to regularly attend events where you have to get all dressed up and speak to powerful people or employers, for example local political meetings or graduate careers fairs. You could also try videoing yourself in a practice interview to see what you look like, or ask your careers service to do it for you.

How you say things

Interviewing people can be boring. Therefore, if you sound like a quiet mouse then the interviewer will be wondering how she's going to stay awake and, likewise, if you're too loud and abrasive she may be planning a quick exit! Either way you won't impress. Follow these guidelines:

- Speak slowly and clearly.
- Sound enthusiastic.
- Modulate your voice so that it goes up and down in tone and volume.

Again, if you're not used to public speaking or communicating with professionals it can be very difficult to just magically adopt the right tone when the pressure is on; therefore, you should get some practice. For example, you could join a society where you will have to appear in public, get involved in presentations at university or get a job in a call centre.

Planning for the big day

So you've planned what you're going to say and you look like a million dollars. What else can you do to prepare?

- Double-check what's involved and the date, time, venue and so on. Plus, see if you need to take anything with you such as a project or a presentation. (Contact the organisation if the details aren't clear.)
- Do your homework so you know as much as possible about the vacancy and what you have to offer.
- Practise answering the questions out loud using your index cards, but don't write the answers out in full, as you will not have access to them on the day!
- Try to find out who's interviewing you and check them out, so you can easily remember their names and refer to their interests.
- Carefully plan your route and itinerary well in advance leaving enough time for unexpected complications.

Telephone interviews

Prepare for telephone interviews by finding a secure landline in a quiet room where you won't be disturbed. It also often helps to stand up and smile while answering the questions because this communicates your enthusiasm. You may also want to bring in some short, clear notes, but avoid bringing in your full answers in longhand as it will be clear you're reading your answers! One tactic is to bring in the brief skills cards described earlier in the chapter.

Dealing with your nerves

Don't be surprised if you're really nervous – this happens to us all, to some extent or other. A good way to deal with your anxiety is to use the adrenalin positively to make sure you are well prepared and 'in the zone'. You can ease your nerves by:

- Arriving at the venue well in advance so you don't have to worry about any delays (and go to a cafe until your turn comes).
- Avoiding coffee and tea (or anything containing caffeine).
- Breathing deeply and slowly.
- Remembering that you have a great deal to offer and they need you as much as you need them.
- Trying to enjoy the opportunity.

After the interview

After you've finished the interview weigh up how you did/how you could improve. While the interview is still fresh in your mind, quickly jot down the questions and answers so you can go over these later, perhaps with a careers adviser.

If you don't get the job, contact the employer and ask how you did. However, don't be surprised if you can't get any useful feedback because it's hard to get nowadays. If you have the courage, why not ask the employer if they could give you some experience to improve your skills – you never know your luck!

Either way, you should stay in touch with interviewers because you never know when they could be useful future contacts.

Finding out more

In this guide

- Promoting yourself effectively – Chapter 9.

On the companion website

- Further examples of how you could demonstrate the more common transferable and technical skills required by employers.
- Further example answers to tricky application form questions.

On the web

The companion website has a number of useful links in this area including interview questions used by specific employers and sectors.

What to do next

Practise practise, practise! Put yourself in the spotlight and practise speaking in public, proving your skills to the cat and undertaking mock interviews. If you're particularly shy you could also find a volunteer role or a job where you have to regularly meet the public.

Summary

- Employers use interviews to find candidates who fit in.
- There are four main types of interview: telephone, one-to-one, group and panel.
- Employers are especially interested in your skills and commitment and, to a lesser extent, your knowledge.
- Answer skills-based questions by outlining your abilities and specific examples.
- Prove your commitment by showing you have researched each role and reflected on why you find it attractive.
- Carefully prepare for your interviews by researching what's required and thinking of ways you can prove your relevant attributes.
- Use positive body language and speak clearly.
- After each interview, reflect on your performance and continue to improve.

Chapter 14

Psychometric tests

"For so it is, O Lord my God, I measure it! But what it is I measure, I do not know."
St Augustine

Contents

What you will gain from this chapter:

- **Decision making:** The ability to choose effective personal strategies for common graduate psychometric tests.
- **Transition learning:** The capacity to accurately demonstrate your personality and abilities during these tests.
- **Self-awareness:** The aptitude to reflect honestly on your ability and improve.

What they are

Psychometric tests are examinations of your mental capacities and processes. Specific assessments have been designed to measure all sorts of traits, from your verbal and numeric reasoning ability to your personality type. They usually take about 20–45 minutes to complete.

A number of example questions are shown throughout this chapter. These are broadly representative of the questions you will face, but to get a true indication of your ability you should ask the employer exactly what tests you will be taking and then practise them.

Who uses them, when and why

All sorts of graduate recruiters use some kind of psychometric test during the application process, but you will generally find that the bigger the employer, the greater the chance they will test you in this way. The main questionnaires used by graduate employers are verbal and numeric reasoning tests.

Recruiters increasingly set online verbal and numeric reasoning tests very early on in the application process, sometimes even before you are asked to complete an application form. This is because it is a cheap and convenient way to sift out large numbers of candidates who don't seem to have the high level of skills required. If you pass the tests at this stage you will probably face them again at the firm's assessment centre, just to make sure you haven't cheated! Other tests may also be conducted at assessment centres, such as personality profiles.

Verbal reasoning tests

These tests appraise your vocabulary, comprehension and ability to identify relationships between words. They can involve a range of questions, but typical graduate tests comprise several passages of text which are each linked to a handful of statements. Your job is to identify whether these statements are 'true', 'false' or you 'cannot say', based solely on what's been written in the text. In other words, you're not being asked whether you think the statements are true, false or you cannot say, but whether or not the text confirms this. It's absolutely crucial that you appreciate this distinction. For example, the following passage describes how internal combustion engines work and asks you to identify whether 'Internal combustion engines are used to power most cars'. The correct answer is 'Cannot say' because the text does not confirm or deny this fact (even though it is actually true!).

Example verbal reasoning question and answer

Passage: The internal combustion engine is an engine in which the combustion of a fuel (normally a fossil fuel) occurs with an oxidiser (usually air) in a combustion chamber that is an integral part of the working fluid flow circuit. The first commercially successful internal combustion engine was created by Étienne Lenoir. The term 'internal combustion engine' usually refers to an engine in which combustion is intermittent, such as the more familiar four-stroke and two-stroke piston engines, along with variants such as the Wankel rotary engine.

Question: Does the passage confirm whether the following statement is true or false, or is it inconclusive?

Statement: Internal combustion engines are used to power most cars.

a. The passage confirms this statement is true.
b. The passage confirms it is false.
(c.) The passage is inconclusive.

A sample verbal reasoning test

Two passages of text are shown below, each one accompanied by four related statements. For each statement, identify whether the accompanying passage confirms it is true, false or inconclusive either way. Give yourself a strict two minutes for each section, and review your answers before moving on.

Answers and short explanations are provided at the end of each section. Two extra questions are provided on the companion website. All the passages are adapted from Wikipedia.

Section 1

Irish setters are a type of gundog. They were bred to trap or 'set' birds for hunters. They are very handsome dogs but tend to be very skittish and require lots of attention. However, they are rarely aggressive and love to live with families who can give them lots of exercise. Unfortunately, they are prone to two disabling and life-threatening conditions: bloat and hip dysplasia.

Males stand from 63 to 69 centimetres and weigh from 27 to 29 kilograms; females reach a height of 60 to 63 centimetres and weigh from 24 to 29 kilograms. They have long luxurious red/chestnut coats that usually feather in places such as the tail, ears, chest, legs and body. Therefore, they require frequent brushing. About 40–70% also have small patches of white hair on their chests. They have a peculiar shape with long ears and legs, deep chests, small waists and abundant winter coats.

1: Irish Setter waists are usually smaller than their chests.
  a. The passage confirms this statement is true.
  b. The passage confirms it is false.
  c. The passage is inconclusive.

2: Irish Setters are also called Red Setters.
  a. The passage confirms this statement is true.
  b. The passage confirms it is false.
  c. The passage is inconclusive.

3: The hair on most Irish Setters feathers in places.
  a. The passage confirms this statement is true.
  b. The passage confirms it is false.
  c. The passage is inconclusive.

4: The majority of Irish Setters have white hair on their chests.
  a. The passage confirms this statement is true.
  b. The passage confirms it is false.
  c. The passage is inconclusive.

Answers

Statements	Answers	Explanation
1	c	The text does not categorically state whether or not Irish Setters' waists are smaller than their chests.
2	c	This is true but it is not stated in the text.
3	a	This is clearly stated in the text.
4	c	The text states that 40–70% have white hair on their chests so it could be a minority or a majority.

Section 2

> Heart attacks are also called myocardial infarctions. They are usually caused by an interruption in the blood supply (ischaemia) to the heart caused by a blockage of a coronary artery, called an 'occlusion'. These occlusions are most commonly caused by a rupture of atherosclerotic plaque in artery walls. The resulting oxygen shortage can cause damage or death (*infarction*) of heart muscle tissue (*myocardium*).
>
> During myocardial infarctions, men often feel sudden chest pain and/or pain in the left arm and neck, shortness of breath, nausea, sweating and anxiety. A sizeable proportion of myocardial infarctions are 'silent', that is without chest pain or other symptoms, and are often confused with indigestion.

5: Ischaemia can cause infarction of the myocardium.
   a. The passage confirms this statement is true.
   b. The passage confirms it is false.
   c. The passage is inconclusive.

6: Men having a heart attack usually feel sudden chest pain which radiates to the left arm or left side of the neck.
   a. The passage confirms this statement is true.
   b. The passage confirms it is false.
   c. The passage is inconclusive.

7: The main cause of myocardial infarctions is an occlusion of a coronary artery resulting from the rupture of atherosclerotic plaque.
   a. The passage confirms this statement is true.
   b. The passage confirms it is false.
   c. The passage is inconclusive.

8: Silent myocardial infarctions just indicate indigestion.
   a. The passage confirms this statement is true.
   b. The passage confirms it is false.
   c. The passage is inconclusive.

Answers

Statements	Answers	Explanation
5	a	This is clearly stated in the text.
6	c	We are told that chest pain is often a side effect of myocardial infarctions but not whether this *usually* happens.
7	a	This is clearly stated in the text.
8	b	The text states that silent myocardial infarctions are often confused with indigestion, not that they indicate it.

Numeric reasoning tests

Numeric tests typically examine your ability to add, subtract, multiply and divide, work with percentages, averages and fractions and interpret graphs, tables and statistics. You are usually allowed a calculator and some paper to calculate the answers.

A sample numeric reasoning test

Take 13 minutes to answer the questions provided below. Answers and explanations are also provided. Another ten-minute test is provided on the companion website.

1. Company A charges £120 per year for each set of the 200 urban traffic lights it cleans for the council, £180 for each of the 400 in the suburbs and £240 for each of the 50 in rural areas. How much cheaper per year would it be to hire company B, which offers to do it for £144 a year for each set of lights wherever they are?
   a. £14,400 b. £93,600 c. £15,400 d. £1200 e. £93,900

Cars sold each year in Bath according to their colour	2007	2008	2009	2010	2011
Red	1500	500	1000	1000	750
Blue	1000	500	250	250	500
White	2000	1500	1500	1750	2500
Other colours	1500	1000	1250	1500	2000

2. In the table above, what percentage of total car sales are red?
   a. 0.2% b. 25% c. 20% d. 25% e. 5%

3. If the number of white cars sold in 2011 had risen since 2010 by the same percentage as blue cars over the same period, how many would have sold?
   a. 1250 b. 3000 c. 2250 d. 3500 e. 250

4. If 20% of the cars with other colours are green, how many cars sold over this period are not blue or green?
   a. 17,950 b. 7250 c. 15,450 d. 18,900 e. 19,800

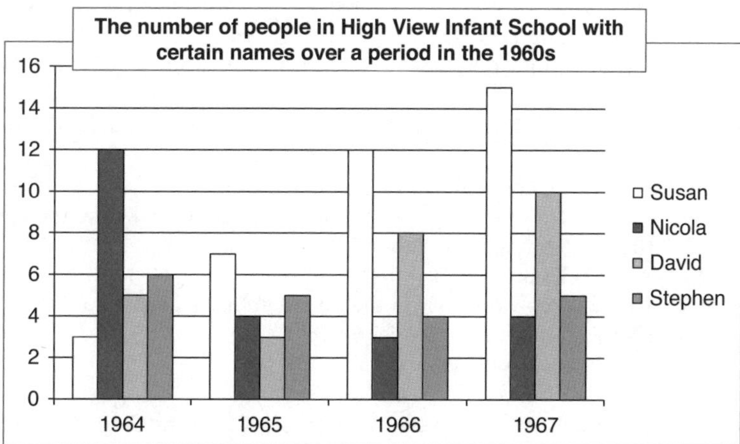

5. Over the period covered by the graph above, how many more children were called Susan than David at High View Infant School?
   a. 11 b. 14 c. 17 d. 37 e. 3

6. If children with these names comprised 20% of the total number of children in High View Infant School in 1964 and 25% in 1967, what is the difference between the total number of children in the school in 1964 and 1967?
   a. 6 b. 32 c. 136 d. 4 e. no difference

7. If there were 120 students at the school in 1965, what percentage were not called Nicola, David or Stephen?
   a. 10% b. 15% c. 90% d. 95% e. Can't say

Your answers

See how many of these 7 questions you answered correctly.

No.	Answers	Explanation
1	a	The existing cost of cleaning the lights per year = (120 x £200) + (180 x £400) + (240 x £50) = £108,000. The cost of cleaning the lights with the new company equals 12 x (200 + 400 + 50) = 144 x 650 = £93,600. Therefore, the saving = £108,000 – £93,600 = £14,400.
2	c	The total number of cars sold = 23,750 and red cars = 4750. Therefore the percentage of red cars = $\frac{4750}{23,750}$ x 100 = 20%.
3	d	500 blue cars were sold in 2011 and 250 were sold in 2010. Therefore, the increase in blue cars sold over this period was 100%. 1750 white cars were sold in 2010. Therefore, the number of white cars that would have sold in 2011 if sales had risen at the same rate as blue cars = 1750 + 1750 = 3500.
4	e	Total sales = 23,750 (already ascertained). Blue sales = 2500. Green sales = 20% of other colours = $\frac{20}{100}$ x total number of other sales (7250) = 1450. Therefore, total non-blue or green sales = 23,750 – 2500 – 1450 = 19,800.
5	a	There are 37 Susans and 26 Davids, so the difference is 37 – 26 = 11.
6	a	In 1964, 26 children had these names. If 26 children were 20% of the total number of children at the school then 100% = 5 times this number = 130. In 1967, 34 children had these names. If 34 children were 25% of the total number of children at the school then 100% = 4 times this number = 136. Therefore, the difference is 136 – 130 = 6.
7	c	In 1965, 12 children were called Nicola, David and Stephen and the total number of children in the school was 120. Therefore, the percentage of children called Nicola, David and Stephen was $\frac{120}{12}$ = 10%, so those without these names = 90%. So, the number of children without these names was 90%.

Chapter 14

Abstract reasoning

These profiles are also quite common at assessment centres. They test your diagrammatic reasoning ability without leaning on your language skills and are therefore often used for more technical roles. You are typically asked to look at a series of diagrams and establish relationships and sequences. For example, in the following illustration you are expected to identify which card comes next. Give it a go! The answer is below.

Example question

Which figure comes next – a,b,c,d or e?

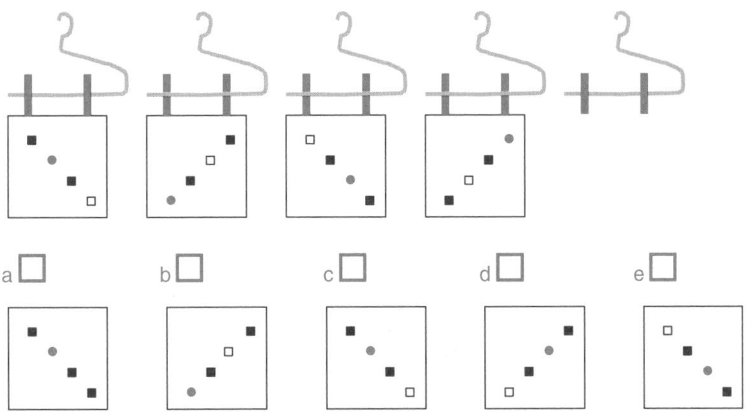

The answer to the problem above is **c** because the sequence is rotating in a clockwise direction and the blue circle and colourless square change places at each rotation.

Verbal/numeric logical reasoning

These tests are less common. They tend to involve written and numeric puzzles much like the puzzle magazines you can pick up at the airport.

Example question

The best player in a team is 5 years older than the youngest. The youngest player in the team is 7 years younger than the oldest. The second oldest is 2 years younger than the oldest and a year older than the third oldest. If the third oldest player is 28, how old is the best player?

a. 28 b. 30 c. 26 d. 25 e. 29

The answer is **e** (29). This is because:

1. If the third oldest player is 28 and the second oldest is 1 year older than her, then the second oldest is 29.
2. If the second oldest is 29 and 2 years younger than the oldest, then the oldest is 31.
3. If the youngest player is seven years younger than the oldest she is 24.
4. If the best player is five years older than the youngest she is, therefore, 29.

Personality profiles

These questionnaires look at your preferred way of doing things and how well you'll fit into a role and organisation. Personality profiles are not as reliable as ability tests so they are generally used just as an indicator of your general personality type along with other pointers such as your behaviour at interview (see Chapter 2). Of course, there is no single personality profile that suits all graduate jobs because different roles require different traits and teams work best when members have different strengths. However, some characteristics certainly suit corresponding occupations: for example, it would probably be advantageous if all air stewards were outgoing and counsellors were friendly!

Some typical questions are shown below. As you can see, you are usually asked to gauge how strongly a range of statements reflect your personal character, from not at all to 100%. This is certainly very subjective and often quite biased but you shouldn't worry about this – just be honest and trust your instinct, i.e. the first answer that comes into your head is usually the most accurate.

Example questions

I am:

- Confident in group situations Fully disagree ☐ ☐ ☐ ☐ ☐ Fully agree
- Good at working independently Fully disagree ☐ ☐ ☐ ☐ ☐ Fully agree
- Good at planning ahead Fully disagree ☐ ☐ ☐ ☐ ☐ Fully agree
- A worrier Fully disagree ☐ ☐ ☐ ☐ ☐ Fully agree

What's the pass mark?

Ability tests are very demanding for two reasons:

- They include numerous questions within a very restrictive time limit.
- They assess your ability in relation to other graduates, not the population in general, so you are usually expected to have better skills than most.

Therefore, don't panic if you struggle. Pass marks vary but you will usually be expected to get a score of at least 70%, i.e. you can make quite a few mistakes and still pass!

Personality profiles are measured according to specific personal traits, typically your conscientiousness, agreeableness neuroticism, openness, and extraversion (CANOE). As shown below, you are typically graded somewhere along a continuum for each of these qualities.

The five personality traits typically measured in a personality profile

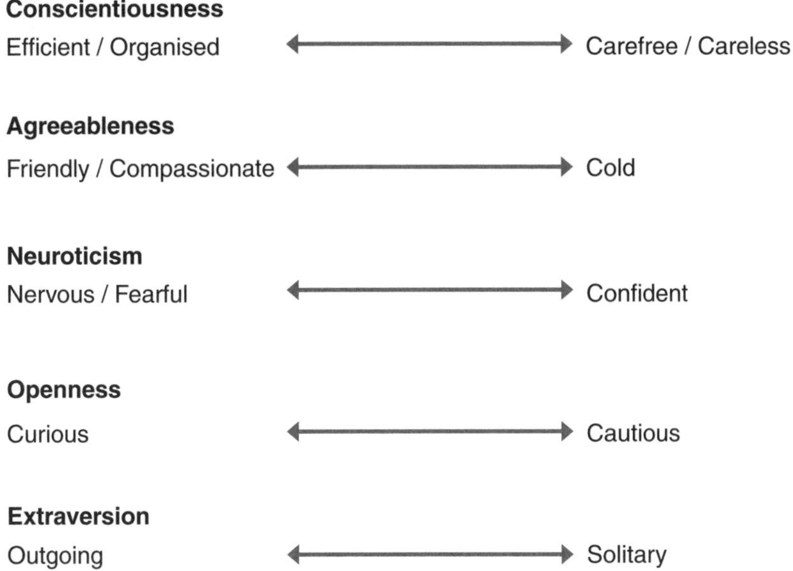

Therefore candidates are generally deemed to have failed personal profiles if they are not perceived to be the character type required or if they have provided inconsistent answers demonstrating either inadvertent mistakes or an attempt to present themselves in a false light.

Common problems and mistakes

Students and graduates fail ability tests for a wealth of reasons such as:

- An insufficient ability, which leads to mistakes and slow progress.
- Panic.
- A mental block.
- The strict time limits.
- Carelessness.
- Misinterpreting the instructions.
- A loss of concentration/being interrupted.
- Unfamiliarity with the type of test (especially for abstract questionnaires).
- Problems with an Internet connection.
- Problems with resources (e.g. paper/pen/batteries in mouse...).
- Lack of confidence.
- Being too careful (and therefore not finishing on time).

In the exercise on the next page, list the specific problems you had with the personality profile and verbal/numeric questions provided earlier in the chapter and read on to see how you can improve.

Self-assessment: So, what's stopping you?

Identify the main problems you had with the personality and ability questions in this chapter.

Your problems with the verbal reasoning test:

- __________
- __________
- __________
- __________

Your problems with the numeric reasoning test:

- __________
- __________
- __________
- __________

Improving your performance

Psychometric profiles

There's little you can do to prepare for these tests. If you're tempted to cheat and try to present yourself in a more positive light, be aware of the following ramifications:

- The tests are designed to identify inconsistencies, and you will be asked trick questions to see if you are telling the truth – it is important that you answer these questions appropriately. For example, if you are asked 'Are you always honest?', you shouldn't fully agree with this statement because we've all told a few lies from time to time! (4/5 will do!).
- You may get the job by pretending that you have an alternative character but this could easily mean that you won't enjoy it, or indeed perform well.
- Recruiters are looking for a range of different personalities so you may be exactly what they're looking for, even with all your little peccadillos!

A good compromise is to answer the questions as the 'best' you – the one you present to your mum and dad!

Ability tests

Many students dread this section of the application process because they fear it will expose an inherent weakness which they can't improve. To some extent this is true, but there are a number of things you can do at the margins to significantly increase your scores; many of these are outlined below.

1 Learn your stuff

An immediate instinct when it comes to improving performance at ability tests is to get lots of practice, but this is only effective if you know what you're doing in the first place! Therefore, your first step should be to fully develop the skills you're being asked to demonstrate – and then rehearse.

Improving your English is a long-term commitment, but it will help in every walk of your life. You can indirectly improve your performance by reading widely. There's no need to consult highly technical material that doesn't interest you – you'll get bored and give up! Find books and newspaper articles that keep you engrossed. You should also get involved in activities and roles where you have to professionally communicate in English. This is especially true if English is not your first language.

It's easier to improve your numeric ability in the short run. You probably haven't needed to carry out basic arithmetic operations at speed for years and have quite likely forgotten the basics – therefore you need to dig out your old GCSE maths books and relearn them. Such a careful approach will definitely bring dividends.

In particular you should have instant recall of the following:

- Basic number facts including times tables, place value (especially from .0001 to a million), squares and square roots, adding two numbers together to make 100 or 1000, multiplying and dividing by .01, 0.1, 10, 100, 1000 and so on, and doubles (e.g. 25 + 25 = 50).
- The correct order to conduct a series of operations (anything in brackets first then division, multiplication, addition and finally subtraction – BODMAS).
- Working out fractions and percentages in your head, on paper and with a calculator.
- Manipulating fractions and percentages in your head, on paper and with a calculator.
- Converting numbers, fractions and percentages in your head, on paper and with a calculator (e.g. 4/5 = 80% = 0.8).
- Calculating basic operations in your head, on paper and on a calculator, e.g. long division.
- Interpreting tables, line graphs, pie charts and block graphs.
- Basic probability and chance.

You should also get used to solving problems in different ways – for example, you should be an expert at the following methods suggested in the Australian Maths Curriculum:

- Draw a picture/diagram.
- Act it out.
- Make a model.
- Guess, check and improve.
- Make a table.
- Spot a pattern.
- Identify and use a mathematical operation.

- Work backwards.
- Work systematically.
- Try a simpler case or break it up into manageable parts.
- Use logic.

With abstract questionnaires it's probably a good idea to gain a clear understanding of how most patterns are created; many of these are listed below:

- An increasing number of symbols.
- A decreasing number of symbols.
- Clockwise rotation.
- Anti-clockwise rotation.
- Colours rotating.
- Colours changing places.
- Moving gaps.
- Numbers undergoing basic operations such as adding and subtracting 10.
- Horizontal variations.
- Vertical variations.
- Diagonal variations.
- Symbols which change shape and/or colour in a set way.

2 Develop a strategy

Once you've learned your stuff, there are two advantages to developing a robust strategy for each of the tests you are going to face. Firstly, familiar routines will calm your nerves on the day, and secondly, you'll know what to do when you're stuck. This applies to the tests themselves and the individual questions.

In terms of the tests themselves, you should get used to the following:

- The equipment you will be using including the computer and calculator.
- The location (if possible).
- Keeping abreast of the remaining time.
- Devoting the appropriate time to each question.
- Speedily checking your answers.
- Knowing which order you will answer the questions (if you have a choice).
- Moving on when you get stuck (i.e. whether you give up on questions and move on or devote more time to getting each answer right).

For many of the questions you need to decide whether you will read the passage first and then the questions, or vice versa. In verbal reasoning tests you also need to find a foolproof way of checking that your answers are based on what is actually written in the text, not your own opinion! For maths and abstract problems it's also wise to get to know how you will choose the appropriate problem-solving method for each question and which techniques you prefer.

3 Practise

Now you know what you're doing, and how you're going to do it, it's time to practise. Look for tests wherever you can find them and focus on the specific branded questionnaires you'll be facing. The recruiter should give you this information along with a few practice questions, but contact them if it's not obvious, then look up the website of the firm that organises the specific test and take it from there. A large number of web-based organisations also offer similar tests for a small fee and many books are available on the subject. Your careers service may well be able to give you access to these guides and may also offer workshops on psychometric tests and practise sessions.

On the day

When the big day comes you should relax and enjoy the challenge. Make sure you've eaten healthily over the last few days, avoid alcohol and get some rest, as your brain works significantly better when it is fresh. If you are attempting the test online, choose the time of day when you're brightest and used to studying – most people do better in the morning, but not everyone.

Check all your equipment is working, powered up and you know how to use it! Get some spare paper and your timepiece in position and kick off!

If you have a disability

There are a number of disabilities which could affect your performance on these tests, such as dyslexia, dyspraxia and autism. The organisations running the assessments will make appropriate adjustments (if you tell them!), but you should also seek help from your university to develop specific strategies to improve your performance.

Finding out more

In this guide

- Passing assessment centres – Chapter 18.

On the companion website

- More example questions.
- Summary of the specific tests used by major UK recruiters.

On the web

On the companion website you will find links to various guides on psychometric tests and example questions provided by the main test publishers including SHL, Kenexa and Saville Consulting.

What to do next

If you still can't get through this stage in the application process, do not despair. Firstly, ask yourself if you've prepared as well as you possibly can – only you know the true answer. If not, get back to the books!

If you really can't do any better you just have to look for a different route into your chosen field, or slightly change your plans. Remember, the big brand names often recruit in this way, but many other organisations don't.

Of course, psychometric tests are primarily designed to see if you can carry out the specific job so, at the end of the day, you should also consider whether this is the career for you. However, don't rush into this decision – thousands of CEOs have no qualifications at all, but plenty of passion!

If you pass the tests, you'll be invited to the next stage in the application process, which may be an interview or a fully blown range of assessment centre exercises. If this is the case, consult the relevant chapters in this guide, and good luck – you're halfway there!

Summary

- Psychometric tests scientifically measure your ability in a range of areas and your personality.
- They are a cheap and efficient way for graduate employers to find high calibre/ appropriate candidates.
- You can improve your performance by learning your stuff, developing a strategy and practising.
- On the day you should be fresh and well prepared.

Chapter

15

Passing assessment centres

"Drawing on my fine command of the English language, I said nothing." *Robert Benchley*

"Students and graduates need to become more savvy about the recruitment process in general and in the need to address organisations' core values when completing applications, you need to separate yourself from the crowd! Therefore, you need to find ways to promote yourself above your competition (other applicants). For example, when attending selection events, such as assessment centres, interviews etc. you need to demonstrate that you are commercially aware by displaying confidence, determination and focus."

Jonathon Field, Managing Consultant, Techsearch

Contents

What you will gain from this chapter:

- **Decision making:** The ability to choose fitting personal strategies to perform well on each of the more common graduate assessment centre activities.
- **Transition learning:** The capacity and confidence to demonstrate that you have the specific skills being sought on each exercise.
- **Self-awareness:** The aptitude to reflect honestly on your ability and improve.

What they are

Assessment centres are the venues where specific job assessments are carried out. Larger organisations often conduct a number of exercises over a few hours or a couple of days; smaller firms may just combine interviews with one or two activities such as a presentation and/or a group discussion. They are expensive operations and are therefore usually conducted at the latter stages of the recruitment process. As such, they are often the final hurdle on the path to a pay packet! The activities can include:

- Interviews
- Psychometric tests
- Group exercises
- Group discussions
- Presentations
- In-tray exercises
- Social get-togethers
- Case studies

Interviews and psychometric tests have been covered in previous chapters, so this section focuses on the remaining activities.

Learning the ropes

Once you've received an invitation to attend an assessment centre, carefully organise your trip and your accommodation (if required). You may also need to update your wardrobe and make sure you're well rested, well fed and well ready!

Your invitation should outline the timetable and the specific set of activities you will undertake, but contact the employer if you have any questions. Information is power, so any details you can find out in advance could give you the edge. For example, you could try to identify who will be interviewing you and what specific type of psychometric tests they'll be using (so you can practise).

You can also chase up various other sources of information on specific assessment centres, as follows:

- Speak to contacts from the organisation or representatives who come to your university/careers fairs.
- Consult the firm's website.
- Ask your careers service.
- Look up blogs such as those on www.thestudentroom.co.uk and www.wikijob.co.uk.
- Google the name of the firm and the word "assessment centre".

On the big day

"Students need to ask us good questions at fairs which show that they have done their research. It also helps to demonstrate personality and opinions, not just knowledge.

Some good tactics for performing well in group exercises are to keep an eye on the time, use open and engaging body language, interact and use the opportunity to demonstrate commercial awareness."

Nicola Snaith, Assistant HR Adviser, Baker Tilly Management Limited

On the day, arrive in plenty of time so you're not in a big panic. Smile as soon as you get through the door and don't stop until you're back on the bus. Warmly greet everyone you meet, try to remember their names and laugh at their jokes. Also, ask intelligent questions and stand out from the crowd without being too overbearing. Finally, establish your passion for the firm and the industry through your questions and your body language.

This positive approach will be easy for some people, but others are less demonstrative, especially when they get nervous. If this sounds like you, prepare for the day by envisioning yourself during the assessments and focusing on how you will practically and clearly convey the key messages you want to get across.

Group exercises

Group exercises are one of the more common assessment centre activities because team skills are so crucial and employers want to ensure that their new recruits don't upset the teams they've already established.

What's involved

Candidates are typically split into groups of five to seven people to solve a specific problem within a set time frame. Most group exercises are paper based but exercises for technical roles may be more hands-on.

Some typical activities are provided below:

- Build a bridge out of straws and paper clips to support a specific object.
- Build a paper airplane that flies the furthest.
- Hire the right person for a fictitious job.
- Pick the 400-metre athletics relay team for the Olympics.

Groups are typically given enough information to make a decision but no guidance on how to proceed – this is totally up to them. Just to add a bit of spice, typical scenarios are usually controversial and designed to inspire debate (see the example below).

What they're looking for

On the whole, there are no right or wrong answers. Employers are actually assessing how effectively you scrutinise the issues involved and engage with the other candidates.

An example

The group exercise shown below is a scenario where you and your team have to choose a new drug (or group of drugs) for the NHS. The key issues in this particular exercise are diverse moral and financial issues, unfamiliar terms and the confusing array of costs.

Your drug of choice

You have 5 minutes to read these instructions and 25 minutes to complete the exercise, after which you will be asked to report your findings.

As a group, you are tasked with choosing a new drug/group of drugs to register for general use in the NHS. Your five options are listed below along with brief information about what each drug treats and what they cost. You have £5 billion pounds (five thousand million) to spend over the next ten years, and must spend it all – which drug or group of drugs do you choose and why?

Flexal (Fibroaximide detrooonium): This is a completely new treatment for acute lymphoblastic leukaemia in children. The treatment is 80% effective, which matches the current medication regimen, and it is cheaper than the existing drug (£100 million over the next five years as opposed to £110 million). However, the tablet has some serious side effects in 1–2% of users which are not present with the existing medication, namely chronic fatigue and migraines.

Gossalder (Elledreinal gysotamine): This new medication is a brand-new treatment for obesity. It alleviates the feeling of hunger and gives more energy to patients thus encouraging them to do more exercise. The treatment is expected to cost £150 million over the next three years but will reduce obesity by 10%. As obesity costs the NHS an estimated £1 billion a year (one thousand million), this could be a massive saving.

Lassitate (Fibro-stenossum): This can be used to replace up to 20% of the genuine blood used in transfusions. There are no marked side effects and the drug is expected to save a million pounds a year, but the costs of incorporating this new treatment are massive because expensive new equipment is required which costs £500 million. This equipment lasts for five years and costs the same as the existing equipment already in place, for which there is already an ongoing budget.

Novelle (Axionmatic indoctrinise): This new drug treats the complications caused by prostrate cancer. It does not replace any drugs but is an additional treatment, which will cost £200 million per year. It will lengthen the lives of 10% of the men who get the disease by two years on average, but quality of life is still poor and ongoing treatment for those with the disease costs £50 million per year. This cancer kills roughly 200,000 people a year in the UK and few new treatments have come to the market in the last 20 years.

Dias (Duocturine exhomerate): This is a new statin which has similar success in reducing cholesterol as the medications already on the market. However, it brings significantly fewer side effects to 10% of the population already on statins (ten million) but is twice the cost of the other treatments. A typical patient's statins currently cost £500 a year.

A possible solution

One way to solve this problem would be to audit the costs and savings of each of these drugs over the ten-year period for which you are responsible so that comparisons are easier.

Once you do this you'll notice that many of the drugs actually constitute a saving, not an extra expense, and you can even agree to all them if you limit the supply of the final drug, Dias, to patients who have already tried the other options. You should probably avoid Flexal, however, because it makes a relatively small saving and you don't know anything about the costs of treating its side effects.

How to prepare

We all have extensive experience of working with other people in teams. Therefore, you can really enhance your success in group exercises by simply taking a step back and evaluating how you generally perform in these situations. It can be very challenging to coldly reflect on your own personal skills in this way but it can also be quite revealing. Three steps to success in group exercises are shown below.

1 Identify your favourite roles

The first step to succeeding in group exercises is to identify the team roles you want to follow. This will give you a style and a structured framework which can be used in all situations. Don't worry if you're not a born leader; good teams require a wide range of personalities and people to take on different responsibilities. After all, it would be no good if everyone in a group wanted to be the boss – you'd never get anything done! In the early 1980s Meredith Belbin[1] defined the various team roles as shown below. In the following exercise, identify your favourite roles amongst the nine alternatives displayed.

- *Plants*: Free-thinking, creative idea generators.
- *Shapers*: Outgoing, enthusiastic individuals who drive the team to achieve.
- *Resource investigators*: Outgoing people who explore opportunities and develop contacts.
- *Co-ordinators*: Confident leaders who are good at clarifying goals, managing projects and delegating tasks.
- *Monitors/Evaluators*: Team members who are able to take a step back and objectively, systematically evaluate progress.
- *Teamworkers*: These diplomatic worker ants go about their roles unnoticed but bring everyone together and keep everyone happy and focused.
- *Implementers*: Efficient, loyal workers who turn ideas into solutions.
- *Completers/Finishers*: Independent souls who want to ensure that everything is done correctly and accurately.
- *Specialists*: Team members who are driven by their interest in a specific subject.

Self-assessment: What are your favourite team roles?

Identify team roles you generally fall into (use Belbin's definitions or your own terms).

My favourite team roles:

- ______________________________
- ______________________________

2 Recognise your specific skills

Once you've reflected on your favourite team roles, the next step is to recognise how you perform them well. Don't just rely on your own opinion to assess yourself, ask your friends, family and colleagues to outline your strengths and weaknesses (but don't hit them afterwards!). For example, you may be proficient at some of the following skills:

- Sharing your ideas positively
- Being open to other people's ideas
- Demonstrating reliability
- Listening empathically
- Speaking up for yourself
- Including everyone
- Being friendly and enthusiastic
- Encouraging others to get involved
- Praising others' contributions
- Addressing people by their names
- Staying calm and upbeat
- Showing inclusive and welcoming body language
- Showing enthusiasm
- Persuading colleagues
- Compromising

In the exercise below identify your top three skills in relation to your favourite team roles, and think of practical, obvious ways you could demonstrate each of these skills to invigilators during the group exercise.

For example, if you're a good 'Shaper' in team situations and you're good at encouraging others, you could focus on using inclusive body gestures and saying things like 'Great idea, Bill' to colleagues just as the employers pass by.

Self-assessment: How do you perform well in teams?

List three obvious ways you demonstrate each of your team skills.

Your favoured team roles	Three specific skills you have demonstrated in the role	Obvious ways you could show these skills to invigilators
	•	•
	•	•
	•	•
	•	•
	•	•
	•	•

3 Practise

As always, the final step to preparation is plenty of practice. You can do this in two ways:

- Try out your skills on your friends and colleagues in everyday situations.

- Have a go at some example group exercises at home or sign up for any workshops at university. An additional group exercise is provided on the companion website and the links at the end of the chapter direct you to many more.

On the day

On the day, enter the room with a handful of strategies to demonstrate your role and impress the employers. Don't try to remember too many tactics as you'll probably forget everything – four or five simple actions or statements will do. For example, if you are a 'Teamworker' (according to Belbin's roles) you could endeavour to undertake the following four tasks:

1 Help colleagues get involved by saying things like 'You and Jenny sound like you've done this before!' and 'Bob – you were saying the same thing as Paul, weren't you?'
2 Cheerfully volunteer for unpopular roles. For example, you could offer to keep an eye on the clock or introduce the group's presentation at the end.
3 Diligently and noticeably get on with your set tasks, making it clear that you are performing a valuable role.
4 Build a good rapport with the leader and proactively offer assistance.

Sit down and introduce yourself to the other candidates – try to remember their names (you may even want to jot them down). Read the instructions carefully and jump in. As time passes, make sure you get involved but remain detached enough to establish your role and mentally tick off each of your successes in carrying out one of your carefully prepared strategies. If your chosen role is not feasible or has already been taken, don't worry – try an alternative role, or just focus on showing off your skills as a teamworker (as defined by Belbin).

Whatever approach you take, be friendly, enthusiastic and open to your colleagues... but avoid the following pitfalls:

- Speaking over other people
- Speaking too much
- Not speaking clearly
- Not listening
- Being too rigid
- Not speaking at all
- Making too little contribution
- Bullying others
- Not standing up for yourself
- Being overly acquiescent
- Not taking the exercise seriously
- Being too formal

Group discussions

Smaller employers often opt for the softer option of a group discussion rather than an actual exercise. In this situation you are typically given a topical issue to discuss which is related to the specific industry and/or role. For example, a banking organisation may ask about the recent scandals or the Forestry Commission may instigate a debate about recent proposals to sell off the UK's public forests. Sometimes you are also encouraged to record your findings and come to a conclusion. Therefore, before you attend a group discussion try to catch up with the key issues currently being discussed in the industry. Of course, you should do this anyway for your applications and interview.

These deliberations are usually less formal than group interviews (see Chapter 13) and any number of candidates may be involved. You should engage with the issues just as you would in a group exercise and prepare the same strategies in order to stand out.

At the beginning of the discussions it can be quite hard to get a word in edgeways, but don't worry. Most of what is said at this stage will be haphazard and ill thought out. Listen to the discussion and, when things get a bit quieter and more interesting, jump in with a well-considered point. Mentally tick off your strategies as you would with a group discussion, listen empathically (e.g. nod your head and agree), keep smiling, praise incisive comments and avoid putting other people down.

Presentations

Just the mention of the word 'presentation' sends spasms of fear into half the population, so this is often the most feared of all the assessment exercises. This section outlines what you can expect, and how you can build confidence and perform well on the day.

What's involved

Employers tend to either ask you to prepare an individual presentation in advance to deliver at the assessment centre or develop an individual or group presentation on the day. They typically give you a specific topic and ask you to speak for just five or ten minutes. They also usually ask you to provide PowerPoint slides or some other visual aid. The audience often comprises the same people who will be on your interview panel, so the two activities are often conducted consecutively. The topic could be related to almost anything, from what skills you've gained in your degree to a current issue related to the industry.

Big smile

Animated delivery

What they're looking for

Employers ask candidates to deliver presentations because, before they set you free on their clients, they want to make sure you're eloquent, confident and engaging. Therefore, they're not focusing on your ability to impart endless information but to get straight to the heart of the issue and effectively communicate the key points. You should never underestimate how boring it is to assess applicants in this way, so the panel will also greatly appreciate it if you can provide some sort of entertainment (within reason)!

Planning and delivering your talk

In order to develop an excellent presentation you need to be clear about what you want to say and how you're going to say it.

In terms of what you say, it's always best to narrow down your remit so you only have one or two key points. This method of communication doesn't lend itself to weighty reams of information and data. If necessary, these can always be provided in a handout. As far as your delivery goes, it is crucial to maintain eye contact, show enthusiasm and engage with your audience.

Some important presentations tips are listed below:

- Speak slowly, clearly and energetically. Be careful – your adrenaline will probably be telling you to go at a 100 miles per hour.
- Avoid just reading directly from your notes or slides.
- Interact with the audience, e.g. through quizzes and questions.
- Use interesting visual displays.
- Present from a comfortable and logical position, e.g. right-handed people should stand to the left of any visual displays so they don't cover them when pointing things out.
- Make sure everyone in the room can read your text – i.e. it needs to be big! PowerPoint slides should use text no smaller than 30 points.
- Use just a few posters or slides (six should do for a five- or ten-minute presentation).
- Use only a few pictures or words on each poster or slide.
- Follow this simple guide: 'Tell them what you're going to tell them, tell them and then tell them what you've just told them.' In other words, always include an introduction and conclusion.
- Face your audience (don't look at your notes or the screen). In fact, try to avoid notes altogether; they can become so addictive that many presenters end up just reading them out loud.
- In group presentations, make sure the handovers are smooth and you maintain pace. Also, if possible, avoid just moving on from one person to another in a sequence – get each member to jump in and out and interact in more interesting ways.
- Keep to the time limit.

Dealing with your nerves

There are a number of strategies you can employ to minimise your nerves:

1 Practise delivering presentations whenever you can.
2 Learn every word and inflexion of your talk off by heart.
3 Repeatedly practise your presentation so you know it fits the time frame.
4 Use simple IT because if it *can* go wrong, it will!
5 Be totally familiar with your subject.

6 Don't say much – just the key point/s will do. Therefore, you should be able to remember your whole talk off by heart.
7 Avoid too many statistics and difficult technical concepts/definitions.
8 Eat sensibly beforehand.
9 Spend some time in quiet contemplation before you step on to the stage, and control your breathing.
10 Take it easy – if you make light of small mistakes then so will the panel!

See a video of an example presentation on the companion website.

Have a look at Guy Kawasaki's '10/20/30' video at www.youtube.com/watch?v=liQLdRk0Ziw for a frank and funny outline of good presentation technique, called 10/20/30.

In-tray exercises

Abstract, theoretical tests can be very informative and revealing but nothing beats putting you in a typical work situation and seeing how you perform under pressure. In-tray exercises perform this function.

You are typically asked to pretend you're in a particular job (not necessarily linked to the one you're seeking) and given an hour or so to deal with about 20 different issues. To help you make your decisions you will usually be given details about the organisation's aims and objectives, its structure, its partners, upcoming events and your specific responsibilities/those of your colleagues. Nowadays, in-tray assessments are often conducted online and are called e-tray exercises.

You will be tested on how appropriately you deal with each of the items in your in-tray. Speed is the key, but you should also demonstrate accuracy, independence, the ability to prioritise, share problems and delegate appropriately (according to the information you've been given about your role).

Take the following steps to maximise your performance:

1 Swiftly read through everything.
2 Identify the tasks that have arisen.
3 Check the dates when the messages were sent.
4 Divide the tasks in terms of those that are important and urgent, those that can be delayed, those that should be delegated and those that should be dropped.

Obviously, you should spend most time on the important and urgent matters arising but avoid looking into things too deeply as you will run out of time. Just focus on the key details. Sometimes, you are asked to justify your decisions at the end of the test; if this is the case, take notes as you go along.

See an example in-tray exercise on the companion website.

Social occasions

All interviews and assessment centres involve important social interaction, but some more than others. Assessment centres often involve a group lunch or dinner where interviewers, managers, partners and clients hope to meet the real you (and like what they see!). In these situations, try to present yourself in the best possible light. You can afford to be a little less formal than at other stages in the recruitment process but don't get carried away. Employers will be looking for engaging applicants who are good communicators.

Obviously, you are at an advantage if you are used to meeting important people in this sort of environment. Novices tend to be too rigid or too lax. Therefore, to prepare, you need to find opportunities to meet people in similar surroundings. You could do this by joining clubs and societies such as church groups, university or council committees, local resident groups and professional organisations.

And finally, dress appropriately and avoid too much alcohol!

Case studies

These are business scenarios typically run by investment banks, management consultants and corporate law firms to see what you'd be like in the actual job. Recruiters in these fields need to make absolutely sure that you have the ability to make decisions and confidently/persuasively communicate your conclusions.

Applicants are usually given information and data related to a typical business decision and given a fixed time limit to come up with appropriate courses of action. Sometimes, further information is also drip-fed, as the time passes. They are usually conducted in teams. When the time is up, the assessors will usually ask you a set of questions about your proposal and will expect you to clearly and persuasively back up your argument.

According to Job Step Prep (www.jobtestprep.co.uk), the following topics are common:

- Strategic decisions in global or local contexts.
- Expansion of departments, acquisition of new companies or products.
- Entrance into new fields of development and product lines.
- Exploring new markets.
- Reconstructing organisational trees (hierarchies).
- Creating advertising campaigns.

Graduates are not usually required to have specific knowledge and experience but it helps to have a good understanding of the jargon used in the industry you are seeking to enter. You may want to look at www.incorp.com/incorp-glossary.aspx.

You can succeed in these activities by:

1 Quickly identifying and focusing on the key issues – much of the information will have little bearing on the case.
2 Analysing the relevant data.

3 Choosing your favourite solution.
4 Preparing positive arguments as to why you have chosen your particular path.
5 Making sure the salient information is at your fingertips.
6 Considering how your analysis addresses common questions.

A major part of the challenge here is dealing with the pressure. Therefore, in order to prepare it can really help to put yourself in this position before the assessment centre and get lots of practice. Your careers service should be able to help out in this regard but you can also find advice and practice case studies on a number of websites, such as the following:

- **Bain & Co:** www.joinbain.com.
- **Boston Consulting:** www.bcg.co.
- **Capital One:** www.capitalone.com.
- **McKinsey:** www.mckinsey.com.
- **Target Jobs:** www.targetjobs.co.uk.

Finding out more

In this guide

- Impressing at interviews – Chapter 13.
- Psychometric tests – Chapter 14.

On the companion website

- Video of example presentation.
- Example in-tray exercise

On the web

On the companion website you will find extra links to assessment centre guides on a range of websites, including the excellent advice from the University of Manchester. Furthermore, you may also find out more about your specific assessment centre at your careers centre, www.thestudentroom.co.uk or by Googling "Assessment Centre" "Name of Organisation".

What to do next

The key skills necessary to perform well in assessment centres are the ability to undertake the tasks confidently and get on with everyone. Therefore, you can prepare for them by practising some of the activities outlined in this chapter and getting experience of the work environment you want to enter. Even a day or two in an organisation or a chat with one of their employees will give you an idea of how to perform.

If you've been to a few assessment centres and not been hired, you need to find out why. Ask the employers for feedback, honestly assess yourself against the organisations' requirements and ask a careers adviser to give you a true opinion of your strengths and weaknesses. Many candidates are rejected because:

- They perform badly. If this is the case, get back to the books and practise!
- They're too quiet and shy. If this is you, try to figure out how you can get noticed.

Summary

- Assessment centres involve a range of recruitment exercises, which could include interviews, psychometric tests, group exercises, group discussions, presentations, in-tray exercises, social get-togethers and case studies.
- You should carefully prepare for the specific tests you will face.
- In group exercises you will be asked to conduct a task along with five or six other candidates and tested on how effectively you scrutinise the issues involved and engage with your colleagues.
- You can prepare for group exercises by identifying your favourite team roles, recognising your specific skills and practising.
- On the day you should clearly demonstrate your top two or three relevant skills.
- You are often asked to conduct a presentation to see if you're up to communicating effectively with colleagues and clients.
- Carefully plan what you're going to say, sticking to just one or two key points.
- Pay heed to how you're standing and the effectiveness of your visual resources.
- In-tray exercises are a great way to see how you cope with pressure.
- Systematically work through your workload and focus on the urgent and important issues.
- In any social interactions, including meals, try to fit in with professionals in the field by loosening up a bit but remaining professional.
- In case studies, focus on the key information and prepare to back up your arguments.

Chapter 16

This job's for you

"If it's your job to eat a frog, it's best to do it first thing in the morning. And, if it's your job to eat two frogs, it's best to eat the biggest one first." *Mark Twain*

Contents

What you will gain from this chapter:

- **Decision making:** The capacity to keep looking for the best career route once you've already started work.
- **Transition learning:** An understanding of how to make the most of new jobs.
- **Self-awareness:** The ability to reflect on your career as it progresses.

What's in a job offer?

Sooner or later a job offer will land on your doorstep. You'll know it's good news because the envelope will contain more than just a brief rejection – it will be packed with paperwork and information about your new opportunity.

The letter of acceptance will probably include some or all of the following documents:

- A provisional offer in lieu of your references and any other requisite documents (see the following section).
- Your proposed pay and conditions.
- Contact details for your new manager/HR.
- An outline of the role (hopefully your formal contract and terms and conditions will be included but the employer does not need to give you these until well after you have started).
- Documentation about the organisation and your department.
- Administrative information about things like IT passwords and ID badges.
- A formal acceptance letter for you to return to HR.
- A health questionnaire.

Your response

1 Once you've called all your family and friends and hugged the dog, let the employer know that you've received their offer. Don't be afraid to share your joy but, if possible, avoid formally accepting the offer until you've read through all the small print and made sure it's right for you. At this stage, you could say something like you are 'happy to accept the offer subject to reading the full terms and conditions'.
2 Carefully read through the documents and highlight anything you don't understand or want to question, plus make sure there are no nasty surprises (such as your start date or your salary).
3 Contact the organisation to check any details you need to clarify. It may be tempting to let things slide at this time but don't – you need to start work with a clear understanding of what the job entails.
4 Once you're clear about the job offer, decide if it's what you want. Don't be afraid to reject the offer if it's not up to scratch, but, in these difficult times, it's probably better to put up with any awkward aspects in the new role rather than reject it outright. After all, once you start in the role, you'll soon have the opportunity to move up into bigger and better things.

If you're badgered to make the decision on the spot, as are many teachers, then you have the right to take the time to also clarify the offer there and then before giving your agreement. If you can't pin them down to the exact pay and conditions, then, more than likely, something fishy is going on. You may want to insist that you have this information before you make your final decision.

Negotiating the deal

If the job is not up to your expectations but you don't want to reject the offer, this could be a very good time to negotiate terms. You may want to discuss issues such as your start date, pay, hours, holidays, training opportunities or a golden handshake. If you do want to enhance your offer, make an argument as to why you warrant this extra investment. For example, you could ask for extra relocation expenses and a higher salary as follows:

> 'Unfortunately, as I live in a country town in Derbyshire my relocation expenses to London will easily dwarf the £500 allowance offered. I propose an extra £500 which will enable me to move all my possessions in good time (including work-related material) to my new home which is in easy commutable distance to the office.'

> 'Thank you for the wonderful offer of a traineeship in London – I am very excited and cannot wait to start. Unfortunately, however, having looked for a flat-share last weekend, I just cannot see how I can move to the capital city and support myself on the provisional salary of £14,500. Therefore, as I have a relevant degree, exceptional experience and the commitment and ability to quickly add value to your organisation, I would very much appreciate it if you could reconsider my initial pay and conditions.'

Whatever you do, though, make sure you negotiate in a positive, friendly manner.

Balancing multiple offers

If you're lucky you may get more than one job offer at once, or even one job offer and an interview the following week for a much better position. The pros and cons of each of your options in this situation are outlined below:

- Accept the first offer you get but keep looking for better roles. The advantage of this approach is that you will have a job to go to and you might even get a better one before you start.

  The advantage here seems to be that you have nothing to lose, but you should be aware that employers tend to be very well connected and the one you've signed up for may well hear about your other applications. Not good!

- Delay formally accepting your original offer until you hear if you've been successful with any other jobs you're seeking. It can be difficult to delay things for very long using this strategy but you could keep your options open by negotiating your original offer whilst waiting for any other offers to come in.

  The advantage of this approach is that you can responsibly secure your favoured role whilst keeping your options open. The downside is that you may lose everything, i.e. the original offer may be withheld because of your delay and no other position may come through.

- Take up the original job offer and withdraw from your other applications.

  The advantage here is that you have been honourable to yourself, the employer and the other candidates with whom you're competing. The disadvantage is that the job you get may not be the job you want.

- Reject the original offer and hope to get a better job in the near future.

The big advantage of this strategy is that you can still hope for the job of your dreams. The disadvantage is that you may never get it!

Whichever route you choose, you should remember that this is only the start of your career, so your initial role will probably quickly change and your pay and conditions will improve. With your newfound experience you could also soon start looking for even better roles. Therefore, any concerns you originally have about a job offer should be balanced against the very real benefit of having a job. A bird in the hand is worth two in the bush!

Preparing for the big day

As soon as you've accepted a job offer you should start preparing for your new lifestyle. This is a major transition so it will really help if you are psychologically, intellectually and practically prepared.

We all have our own unique psychological strategies for dealing with major events and the fact that you've got this far means you're probably doing OK. However, whether you breeze through life or meticulously plan every step, you should take some time to mentally prepare for what's in store. Therefore, before turning up for your first day, reflect on how others see you in the workplace and put steps in place to address any weaknesses. For example, it's never acceptable to be late, so plan on getting to work earlier than anyone else – this will get you noticed.

In order to minimise the stress of your first day, you may also want to visit the organisation beforehand and have a chat with your new boss. Feel free to ask.

Fitting in a social life can be difficult at first. Some new workers stop going out altogether and don't get a chance to blow off steam, whilst others continue to stay out all night and can't stay awake at work. Either way, this will not help you get on. Try to fit your social life around your work instead of vice versa and make sure you're having enough fun, but not too much! Remember the following guidelines:

- Your new job isn't just a means to paying the rent; it's a chance to start your quest for a fulfilling and successful future.
- Success is not just about carrying out the tasks you've been given; it centres on taking responsibility and proactively looking for opportunities to develop.
- You need to be professional, i.e. on time, well mannered, well dressed, friendly and co-operative.
- You're still allowed to have fun!

Don't panic about the intellectual challenge presented by your first graduate role – it's rarely as difficult as you may imagine and employers are keen to guide you through. However, you should show your enthusiasm by contacting the organisation beforehand and asking how you can prepare for your first assignments. This may involve reading around a particular topic, researching current trends and/or researching the organisation's policy and practice. This will impress your new employers and take the heat off your first few weeks in the job.

In terms of practical preparation, it can really help to comprehensively sort out your new domestic arrangements before your start. For example, you don't want to be living on a friend's floor and looking for a flat-share whilst you're embarking on such an important journey. Some of the measures you may need to arrange are as follows:

- A quiet, convenient place to live.
- New clothes.
- Your journey to and from work.
- Cooking arrangements.
- Washing/cleaning arrangements.
- Emotional support.
- Banking facilities and cash.

Day one and induction

On your first day you'll be very nervous but, amid all the greetings and handshakes, take a moment to congratulate yourself on this auspicious achievement. It's important to retain perspective when the pressure is on at work and retain your self-esteem. This will give you the confidence and drive to succeed.

Get there in good time and share your joy and excitement with everyone you meet. This will both serve to boost your enthusiasm and build a favourable impression with co-workers.

Induction is a set of activities which employers design to introduce new employees to their colleagues and prepare them for their role. In some organisations this will involve a quick handshake before lunch, whilst in others there will be extensive meetings and consultations. You can maximise the benefits of this period by clearly defining your tasks and line of management. Good work relationships are fundamental to your success so, during your first few days and weeks, you should get to know everyone's names and make sure you spend some time with key colleagues and clients.

Part of your induction will probably involve a work plan for your first few months at the firm. Try to engage one hundred per cent with this initiative and endeavour to include your personal aims and objectives along with the organisation's. For example, if you want to learn a new technique or process, but it's not in your schedule, ask your boss to include it. They will respond positively to your proactive approach.

Making a success

You can't guarantee success but good things come to those who work hard, get on with colleagues and show enough enterprise. The following guidelines are adapted from a previous Palgrave guide[1]:

- Ask questions if you are unsure, and keep asking until you understand the answer.
- Meet all the conditions of your contract, for example timekeeping, attendance, confidentiality, disciplinary code, health and safety.
- Contribute to the team effort in all tasks, including the menial ones.
- Meet objectives set, including the timescales – if in difficulty raise issues before deadlines.

- Be respectful but not subservient.
- Recognise knowledge and experience in others – don't be a know-all.
- Continue to develop your listening and communication skills.
- Recognise the dress code.
- Keep your own counsel and don't be too trusting – you are now entering a political, business world, where people have their own agendas.
- Avoid becoming entrapped in office politics.
- Be good-humoured – be ready for 'leg pulling', which will be well meant.
- Treat people at face value unless they demonstrate that they are not sincere.
- Be principled: have the courage of your convictions but be ready to learn the art of compromise.
- Always act honestly, with integrity and within the law.
- Own up to your own mistakes and don't compromise others.
- Learn from your mistakes – you will make them, but try not to make the same mistake twice.
- Avoid any form of harassment or discrimination.
- If the organisation offers a mentor (a manager who is given the task of supporting you), speak to them regularly but don't abuse the privilege.
- Treat people with respect and consideration (remember, you are always networking); you may need their help or support in the future.
- Where constructive criticism is given, accept it with good grace and use it in your personal development.

Moving on up

Human nature is such that we're never satisfied with what we've got, so, as soon as you get a job, you'll probably want a better one. There's nothing wrong with this ambition as long as you can maintain a balance whereby you work well in your current position but continually strive for more. Here are some strategies:

- Just reliably do your job.
- Develop your skills and maintain your commitment.
- Proactively look for better ways to benefit your employers.
- Find ways to get more involved in the tasks you enjoy, and those of a higher level.
- Energetically engage in your personal development and strive for promotion.
- Look for similar work at a different organisation where you may be more fulfilled/there may be more opportunities.

Moving on?

Sometimes it can be a good idea to move into a new organisation or even a new role. The key advantages of such a transition are that you may find a more fulfilling role with higher pay, more opportunities to develop in the future and a fresh start. On the downside, the new job/role may not turn out to be as rosy as you thought and you'll have to build new networks and contacts at work. Therefore, if you want to move on, don't rush into it. Make sure you objectively compare the true opportunities at your existing workplace with those at any new organisations – don't just jump because you're bored.

If your chosen role is the problem, don't panic. The current graduate and recruitment market is set up to enable you to move on without any fuss. Follow the strategy outlined below:

1 Identify what you don't like about your current role.
2 See if there are opportunities to eradicate these aspects of your job at your current workplace or with a new employer.
3 Examine similar jobs in your sector that could be more fulfilling. For example, if you're a medical researcher, maybe you would prefer to be a medical writer; if you're a teacher, you could consider home tutoring.
4 Re-examine the whole cornucopia of graduate roles. Your degree, experience and skills will make you very attractive to employers in numerous fields, whether or not they are connected to the work you're doing (see Chapter 2).
5 Speak to people about all your research, including your mentor at work.
6 Make a decision.
7 Plan your next moves so you can hopefully make a smooth transition. For example, you could stay in your existing role while you develop specific skills, apply for jobs and go for interviews (if you're moving on).

Getting back in the game

“I graduated with a BA Honours in Economics in the early 1990s, which was in a time of recession, so graduate jobs were difficult to find. I found myself unemployed for several months, and therefore I had to settle for any job I could get. I started my working life in the stockroom of a well-known record store. I remained with this company for twelve years, progressing to supervisor level, and then to a role within Accounts Payables at Head Office. This was a job I thoroughly enjoyed even though the salary was never on a par with some of my graduate friends.

Unfortunately, I had to leave this company to relocate to my home town as a result of divorce, so I could look after my young daughter. At this stage I accepted job roles for which I was overqualified because I lacked confidence. Over time, however, I have gained extra vocational qualifications in accounting which have been funded by my current company. I have also tried to develop in my current role and take on new tasks that will gain me new skills. This will hopefully enable me to pursue my career in the very near future.

Looking back, my degree has not added any value to my working life. In hindsight, it might have proved more worthwhile if I had gone on to an apprentice role straight after school, which would have provided me with valuable skills to compete in the job market. I cannot remember being offered any useful advice from the Careers Office at the university, but maybe I didn't make full use of the service either. The main problem was when I had completed my degree; I had no real sense of what I wanted to do, and did not investigate all possible avenues.

My main advice would therefore be to firstly identify what career you would like to pursue and then view all options on how to achieve this.”

Penny Maynard, Economics Graduate

> Sometimes careers just ebb and flow. All I ever wanted to be was an Army Officer. I applied for and received an Army Scholarship when I was 16. With that came a career in the army to age 55. By the time I was 22 I was injured and my career in the army looked to be over. I decided to qualify as a barrister as an alternative and by the time I was 25 I was practising in the courts. This was now to be my chosen career. Because I knew something of the military I often found myself in the Military Courts dealing with Courts Martial. In one of those I found myself representing a soldier charged with manslaughter. The incident happened in Iraq but he had been sent there without proper training and it wasn't his fault. He was acquitted despite an attempt to cover up his lack of training. I was furious; I could have been that soldier. So I decided to stand for Parliament. Someone who was to have fought a Yorkshire seat – just the sort of seat I wanted – decided to stand down and so a new candidate was needed. Dewsbury is the only seat I have ever applied for and the 2010 election is the only election of any kind that I have fought. I am now an MP! I have no idea what the future holds but I am sure it holds something!
>
> *Simon Reevell, MP*

Graduates can often drift for years in unfulfilling roles, wondering what the point was of doing a degree in the first place. In this situation, you can also lose your self-esteem, drive and ambition. If this sounds like you, you need a dose of reality. Graduates earn more than non-graduates and if you haven't achieved your aims in life then it's almost certainly not down to your particular qualifications.

In this situation, take the time to sort out any issues that are holding you back and restart your journey, one step at a time. For example, you could start by looking for any opportunities where you currently work or sign up for some further training.

No one is pretending the journey will be easy, but you'll soon start overtaking graduates who've yet to experience many of the harsher lessons of life. Also, don't hesitate to talk to people such as friends, family and careers advisers at your old university (even if they're younger than you!).

Finding out more

In this guide

- Help! Where do I start? – Introduction.
- Choosing a role – Chapter 2.
- Planning your journey – Chapter 3.
- Targeting your CV – Chapter 10: see Example CV4.

On the web

Find links to advice on changing or improving your career on the companion website.

What to do next

The key thing to realise when you get your first graduate job is that this is the start of your journey, not the end. Your days of developing your skills, networking, getting experience and promoting yourself are not over – they're only just beginning. You've managed to get your foot in the door, so well done! But now you've got to get past the threshold and turn a promising career into a real success.

So, keep looking for new horizons, and find ways to make them happen.

Summary

- Job offers include provisional offers of work and a host of documentation including details of your start date and your pay and conditions.
- You should respond by celebrating, then provisionally accepting the offer, reading through the small print, checking any details and, if necessary, negotiating the deal.
- There are several ways to balance two or more offers until you can decide which one to take but they all have advantages and disadvantages – don't get too greedy or you might lose everything.
- Prepare psychologically, intellectually and practically for your first day so that you can devote all your attention to your new job.
- When you start your new role pay special attention to building strong relationships with your colleagues and clients and maintaining a professional outlook.
- The current graduate employment and recruitment market allows you to easily move onwards and upwards in your career, but you need to take control of your next steps.
- It's never too late to get your career back on track if you've been drifting for a long time. Just look for your new path and strategically focus on developing your skills and experience.

Part

IV

ENTREPRENEURSHIP

One exciting employment option for students and graduates is to set up your own business and work for yourself. In fact, recent studies by the National Centre for Social Research and RBS[1] have found that, in 2010, almost 30 per cent of people in their twenties have seriously considered working for themselves and 8 per cent have actually done so.

This section of the guide is a short introduction to entrepreneurship which will help you:

- Decide whether self-employment is right for you.
- Identify some interesting business ideas.
- Get things going.
- Secure appropriate help.

Chapter 17

Becoming an entrepreneur

"God helps those who help themselves." *Proverb*

"I decided to run my own business and came up with an idea when I briefly returned to the UK for a few months in 1999. I had been a supply teacher in London for many years and understood the ins and outs of the industry. I also knew that agencies relied on teachers from countries like South Africa, New Zealand and Australia. Therefore, I figured out that I could procure teachers for them in Western Australia, where none of the existing agencies had offices. I approached a range of organisations and my old employer agreed to work with me. I spent the next two years sitting on the beach in Fremantle finding teachers when I felt like it.

I enjoyed being my own boss but I hated all the paperwork and the worry over not knowing if I could pay the rent each month. I didn't plan this venture in any way and relied on my creativity to face any issues when they arose. After about six months I figured out that my future relied on building a closer relationship with the universities in the area and recruiting new graduates. If I had just thought about things a bit more deeply when I started I might have worked this out much sooner."

Steve Rook, author of this guide

Contents

What you will gain from this chapter:

- **Decision making:** The ability to decide if entrepreneurship is right for you and choose an appropriate business.
- **Opportunity awareness:** The chance to investigate a range of entrepreneurial ideas.
- **Transition learning:** An idea of the skills you'll need to succeed as an entrepreneur.
- **Self-awareness:** The ability to link this career option to your relevant personal attributes.

Enterprise and entrepreneurship

The words 'enterprise' and 'entrepreneurship' are often conflated and confused, therefore, before we go any further, it's important to define what we mean by each term.

In this chapter and the following, 'enterprise' will relate to your ability to proactively solve problems and find opportunities in any walk of life, whereas 'entrepreneurship' will strictly refer to the process of launching a risky new venture that could lead either to a profit or to a loss. A further glossary of terms, jargon and acronyms used in this sector is provided at the end of Chapter 18.

The pros and cons of entrepreneurship

On the positive side, the common attractions of entrepreneurship are:

- The potential for great rewards.
- Being able to work around other commitments (e.g. study).
- Getting some experience for your CV.
- Developing necessary skills.
- Using your creativity.
- Being in control of your own destiny.
- Avoiding mundane tasks and miserable managers.
- Working in your chosen area.
- Following your dreams.
- Independence/being your own boss.

On the other hand, you'll also probably have to face the following trials, at least until you get your business up and running:

- Financial risks.
- The insecurity of living by your wits and not earning a fixed wage.
- Never knowing what's around the next corner.
- Mountains of paperwork.
- The need to become a business expert.
- Staying one step ahead of the competition.
- 24-hour personal responsibility.
- Long hours.

The skills you'll need

In general, you'll need the following attributes:

- Enterprise and the ability to innovate.
- Enthusiasm and commitment.
- The willingness (and capacity) to work hard.
- The ability to deal with pressure and stress.
- The flexibility and adaptability to deal with a wide range of issues and problems.
- Stamina.
- Self-discipline (will you be able to get out of bed every Monday morning?).
- The capacity to learn from new experiences.
- The ability to communicate and build networks.
- A thick skin – especially the facility to cope with setbacks and rejection.

Is it right for me?

Unfortunately, when you're starting out it can be quite hard to identify whether you'll enjoy self-employment and whether you'll be any good. This is because we're all unique, it's such a novel experience and there are so many potential business models.

One way to go about making a decision about whether or not to set up your own business is to compare your favourite business idea with your preferred occupation and see which one inspires you more. You can do this in the exercise below by evaluating each of your options in terms of your personal skills, interests and motivations.

Self-assessment: Your career shortlist

List your key skills, interests and motivations and identify whether each specific attribute is more closely matched to your favourite occupation or working for yourself.

Your attributes	Which is the closest match?	
	Your favourite occupation	Working for yourself
Your skills (what you're good at)		
Your interests (what you enjoy doing on a day-to-day basis)		
Your motivations (what you want from life)		
TOTAL		

Coming up with ideas

Of course, in order to set up your own business you have to think of something to sell. Don't feel you have to come up with some amazingly creative new idea – you just need to deliver a good or service that some people will buy instead of (or as well as) the main product on the market. For example, you could establish a fancy dress shop or a tablet repair shop for students.

Seven of the more common business idea generators are outlined below. Use these strategies to come up with some possible options in the following self-assessment exercise.

Self-assessment: Your business ideas

Use the approaches outlined below to come up with three exciting business ideas.

Your business ideas
•
•
•

Focus on your skills, study and experience

Businesses generally stand a much greater chance of success when entrepreneurs know what they're doing and understand the market. For example:

- If you gained good grades at university you could help struggling students with their essays.
- Overseas graduates could share their knowledge and experience with the families of students back at home who are considering coming to the UK.

Research growth markets

Even in the middle of a recession many sectors and businesses will be growing. Do your research to identify strong, successful industries and consider whether you can add value. For example, up to 2012, strong UK sectors included oil and gas, aerospace and the automotive industry. There have also been recent gains in alternative therapies and organic produce.

This approach can be especially effective if you look out for markets that are inefficient and outdated and where there is minimal competition in terms of major brands and large suppliers. For example, services such as bicycle messengering in smaller cities, IT repairs for older people and posh dog-grooming centres (dog ownership is also currently on the up).

You can identify sectors of the economy that are growing at any one time through a range of resources including Prospects at www.prospects.ac.uk/sectors.htm.

Look at common business start-ups

Another way of finding potentially successful business ideas is to see what other new entrepreneurs are doing at the moment. For example, there is currently a plethora of new businesses seeking to address greener energy solutions. Could you turn your hand to this? You can find out about new business initiatives by popping into your university's enterprise centre, contacting professional organisations, noticing who's winning entrepreneurship awards and looking at adverts in local papers/web banners.

Use new technology

Throughout history new technology has led to a wealth of commercial opportunities. Nowadays, most new technologies are connected to IT and communications and numerous opportunities have opened up in these sectors including:

- *Designing apps* – Try to think of apps that would help you at work or during your hobbies. For example, if you like gardening, how about an app that uses a phone's camera facility to identify plants and then provides instructions on how they should be looked after?
- *Designing bespoke websites.*
- *Facilitating search engine optimisation* – Helping small businesses improve their online presence.
- *E-commerce* – Selling your own good or service either on your own website or through a market such as eBay.
- *Blogs* – Constructing blogs and forums that attract advertising revenue.
- *Social media spin-offs* – Come up with a niche new social network such as a lifestyle portal for local lesbians (it will probably help if you're a lesbian!).

Find niche organisations

These are numerous businesses which target small specific markets that major companies or public sector bodies cannot fully exploit: for example, setting up a corner shop that focuses on the specific needs of local communities, hawking revamped bicycles to students and selling traditional formal clothes to UK Muslims. One good way to identify appropriate niches is to simply identify major goods and services that aren't sufficiently targeted at you, your friends or your family. For example, if you're Jewish, can you get hold of good kosher food where you live? If you're bigger than Kate Moss, can you find any cool clothes that fit? If you're a female who loves hunting and fishing, can you get appropriate gear? The Internet gives you a great opportunity to focus on such small specific markets because you can trawl a much wider region to find enough customers.

Look overseas

Anyone who's travelled will have seen that there are thousands of business ideas that aren't exploited here in the UK. Why not look for ideas on your next holiday or transfer a money-making venture from your original country? For example, you could set up a fleet of minibus taxis (prevalent throughout Asia) to transfer groups of students from campus to popular student areas for a pound or two each trip.

Solve your own problems

Simply ask yourself what would make your life easier, more fun or less of a worry and think of how you could create the relevant good or service. After all, if you can find answers to your personal dilemmas, then others in the same situation will probably be prepared to pay. For example, if you can't meet Muslim girls or boys in the normal venues on campus, why not set one up? If your dog runs away every time you take him for a walk, how about marketing a cheap GPS collar with its own app? If you can never afford to stay anywhere on your travels, why not set up a business where students can rent out their couches?

Finding out more

In this guide

- Choosing a role – Chapter 2.
- Getting your business started – Chapter 18.

On the companion website

Further case studies from current entrepreneurs.

On the web

Various Internet links on entrepreneurship can be found on the companion website, including local and regional entrepreneurship societies.

What to do next

You can find out what it's like creating your own business by reading books on the subject (such as *Anyone Can Do It: Building Coffee Republic from Our Kitchen Table*[1]), but you also need to speak to new entrepreneurs who have actively made the decision to proceed. You should be able to find good contacts through your current or previous university, especially if they have an enterprise centre.

If you think that this is the path for you, turn immediately to the next chapter on getting a business started and identify what you need to do to turn your ideas into reality.

If you're not sure this is the right track just now, why not look for a career in a favourite sector and plan to set up on your own when you know more about what you're doing?

Summary

- Enterprise is a general skill centred on initiative. Entrepreneurship is the process of setting up a business.
- There are many positive aspects to setting up your own business, such as the freedom to chase your own dreams, but there are also numerous challenges, such as increased risk and hard work!
- Different businesses require different skills but they all need passion and commitment.
- All career paths confer both positive and negative features. Therefore, one way to determine whether self-employment is the right path for you is to compare it to the other career options you're considering in terms of your skills, interests and commitments.
- There are numerous ways to come up with new business ideas including looking for ventures linked to your skills, researching growth markets and identifying niches.

Chapter

18

Getting your business started

"Don't open a shop unless you like to smile."
Chinese proverb

Contents

What you will gain from this chapter:

- **Decision making:** An introduction to defining your customer, finding a market, choosing a business structure and planning your first steps.
- **Transition learning:** An appreciation of what it takes to run a successful business.
- **Self-awareness:** The practical facility to identify your entrepreneurial instincts and skills, then use them and constantly improve.

Defining your customer

Once you've come up with some possible business ventures, it's time to develop your ideas, test them and get going. The first stage in this process is to clarify who you think will buy your product, i.e. your target customers. This is called market segmentation. Such focus is crucial because you can only focus on the specific requirements of your customers when you know who they're likely to be!

It may seem counterproductive to narrow down your planned market before you've even started doing business but this will allow you to design something that's attractive and sellable to a specific audience. You need to consider aspects such as the age of your potential customers, their sex, social class, race and level of education, as all these things will affect how you market your product. Try to be selective without being too limited. For example, it may benefit you to focus on young male Asian Muslims in Bradford, but not single white females from Brighton called Jenny! In the exercise below, define three characteristics of your target customers for one of your own business ideas.

Self-assessment: Picturing your customers

What are your customers like?

Your business idea:
Characteristics of your target customers
•
•
•

Finding your market

Once you've classified your target customers you need to develop and market your business with them in mind. Marketing comprises everything involved in getting your merchandise to market and selling it. Therefore, the process is traditionally outlined in terms of the following four elements: *product* (an exact description of what you're selling), *promotion* (publicising and advertising what you have to offer), *price* (what people will pay) and *place* (where the product is made and how it's distributed). You need to ensure that each of these 'four Ps' is appropriately developed with your specific customers in mind. The following sections outline how you can do this.

Product

The product or service you're developing should fit the exact needs of your planned customers – not yours or indeed those of the technology you are using! It can be very difficult to put yourself in other people's shoes in this way, but it needs to be done if you want to make any sales. For example, you could tailor two of the products and services outlined in the previous chapter as follows:

- *Student minibuses*: If you decide to cater for clubbers you could have colourful, loud buses which pick customers up from the student union and local pubs/clubs. For international students you could have posh wagons that leave from student halls. Regular customers could be picked up on busy corners and long-distance commuters could book seats and be collected from their homes every day.

- *GPS pet collars/implants*: If you cater for owners of professional animals you'll need to produce an extremely safe, well-engineered (and expensive) product. For customers who have more money than sense then you'll undoubtedly have to make your collars very shiny and attractive and everyday people will require a cheap alternative which should probably be available in popular shops and supermarkets.

Now it's your turn: Consider how you could tailor the business idea you outlined in the previous exercise to the customer characteristics you've defined.

Self-assessment: Targeting your product

How could you design your product or service for your customers' needs?

Your business idea:
How you could target your product or service at your specific customers
•
•
•

Promotion

Another benefit of focusing on the needs of your specific customers is that you can develop a targeted publicity and advertising campaign. Publicity is all about raising your profile; you can do this in a number of ways, such as:

- Entering enterprise awards.
- Attracting media attention.
- Networking.
- Finding partners who will actively raise your profile (if you will reciprocate).
- Maintaining a high web and social media profile.
- After-sales service (e.g. look at how organisations like Amazon target previous customers with targeted product suggestions).

You should also find creative ways to promote your ideas that are linked to your specific product or service, for example:

- If you're opening a student fancy dress shop, why not organise a fancy dress party during freshers' week?
- If you plan to help people mend their phones and tablets, maybe you could offer your technical skills free to a university service (such as the careers service).

Advertising also needs to be targeted. For example, local services such as student cafés and academic support would probably benefit from initiatives such as flyers, sponsorship of student societies, promotions in the local media and dynamic activities such as free product placement at major university events. However, campaigns like this will be largely useless if you're running some sort of e-commerce activity and all your potential customers are in Brazil! In this case, you should probably focus on web banners, blogs, forums, social networks and search engine optimisation.

Price

The equation for working out how to price your product is quite complicated. You need to consider factors such as:

- Your costs.
- You salary and profits.
- What your customers can pay and what they're prepared to pay.
- Incentives for repeat trade.
- How much your competitors are charging.
- The price sensitivity of your product/service.

Place

Of course, all the above is just theory if you haven't figured out:

- Where you're going to get your raw materials.
- How you're going to transport them to your site.
- Where you're going to be based.
- How you're going to put together your product or service.
- How you're going to get it into your customers' hands.
- How you're going to be paid.

These logistical issues can be very expensive but, at each stage, you can minimise your costs. For example, if you're providing a free magazine for black and Asian students at your university you could build a partnership with a local printer to keep costs down, store them in your garage and deliver them yourself to local shops and societies.

Testing your market

Good market research can give you a clear perspective on how to market your product. It isn't just about finding out if your idea is popular; it should also focus on the commercial viability of your particular product or service and how it should be designed to deliver maximum impact. You can start by investigating the market size (the money spent on similar products by your target group), the share of the market you're likely to win and recent trends in that sector. Then, you can look for effective ways to differentiate your product or service from those of your competition. For example, you could look into what customers are seeking in terms of appearance, delivery time, performance and quality.

Market research

Market research usually involves web research, direct contact and pilot studies.

Web research

You can research business sectors and market trends on the following websites:

- Prospects: www.prospects.ac.uk – Look up the job sectors section.

- Relevant professional organisations (see the companion website).
- The Office for National Statistics: www.ons.gov.uk.
- Business Link: www.gov.uk.
- The Confederation of British Industry: www.cbi.org.uk.
- The Association of Graduate Recruiters: www.agr.org.uk.
- Media related to your field, e.g. *What Car* magazine (www.whatcar.com) / *British Naturism* magazine (www.bn.org.uk).
- Your competitors.
- Your local Chamber of Commerce (see www.britishchambers.org.uk/contact-the-bcc/interactive-chamber-map).
- Business directories such as www.yell.co.uk and those available from your local Chamber of Commerce.

You can find out statistical information about people (demographics) and their habits and values (psychographics) on these sites:

- Zoopla: www.zoopla.co.uk – See the information on 'Area Stats'.
- Caci: www.caci.co.uk/acorn-classification.aspx – See the ACORN classifications, which are geographically focused demographic segments of the UK's population.
- Index Mundi: www.indexmundi.com – International demographics.
- Demographics Online from Experian: www.demographicsonline.com – Business-related demographics and psychographics for the UK.
- The Office for National Statistics: www.ons.gov.uk.
- UK National Statistics: www.statistics.gov.uk.
- Just Google your business idea.
- Google "demographics of the ... sector".

You should also get involved with other online tools such as relevant forums and discussion boards.

Talking to real people

Start by getting in touch with agencies that help small businesses in your area. Your university's enterprise centre should be your first port of call but there are numerous other bodies that can help – see the 'Finding out more' section at the end of this chapter. You could also speak to:

- People in your market segment.
- Distributers and retailers.
- Customers at trade fairs.
- Sales representatives of organisations in your chosen sector (why not pretend to be a customer and ask really tricky questions?).

Pilot studies

Try to sell your product in a small trial to test your ideas. This will also give you a chance to correct any problems before you hit the market at full speed. For example, if you decide to sell bicycles to students, you could advertise them at freshers' week and offer free personal delivery.

Test your business ideas in the exercise below.

Self-assessment: Testing your market

List some specific resources you could use to assess your intended business.

Your business idea:
How you could measure…
Your market size: ____ Your possible market share: ____ The buying habits of your market segment: ____ ____ ____ What your customers think of your business idea: ____ ____ ____

Choosing a business structure

Once you've adapted your product appropriately and tested your market it's time to get out there and turn your dreams into reality. You can do this by choosing a business structure and signing up. New entrepreneurs in the UK are usually attracted to the business types shown in the table below.

Some popular business structures for new entrepreneurs

Business structures	Advantages	Disadvantages	How to register
Sole traders: One-person businesses where the owner receives all the profits and has unlimited liability for losses and debts.	• Relatively few regulations • Complete control • Option to raise funds publicly or privately	• Lack of confidence from investors • Increasing personal liability as the business grows	Just register that you're self-employed with HMRC. Profits are classed as income.
Ordinary partnerships: Organisations of two or more people (or businesses) in which each partner is fully liable for the full overall debts.	• Simple and flexible	• Each partner may be liable for all the debts • Larger organisations may not deal with you	One of the partners registers with HMRC for self-assessment. You should draw up a partnership agreement.

Business structures	Advantages	Disadvantages	How to register
Private limited companies: Companies with only a few shareholders and shares are privately transacted (not through a stock market).	• Shareholders are not responsible for debts • Access to finance through shares • More favourable tax regime than for sole traders	• The need to file accounts annually with Companies House • All profits must be shared	Register at Companies House (www.companieshouse.gov.uk). File company tax returns to HMRC.
Public limited companies: Companies where shares are sold on the public market and shareholders have limited liability for debts.	• All members have limited liability • Great potential to raise funds	• Little control over who buys or sells shares • Costly to set up • Inbuilt resistance to change	Register at Companies House and file company tax returns to HMRC.
Community interest companies (CIC): A new business structure for social enterprises where founders are given a separate legal identity to their limited companies.	• Assets and profits can only be distributed if allowed by law – giving confidence to ethical investors	• More difficult to set up • Must publish an annual community interest company report	Same as limited companies but regulator has the power to make sure you are helping the community.

Numerous other business types are available such as private unlimited companies, limited partnerships, co-operatives, offshore companies and limited liability partnerships. Find out more on www.startups.co.uk. You may also want to consult a solicitor or accountant to make sure you're doing everything by the book.

Legal/tax issues

Once you've set up your business there are various other legal and tax issues you will need to consider. These are summarised below.

Intellectual property

Make sure you're not copying and using any unique creative products/industrial secrets that are owned by others (without their express permission). This includes endeavours such as design features, text, artwork, logos, trademarks and patents. You should also make sure that your ideas are protected. Find out more at the Intellectual Property Office (www.ipo.gov.uk).

Tax

Sign up for the appropriate tax regime for your type of business (including VAT) and keep your records in order. You may also want to employ an accountant to make sure you're following the correct procedures and to minimise your liability. If you're employing anyone, you'll also need to sort out their tax through PAYE and National Insurance. You can find out which taxes you should be paying, and how to register, on Her Majesty's Revenue and Customs (HMRC) website at www.hmrc.gov.uk. In the meantime, keep hold of all your receipts!

Licences

Depending on what you're selling you may also require a licence – these are usually provided by your local council. Business Link has an excellent tool to help you identify any licence you may require at www.gov.uk.

Insurance

Your business will also need various forms of insurance, such as public liability and business equipment cover. Business Link also has useful resources on risk management at www.gov.uk.

Financial planning and forecasts

Obviously, finances are a major concern for most people starting a new business (except perhaps Roman Abramovich!). This section shows you how to forecast your costs, income, profits and losses and accurately keep track of them so that you can make sound decisions about the future and enhance your chances of success.

Set-up costs

Your first task is to carefully work out how much money you'll need to set up shop and start trading. Depending on the nature of your business this could involve paying out for things such as:

- Product development.
- Machinery and equipment.
- Staff.
- Training.
- Designing a website.
- An office/warehouse/retail outlet.
- Paying bills and wages until the receipts come rolling in.

These costs can be astronomical if you just jump in with your chequebook and start buying the best products and services on offer but, with a little thought, you can make substantial savings, at least until you start earning enough money to reinvest. For example, you could:

- Set up your office in the free facilities (often called incubators) that may be available from your university's enterprise centre or other local agencies (see the list of resources at the end of the chapter).
- Trade from your own bedroom and store things in the garage.
- Rent the equipment you need or buy it second-hand.
- Hire interns over the summer from your local university (including someone to set up your IT and sales strategy).
- Train yourself on the Internet and attend free courses (see the links at the end of the chapter).

- Distribute your own goods from the back of your car.
- Promote and advertise your goods and services yourself.
- Shop around!

In the exercise below, list the key resources you'll need to set up your business and work out how you can get them as cheaply as possible. This will help you calculate the funds you'll need just to get going.

Self-assessment: Minimising your set-up costs

List the costs you will incur in setting up your business and outline how you can minimise your outlay.

Your business idea:		
The resources you'll need	How you can get them cheaply	What they will cost
		£
		£
		£
		£
		£
	TOTAL	£

Ongoing costs

Once you commence trading you will start incurring extra, ongoing costs. These flexible costs will rise according to how much you sell, but the marginal costs of producing and selling each extra unit will gradually fall because of the economies of scale. In other words, the more you sell, the lower your average costs. For example, if you make music, it will probably cost hundreds of pounds to produce your first compact disc (including equipment, studio time, production etc.), but your second one will probably only cost 50p! Therefore, your average costs depend heavily on the number of units you can sell.

Some of the major marginal costs faced by most new businesses are listed below:

- Payments to suppliers: Raw materials/wholesale products.
- Promotion and advertising.
- Purchases: Everything from raincoats to networking lunches.
- Wages/professional fees: Pay for your staff and accountants, lawyers etc.
- Tax: Including PAYE and NI for your staff, VAT and your income/business taxes.
- Rent and rates.

- Electricity/gas.
- Car costs/travel.
- Telephone: Office and mobile.
- Stationery.
- Logistics/postage.
- Repairs: Especially important if everything is old and rusty!
- General expenses.
- Capital: Better machinery, equipment and IT.
- Bank interest and charges.

Forecasts

Once you've calculated your potential costs, sales and income you can produce monthly financial forecasts for your first year or two of trading. These will help you gauge the success of your business as you proceed and they can be carefully assessed by interested investors. You can see example cash flow, profit and loss and balance sheet forecasts on the companion website.

Finding the funds

Of course, starting a new business can be expensive and risky but intrepid entrepreneurs, with impressive business plans, can still access a number of sources of funding, many of which are listed below:

- Your mum, dad and uncle Eric.
- Keeping your 'day job' (i.e. set things up while you're still working).
- Business 'angels': Wealthy individuals who invest in new businesses for a percentage of the returns. Find out more on the websites of the UK Business Angels Association at www.ukbusinessangelsassociation.org.uk and the Angel Investment Network at www.angelinvestmentnetwork.co.uk.
- Bank loans.
- Bank overdrafts.
- Local, national and European government grants: See the Business Link website at www.gov.uk, Idox at www.j4b.co.uk and Grants Net at www.grantsnet.co.uk.
- Soft loans: Loans with favourable terms often available from local authorities, Local Enterprise Trusts (see www.theenterprisetrust.org) and professional organisations (see the companion website for a list).
- Charities (such as the Prince's Trust at www.princes-trust.org.uk).
- Community Development Finance Institutions (see www.cdfa.org.uk).
- Crowdfunding: Securing funds from a multitude of investors – usually arranged through websites such as www.kickstarter.com, www.fundingcircle.com, www.pleasefund.us and www.crowdfunder.co.uk.

Lenders will expect you to demonstrate your CAMPARI, i.e. your **C**haracter and **A**bility, the **M**argin you will earn, the **P**urpose for the loan, grant or gift, the **A**mount you need, how you will **R**epay what you owe and the **I**nsurance or collateral you are able to provide.

Business plans

Once you've identified your market and set up an appropriate business structure, it's time to formally draw up your plans for the coming years. This will give you confidence that you can achieve your aims, help you avoid getting bogged down with day-to-day problems, monitor your progress, impress investors and find the funds you'll need to get up and running.

Because business plans are so important, you should put a great deal of time and energy into making sure yours is positive, comprehensive (but concise), engaging and realistic. You can find out more about what you need to incorporate through the resources listed at the end of the chapter and get help from Business Link (www.gov.uk), accountants or financial advisers.

What you should include

There is no universal business structure since no two businesses are the same, but you should include the following elements:

1. **A cover page:** Show your business's name, contact details and the date the plan was prepared.
2. **An executive summary:** A persuasive one-page summary of your venture.
3. **A table of contents.**
4. **An outline of your business and product/service:** More details including an outline of your business structure, what your product does, how it will benefit customers, why it's distinct from similar merchandise already on the market, how it will be developed and updated and how the business has performed so far.
5. **Details of your management and staffing:** Summarise your personal, academic and business achievements, relating them to your business, and do the same for your colleagues and staff. Include specific information relating to staff training and any services you may outsource.
6. **Market intelligence:** Include details of the size of your market and the share you are planning on gaining, your likely customers (including demographics and psychographics), your competitors (and how they will react to your entry), how the market has performed in the past, current trends and future potential.
7. **Your sales strategy:**
   - How/Where/Who will sell your product or service, e.g. through the Internet, direct mail, telephone, third parties or your own retail outlet.
   - Your pricing structure.
8. **How you will use the Internet (e-commerce):** Provide technical details of how will you use the world wide web to support your business, including everything from ordering raw materials, selling your merchandise and after-sales service.
9. **Your operational details:** Provide information on where you will be based, your suppliers and the equipment and machinery you'll be using, including any information technology.
10. **An analysis of your finances:** Provide forecasts for costs, earnings and profits for your first trading year and use them to justify any extra funds you are after. Include specific details about what you will do with any cash injections.
11. **A risk assessment:** Describe any potential problems you may face and how they will be overcome. You may want to do this through a SWOT matrix where you analyse the following aspects of your product or service:

- Its strengths (how it's superior to those of your competitors).
- Its weaknesses (its limitations compared to your competitors).
- Your opportunities (positive external factors in the sector/market).
- Your threats (negative external factors).

Find more details on conducting a SWOT matrix at www.businessballs.com

12 **A picture of your long-term prospects:** End your business plan on a positive note by describing your plan for the next five years and how this will be achieved. Focus on anticipated returns and whet investors' appetites by indicating what they will earn if the business is floated or sold.

A one-page business plan

If you're not quite ready to put together a full business objective at this stage then a shorter, more concise plan can be a good stepping stone. Construct your sleek strategy in the exercise below.

Self-assessment: A one-page business plan

Answer the following questions to develop a short, focused business plan.

Your business name:
What is your product/service? ________ What resources will you need to put it together? ________ ________ ________ Where will you be based? ________ ________ Who's going to buy it? ________ ________ How will they find it useful? ________ ________ What will you sell it for? ________ ________ How will you organise payment? ________ ________ What other sources of income does it enable? ________ ________ How will you attract customers? ________ ________ What income will constitute success? £ ________ What do you still need to find out? ________ ________

Glossary of terms used in the sector

If you're going to start a new business or do any further research, you should get a handle on the terms and phrases that are used in the sector, such as:

accounting year end: Each 12-month anniversary of when a company is incorporated, at which time all entries must be adjusted in order to prepare financial statements.

affiliate: A partner organisation or a business that links to your website for their own marketing benefit.

assets: Any valuable tangible or intangible economic resources that can be bought or sold.

balance sheet: A brief summary of a company's assets, liabilities and equity on a specific date (often the end of the financial year).

banner: A web advert that acts as a gateway to your site.

brand: This can either be a unique variation of a good/service (for example, Nike is a brand of sportswear) or the specific symbol that identifies a unique variety of a good/service (for example, the Nike 'tick' shown on the company's apparel).

business angels: Private investors in small businesses.

business plan: A formal outline of a business's goals and how these are going to be achieved.

business start-up: Newly established enterprises still in a state of development (particularly in the digital field).

business strategy: A statement outlining how a business intends to succeed, including what's being offered, the needs of customers, how it will beat the competition and remain profitable in the long term.

cash flow: The amount of money that has moved into or out of a business, usually over a fixed period.

click-through: Clicking on an online advert.

Companies House: UK body responsible for forming and dissolving public companies.

digital marketing: Online advertising.

direct marketing: Advertising delivered directly to the customer, e.g. texting, emails, fliers, catalogues and promotional letters.

domain registration: Claiming ownership of a specific website address.

e-commerce: Business transactions over electronic systems such as the Internet.

economies of scale: The tendency to incur lower average costs when you produce more (to an optimum point when they start to rise again).

Enterprise Zone: Regions in the UK where taxes and regulations are relaxed to encourage entrepreneurs.

fixed costs: Basic business costs that are accrued whatever the level of sales.

flexible costs: Business costs which vary according to how much you produce.

franchising: Piggybacking on another organisation's business model whereby an owner of a business grants a licence to another person (or business) to use their idea.

gross: Before deductions (such as tax).

hits: The number of times a server is asked to upload particular web pages and their associated elements such as images, JavaScript and Cascading Style Sheets. Therefore, a single view of one web page will create a variable amount of hits.

impressions: The number of times a web advert is displayed.

incorporation: Setting up a company.

incubator (in this context): Space and resources such as IT and phone lines provided for free or at low cost to business start-ups, especially within universities.

intellectual property: Any creative endeavour that's considered to be the property of its creator.

lifestyle business: Businesses designed to fit around your existing life.

Local Enterprise Agencies: Local bodies offering free support for entrepreneurs.

logistics: The process of getting your product or service to the customer including production, packaging and transportation.

marginal costs: The costs of producing one more unit.

market research: Information gathering about markets and customers.

market segmentation: Targeting the needs of specific groups of customers.

marketing: Everything involved in creating and selling a product or service that attracts and keeps customers, such as product design, advertising, and how and where it's sold.

marketing mix: The four Ps of marketing, i.e. product, promotion, price and place.

meta tags: Information contained in the coding of web pages which describes issues such as who wrote them, what they're about and targeted keywords to describe their content. These keywords have a crucial role in the prominence of individual sites in web searches.

National Insurance: Contributions paid by workers, employers and the self-employed towards the costs of state benefits.

net: After deductions (such as tax).

niche market: A market subset at which a particular product or service is targeted.

page views: The number of times a server is asked to upload particular web pages but not their associated files (see **hits**).

patents: New, useful and non-obvious processes, machines or articles which have been registered with the state. They typically convey exclusivity in making, using and selling the product or service for a fixed period.

pay-per-click: A method of payment whereby online advertisers pay the owners of a host website a fixed amount each time their advert is clicked.

point of sale: Where goods and services are transacted for hard cash – for example, cash registers, credit/debit card machines, computers and mobile phones.

seed funding: Early funding for a new business to sustain it until it grows and can support itself.

small business: These are businesses (usually sole traders, privately owned companies, or partnerships) with fewer than 50 employees.

social enterprise: A profit or non-profit organisation devoted to enhancing environmental and human wellbeing.

trademark: Unique symbols which indicate the source of particular products and services (see **brand**).

variable costs: The costs incurred by an organisation that rise according to how much they produce.

venture capital: Financial capital provided to businesses in return for a share in equity. Business angels (see above) are more likely to support new businesses.

web traffic: The total data sent and received by websites as determined by the number of visitors and pages viewed.

Initialisms and acronyms

B2B	Business-to-business (commercial transactions between businesses)
B2C	Business-to-customer (commercial transactions between businesses and customers)
HMRC	Her Majesty's Revenue and Customs
NI	National Insurance
P&L	Profit and loss
PAYE	Pay As You Earn tax contributions paid by most employees
PO	Purchase order
QTD	Quarter to date
SME	Small and medium-sized enterprises (organisations with fewer than 250 employees)
S_t	Sales (during time period t)
SWOT analysis	A formal assessment of a project's strengths, weaknesses, opportunities and threats
VAT	Value added tax
YOY	Year on year
YTD	Year to date

Finding out more

In this guide

- Becoming an entrepreneur – Chapter 17.

On the companion website

- Links to professional organisations in a range of sectors.
- Example cash flow, profit and loss and balance sheet forecasts.

On the web

On the companion website you'll find a number of up-to-date links to a range of websites on entrepreneurship including local and regional entrepreneurship societies, the National Enterprise Network, Young Enterprise and Startups.

What to do next

This chapter has been designed to help you explore setting up a business. If you want to look into it further, you could consider the following:

- Study entrepreneurship/enterprise on your current course.
- Sign up for a relevant Masters.
- Talk to people at your university's enterprise centre.
- Use the links listed to meet entrepreneurs in your area.
- Undertake more in-depth research into starting up a business and your chosen sector.
- Get going!

Summary

- The first step to developing a new business is to define your target customers.
- Once you've done this you can plan your marketing strategy, i.e. the specifications of your product, how you will promote it, what you'll charge and where you'll be based.
- You can test your product through web research, talking to people in the industry and conducting pilot studies.
- Once you've defined your market you should decide on an appropriate business structure such as sole trading, an ordinary partnership or a private limited company.
- You also need to consider legal/tax issues such as intellectual property, tax, licences and insurance.
- Financial planning is very important as it gives you a guide to how you will progress and helps investors understand your business.
- Once you've established your planned price, costs and sales you can develop cash flow, profit and loss and balance sheet forecasts.
- A wide range of organisations fund new businesses, from relatives to business angels and banks.
- Once you've researched your new business in detail you can draw up a business plan to help you keep on track and attract investors.
- Entrepreneurs often need to learn a whole new business language – many of the terms used are included here in a glossary.

Chapter
19

Troubleshooting

"Successful people are simply people who learn to solve their problems ... they are not people without problems." *Unknown*

Contents

What you will gain from this chapter:

- **Decision making:** The ability to face up to what's holding you back in your career.
- **Opportunity awareness:** A reminder to follow your dreams.
- **Transition learning:** A renewed appreciation that career planning is an ongoing lifetime process.
- **Self-awareness:** The capacity to challenge your career strategy and progress.

If at first you don't succeed

This guide has been designed to be a constant companion on your path into a graduate career. However, this journey is not a straightforward trip from A to B but a continual, lifelong process of making decisions, seeking out opportunities, learning how to get on and reflecting on your abilities and aspirations. This is demonstrated by the DOTS model shown below, as recreated from Chapter 1.

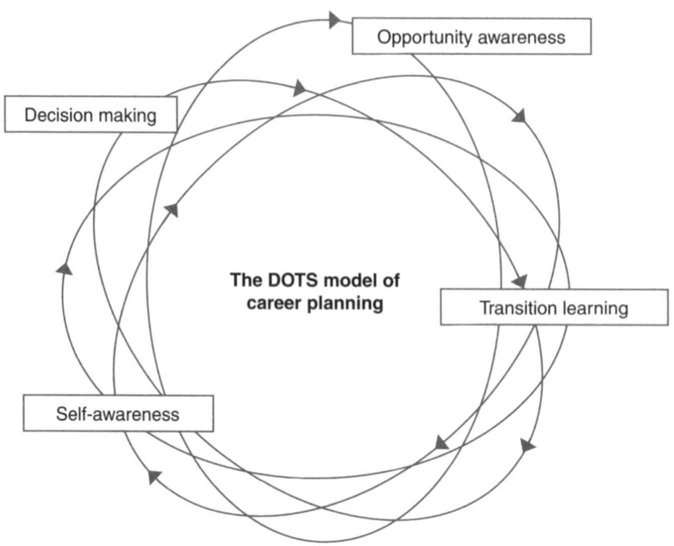

Therefore, you shouldn't feel overly disappointed if you've read the whole of this guide but still haven't found fulfilment. Just identify the positive steps you've actually been able to take (however small) and determine how you can keep moving forward. For example, if you're still not sure about what role to pursue after university, turn to Part I, 'Finding your way'.

If you just can't pinpoint what's holding you back you could also reconsider the issues you identified in the DOTS self-assessment exercise in Chapter 1 (p. 12) and see if this helps you identify what to do next. Try this in the exercise below:

Self-assessment: Your DOTS problems?

What are your key problems with each aspect of the DOTS model? Include any unresolved concerns from Chapter 1 and any new issues you've discovered.

The DOTS architects of growth	Where you struggle with each one	Where you can find help (in this guide or elsewhere)
Decision making		
Opportunity awareness		
Transition learning		
Self-awareness		

Some common concerns

Some of the more common problems faced by students and graduates are outlined below with advice on what you can do in each situation. Further frequently asked questions related to each chapter in this guide can be found on the companion website.

Self-reflection like this can be very challenging, but you should persevere because it's usually the best way to get back on track. You may also want to discuss the issues involved with a careers adviser from your current or former university's careers centre (or your local university) – just give them a call.

I still don't have a clue what to do next because everything's got on top of me!

Like any project, career planning can be daunting and, sometimes, overwhelming. This is quite natural because there are just so many factors to consider and you're bound to get snowed under from time to time. Therefore, you need to take the pressure off yourself, stand back from your problems and systematically plan your way forward one step at a time. Review the first three chapters in this guide and take your time over the activities.

None of the occupations I've found seems that fulfilling

The first step to answering this common query is to identify why you're not finding any attractive-looking positions. Three of the more common factors restricting a successful job search are listed below – which ones are holding you back?

- *You're not looking widely enough*: The majority of graduates don't look further than the obvious options such as teaching, accountancy and the various graduate training programmes. In fact, these popular careers constitute only a tiny fraction of graduate destinations in full. There are less well-known roles such as flying planes, managing national parks and designing dresses.
- *You're looking for jobs not a career*: Most of the time, you'll have to gradually work your way into your chosen role via activities such as voluntary work, alternative roles and postgraduate study.
- *You're not taking things seriously enough*: Have you searched widely enough?

Whatever's holding you back, don't put yourself down. In fact, you have to do exactly the opposite. Take time over the exercises in Chapter 2 and allow yourself to dream. There are probably millions of wonderful roles out there that will suit you down to the ground – you just need the confidence to look and turn your dreams into reality.

What if I haven't got a 2.1?

An ever-increasing number of graduate employers require a 2.1. You have various options if you don't fall into this lucky group:

- Apply before you graduate and state an expectation of a 2.1 – you may be lucky and still get in with lower grades.
- Contact the organisations and ask if you can still apply as you have a good reason for your failure to achieve the grades you expected. Don't just enter your lower degree classification into the normal application forms because they will probably be immediately rejected, probably by a computer!

- Look for employers in your chosen sector who aren't so grade sensitive (usually the smaller ones who don't advertise their positions so aggressively).
- Get so much experience that you can't be refused.
- Look for any old job in the sector you want to enter and work your way up into the job you want.
- Try a different role for a while.

See Chapter 3.

I can't find any jobs in my chosen field

The number of graduates has increased tenfold since the early 1960s but so has the number of graduate jobs. Therefore, there are still plenty of opportunities. The recession has recently slowed things down but not appreciably.

However, the route into graduate careers has changed markedly. A far smaller percentage of students go directly into traditional graduate training programmes and graduates often have to tread long and circuitous paths to get to their career destinations.

Therefore, if you can't find any jobs, there are probably still paths into your chosen career which are less direct and obvious, so you'll have to be more creative. For example, if you can't find roles as a dietician, maybe you could do some specialised training, look abroad or develop your skills in a related field (such as counselling) until the job market recovers. See the first three chapters of this guide.

I apply for loads of jobs but no one wants me!

This could be down to any or all of the reasons outlined below:

- *Your applications aren't up to scratch*: The vast majority of application forms and CVs are rushed, untargeted and full of spelling/grammar mistakes – what about yours? If you can see room for improvement, look at Part III of this guide and take it from there. Remember: it is not a numbers game – you should be spending 20 hours or so on each CV or application form.
- *You don't have the attributes required*: If you are missing some of the crucial skills required in your chosen occupation, you might want to take some time to develop them in a voluntary position, a postgraduate course or in a less competitive position. See Chapter 3.
- *You've just been unlucky*: Employers often have to sieve through hundreds of applications and can dismiss them for the most unlikely reasons – so persevere.
- *The employers don't know you*: You'll probably stand a much greater chance of getting an interview if you know the employer, so start networking and trying to get to know some key people in the sector – see Chapter 5.

I think I need to take up some further study but I don't know what to do

Further education will give you extra skills, contacts and experience and therefore can be very beneficial in your career journey. However, many employers ascribe much more importance to employment experience. For example, the average graduate development programme at a blue-chip employer will look favourably on internships but give very little credit for a Masters, or even a PhD.

Therefore, if you are considering a Masters, or any form of further study, make sure it's part of a focused strategy to get into a specific career (not the other way around). Take more time over Chapter 2 and see what careers are linked to your favourite courses.

I've been doing nothing for a few years; does this mean I'm on the scrap heap forever?

No, it certainly doesn't! Your degree will always indicate that you are a skilled and committed person, but it's only the start – you also need experience. Therefore, you should take stock of where you are, where you want to be and how you can get there.

Don't dismiss your existing experience so readily as it will be valuable to employers even if you haven't had a typical graduate role. For example, if you've been a homemaker for a few years, you will be able to demonstrate your ability to manage and organise your time.

Your next steps could include further training, more experience, voluntary positions or anything else that will help you move on. See Chapters 3 and 16 for more help.

Keeping your eyes open

In his song 'Beautiful Boy', John Lennon wrote: 'Life is what happens to you when you're busy making other plans.' You should remember these lyrics as you plan your career. In other words, as long as you're busy and focused on getting to the next stage in life, other interesting avenues will inevitably present themselves. You need to keep your eyes open to take advantage of these opportunities. For example, if you've always wanted to be a navy diver but you really enjoyed diving in Thailand over the summer, why not reconsider your naval career and set up your own dive school on some exotic beach?

Once again, good luck and enjoy the trip!

Notes

1 Understanding employability and career planning

1 J. Hillage and E. Pollard, *Employability: Developing a framework for policy.* Research Report RR85, Department for Education and Employment, November 1998.
2 B. Law, 'Career-learning space: new-DOTS thinking for careers education', *British Journal of Guidance and Counselling*, 27 (2) (1999), pp. 35–53.

2 Choosing a role

1 www.prospects.ac.uk/what_do_graduates_do.htm.
2 See www.hefce.ac.uk.
3 Career ideas adapted from P. D. Tieger and B. Barron-Tieger, *Do What You Are* (Little, Brown and Company, 1995) and www.personalitymax.com and www.personalitypage.com.

5 Effective networking

1 www.highfliers.co.uk/download/GMReport12.pdf.
2 www.highfliers.co.uk/download/UKGCSurvey2011.pdf.
3 www.prospects.ac.uk/latest_news_graduates_missing_out_on_jobs_with_smes.htm.

7 Taking time out

1 An album by Timothy Leary in 1967.

15 Passing assessment centres

1 See www.belbin.com.

16 This job's for you

1 D. Littleford, J. Halstead and C. Mulraine, *Career Skills: Opening Doors into the Job Market*, Palgrave Study Skills (Basingstoke: Palgrave Macmillan, 2004).

Part IV: Entrepreneurship

1 See Generation Enterprise, Action and Research Centre, www.thersa.org.

17 Becoming an entrepreneur

1 S. Hashemi and B. Hashemi (2002) *Anyone Can Do It: Building Coffee Republic from Our Kitchen Table: 57 Real-life Laws on Entrepreneurship* (Oxford: Capstone, 2007).

References and further reading

Downloads

The Association of Graduate Recruiters, The Graduate Recruitment Surveys between 2008 and 2013, www.agr.org.uk (downloaded throughout 2011 and 2012).

The Association of Graduate Recruiters, The AGR Briefing Paper Series between 2008 and 2013, www.agr.org.uk (downloaded throughout 2011 and 2012).

CBI, Economic and Business Outlooks between February and May 2011, www.cbi.org.uk (downloaded 2012).

High Fliers Research Ltd., Graduate Market Annual Surveys for 2011 and 2012, www.highfliers.co.uk (downloaded 2012).

High Fliers Research Ltd., UK Graduate Careers Surveys for 2011 and 2012, www.highfliers.co.uk (downloaded 2012).

Real Prospects, Graduate Market Trends between 2008 and 2013, www.hecsu.ac.uk (downloaded throughout 2011 and 2012).

Warwick Institute for Employment Research Bulletins between 2006 and 2011, www2.warwick.ac.uk (downloaded 2012).

Books

Barrow, C. (2011) *Starting a Business for Dummies*, 3rd edn. Chichester: John Wiley and Sons, Limited.

Birchall, M. *The Times* (2011) *Top 100 Graduate Employers*. London: High Fliers Publications Ltd.

Bolles, R.N. (2013) *What Color Is Your Parachute: A Practical Manual for Job-Hunters and Career-Changers*. New York: Random House.

Bright, J. and Earl, J. (2011) *Brilliant CV: What Employers Want To See and How to Write It*, 4th edn. Harlow: Prentice Hall.

Butler, T. and Dane, M. (2007) *Reflections on Change 1967–2007*. Sheffield: Association of Graduate Careers Advisory Services.

Byron, M. (2010) *The Graduate Psychometric Test Workbook*. London: Kogan Page.

Cottrell, S. (2013) *The Study Skills Handbook*, 4th edn. Basingstoke: Palgrave Macmillan.

Cottrell, S. (2010) *Skills for Success: Personal Development and Employability*, 2nd edn. Basingstoke: Palgrave Macmillan.

Done, J. and Mulvey, R. (2011) *Brilliant Graduate Career Handbook*. Harlow: Pearson Education.

Dunning, D. (2010) *What's Your Type of Career? Find Your Perfect Career by Using Your Personality Type*. London: Nicholas Brealey Publishing.

Gothard, W. (2003) *Theories of Career Development and Models of Guidance*. Reading: University of Reading School of Health and Social Care.

Griffith, S. (2011) *Work Your Way Around the World*, 15th edn. Richmond, Surrey: Crimson Publishing.

Griffith, S. (2011) *Your Gap Year: The Most Comprehensive Guide to an Exciting and Fulfilling Gap Year*, 7th edn. Richmond, Surrey: Crimson Publishing.

Guillebeau, C. (2012) *The $100 Startup: Fire Your Boss, Do What You Love and Work Better To Live More*. Basingstoke: Pan Macmillan.

Hodgson, S. (2012) *The A–Z of Careers and Jobs*, 19th edn. London: Kogan Page.

Jenner, S. (2000) *The Graduate Career Handbook: Make the Right Start for a Bright Future*. Harlow: Pearson Education.

Johnson, L. (2011) *Start it Up: Why Running Your Own Business Is Easier Than You Think*. London: Penguin.

Kumar, A. (2007) *Personal, Academic and Career Development in Higher Education: Soaring to Success*. Abingdon: Routledge.

Lees, J. (2010) *How to Get a Job You'll Love*, 6th edn. Maidenhead: McGraw-Hill.

Littleford, D., Halstead, J. and Mulraine, C. (2004) *Career Skills: Opening Doors to the Job Market*. Basingstoke: Palgrave Macmillan.

Paton, N. (2010) *The Complete Career Makeover*. London: Guardian Books.

Phillips, C. (1996) *First Interviews – Sorted*. London: GTI Specialist Publishers.

Phillips, C. (1996) *Making Wizard Applications*. London: GTI Specialist Publishers.

Phillips, C. (1999) *No Idea About a Career*. London: GTI Specialist Publishers.

Pryor, R. and Bright, J. (2011) *The Chaos Theory of Careers: A New Perspective on Working in the Twenty-First Century*. Abingdon: Routledge).

Redmond, D. (2010) *The Graduate Jobs Formula: How to Land your Dream Career*. Richmond, Surrey: Trotman Publishing.

Rickman, C.D. (2011) *The Small Business Start-Up Workbook: A Step-by-Step Guide to Starting the Business You've Dreamed Of*. Oxford: How to Books Ltd.

Rook, S. et al. (2010) *Legal Skills*. Basingstoke: Palgrave Macmillan.

Shepherd, A. (2010) *Real Prospects Directory 2010/11*. Manchester: Graduate Prospects.

Thorpe, P. (1997) *Small Business Street Smarts*, 4th edn. Sydney:The Advertising Department.

Tieger, P.D. and Barron, B. (2007) *Do What You Are: Discover the Perfect Career for You Through the Secrets of Personality Type*, 4th edn. New York: Little Brown and Company.

Weinmann, E. and Lourekas, P. (1999) *Photoshop for Windows and Macintosh*. Berkeley, CA: Peachpit Press.

Williams, L. (2000) *Readymade CVs: Sample CVs for Every Type of Job*, 2nd edn. London: Kogan Page.

Williams, S. (2011) *Business Start Up 2010: The Most Comprehensive Annually Updated Guide for Entrepreneurs*. Harlow: Pearson Education.

Research papers and journals

Bimrose, J., Brown, B., Barnes, S. and Hughes, D. (2011) *The Role of Career Adaptability in Skills Supply*. Warwick: Warwick Institute for Employment Research.

Cox, A., Hogarth, T., Usher, T., Owen, D., Sumption, F. and Oakley, J. (2009) *Impact of Recession on the Labour Market in the South East*.Research Report, Learning and Skills Council and South East England Development Agency.

Greenbank, P. (2010) *Initiating Change in Career Decision-Making*. Manchester: Higher Education Careers Services Unit.

Higgins, H. (2010) *Graduate Career Stories*. Manchester: Higher Education Careers Services Unit.

Higgins, H. (2010) *The Best Graduate Employers as Rated by Graduates*. Manchester: Real Prospects.

Leitch. (2006) *Prosperity For All in the Global Economy: World Class Skills*. London: Her Majesty's Stationery Office.

Mason, G. and Hopkin, R. (2011) *Employer Perspectives on Part-Time Students in UK Higher Education*. Manchester: Higher Education Careers Services Unit and London: Department for Business, Innovation and Skills.

Meager, N., Martin, R. and Carta, E. (2011) *Skills For Self-Employment*. Brighton: Institute For Employment Studies.

Mok, P. (2006) *Graduates' First Destinations by Age, Ethnicity and Gender: DLHE Survey Analysis*. Manchester: Higher Education Careers Services Unit.

Purcell, K., Elias, P. et al. (2009) *Plans, Aspirations and Realities: Taking Stock of Higher Education and Career Choices One Year On*. Findings from the Second Futuretrack Survey of 2006 Applicants For Higher Education. Manchester: Higher Education Careers Services Unit.

Purcell, K. and Elias, P. (2004) *Seven Years On: Graduate Careers in a Changing Labour Market*. Manchester: Higher Education Careers Services Unit.

Purcell, K., Elias, P. et al. (2005) *The Class of '99: A Study of the Early Labour Market Experiences of Recent Graduates*. Manchester: Higher Education Careers Services Unit.

Wilson, R., Homenidou, K. and Gambin, L. (2008) *Working Futures 2007–2017*. Warwick: Warwick Institute for Economic Research.

Index